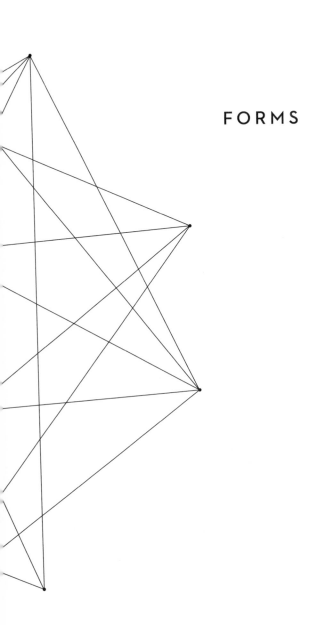

FORMS

FORMS

Whole, Rhythm, Hierarchy, Network

CAROLINE LEVINE

PRINCETON UNIVERSITY PRESS

Princeton & Oxford

Copyright © 2015 by Princeton University Press
Published by Princeton University Press
41 William Street, Princeton, New Jersey 08540
In the United Kingdom: Princeton University Press
6 Oxford Street, Woodstock, Oxfordshire OX20 1TW

press.princeton.edu

Jacket images, from top to bottom:
Empty prison cell © Damin Klimek/Thinkstock; detail of U.S. postal scan code;
detail of *Jane Eyre*, 1847; American flag; detail of Grizzly roller coaster
© Marcrut/Creative Commons.

Library of Congress Cataloging-in-Publication Data

Levine, Caroline, 1970–
Forms : Whole, Rhythm, Hierarchy, Network / Caroline Levine.
pages cm
Summary: "*Forms* offers a powerful new answer to one of the most pressing
problems facing literary, critical, and cultural studies today—how to connect form
to political, social, and historical context. Caroline Levine argues that forms organize
not only works of art but also political life—and our attempts to know both art
and politics. Inescapable and frequently troubling, forms shape every aspect of our experience. But forms don't impose their order in any simple way. Multiple shapes, patterns, and
arrangements, overlapping and colliding, generate complex and unpredictable social land-
scapes that challenge and unsettle conventional analytic models in literary and cultural studies. Borrowing the concept of "affordances" from design theory, this book investigates
the specific ways that four major forms—wholes, rhythms, hierarchies, and networks—
have structured culture, politics, and scholarly knowledge across periods, and it proposes
exciting new ways of linking formalism to historicism and literature to politics. Levine
rereads both formalist and antiformalist theorists, including Cleanth Brooks, Michel
Foucault, Jacques Rancière, Mary Poovey, and Judith Butler, and she offers engaging
accounts of a wide range of objects, from medieval convents and modern theme parks to
Sophocles's *Antigone* and the television series *The Wire*. The result is a radically new
way of thinking about form for the next generation and essential reading for scholars
and students across the humanities who must wrestle with the problem of form and
context"— Provided by publisher.
Includes bibliographical references and index.
ISBN 978-0-691-16062-7 (hardback : acid-free paper) 1. Literary form.
2. Form (Aesthetics) 3. Form perception. 4. Cultural fusion in literature.
5. Literature and society. 6. Criticism. I. Title.
PN45.5.L48 2015
801'.95—dc23   2014006211

British Library Cataloging-in-Publication Data is available

This book has been composed in Sabon Next LT Pro and Neutraface No. 2

Printed on acid-free paper. ∞

Printed in the United States of America

3 5 7 9 10 8 6 4 2

FOR JON

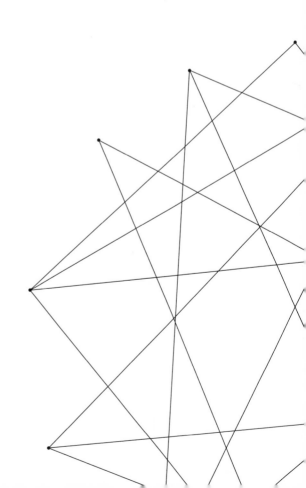

INDEX 169
NOTES 151
VI THE WIRE 132
V NETWORK 112
IV HIERARCHY 82
III RHYTHM 49

CONTENTS

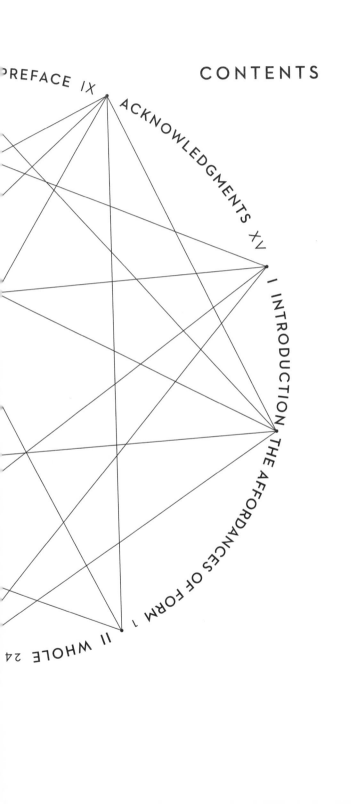

PREFACE IX

ACKNOWLEDGMENTS XV

I INTRODUCTION

THE AFFORDANCES OF FORM 1

II WHOLE 24

PREFACE

My father was a liberal humanist and a historian of ideas. He often read literary writers: he wrote on Pope and Swift. He believed that scholars should strive to understand the intentions of authors as they responded to contemporary concerns and debates. To our mutual dismay, I didn't find this approach particularly exciting. I wanted to track subtle arrangements of words and images interwoven through literary texts. When I first went to college and fell in love with poststructuralist ways of reading, my father was amused and skeptical. He would challenge me to defend "ahistorical" literary studies in debates that went on for hours. I would argue that patterns of language came before us, preceding and creating subjects; he would insist that human agency and intention were primary, shaping any utterance we make. The debates themselves were pleasurable, but he never convinced me—or I him. I wish Joseph M. Levine were alive to read this book. He would cheerfully disagree with every argument in it.

It was something of an irony for me when literary studies took a historical turn. By the time I'd graduated from college in the early 1990s, historicism was clearly displacing deconstruction as the dominant model for the field. This felt like a narrowing of the intellectual world to me, a stifling. Deconstruction had encouraged a kind of intellectual pyrotechnics; my teachers had performed readings so dazzling that a physical thrill would run through me. Now we were being asked to situate literary objects in thickly described, local contexts, with an attention to Parliamentary papers and conduct manuals. I found it dreary. And yet, the ethical arguments that the New Historicists were making had power. Deconstructive approaches might be exciting, but they were increasingly called self-indulgent; historicism might feel laborious, but it was about power and injustice—serious business. Difficult new disciplinary questions took shape for me. If conduct books contributed as much as poems to a given culture, then why wouldn't I become a historian like my father? And if social justice should be my goal, then could I justify a lifetime of studying literature?

Feeling ambivalent about literary studies, I went off to Birkbeck College, part of the University of London, to think and read for a few years, but probably not, I thought at the time, to pursue an academic career. At Birkbeck, every scholar was a Marxist of one variety or another. All of my teachers insisted on historical methods with a political urgency that was new to me—and compelling.

The traditional Marxist attentiveness to long processes of change was especially helpful. When I expanded my attention beyond immediate local contexts, I grasped the massive and manifold disruptions that profound economic shifts had brought: the prolonged industrial revolution that moved huge numbers of people out of rural areas and into crowded cities, fundamentally reshaping social relationships and rapidly accelerating environmental devastation; the competition among European nations for new markets that uprooted and impoverished whole peoples, sometimes eradicating their languages and recasting their values as backward in a dominant story of European progress, a story that I now saw had shaped my father's work and my own childhood values. I understood for the first time how claims to artistic universality and transcendence had been used over and over as political bludgeons and how cultural objects had been crucial participants in the making and remaking of the political world. There was no way for me to pass this off as uninteresting or irrelevant.

Back in the United States, fitted out with a Birkbeck PhD and a new academic job, I realized with embarrassment that my eccentric education had somehow allowed me to skip over any serious reading of Michel Foucault. When I finally read *Discipline and Punish*, it came as a stunning revelation. It remains my single favorite work of theory. Foucault prompted in me an unsettling series of questions about revolutionary politics. Radical political movements had shown themselves capable of squelching the concerns of women, men of color, and queers, as Foucault himself saw first-hand in the French Communist Party of the 1950s. He came to argue that when revolutionaries imagined newly just distributions, they were also envisioning new social orders, sets of standards to govern relations among bodies, ideas, and resources. Even the most radical new arrangements could entail their own painful, oppressive normalizations and exclusions. "Every power relation is not bad in itself," Foucault said in an interview, "but it is a fact that always involves danger."[1] *Discipline and Punish* showed how even seemingly ordinary arrangements of space and time permitted certain circulations of power, while foreclosing others. It was Foucault, then, who suggested to me for the first time that organizations and arrangements were the main means by which power worked: politics was a matter of imposing order on the world.

It never occurred to me not to call these ordering principles *forms*. I, who had always been drawn to patterns and structures in and across texts, immediately grasped social experience in the same terms, using what seemed to me the same habits of thought, the same methods. I wrote a book about a temporal pattern that organized both narrative suspense and the scientific method in the Victorian period, and followed this with a book about structural tensions between avant-garde artists and democratic states. I understood all of these as forms.

It took me a long while to realize that this use of the term was not intuitive to other literary critics, who typically equated form with genre, or saw form as the exclusive domain of aesthetics. Form, for many literary readers, was precisely that which *distinguished* art objects from ordinary life. More and more this seemed to me arbitrary and misleading: if we were interested in containers and enclosures, then why not analyze prison cells or national boundaries, and if we wanted to understand patternings of time, then why not focus on factory routines? All of these were designed arrangements— deliberately crafted to impose order—just like art objects. Even those exciting critics who were challenging dominant practices of historicism with a renewed attention to form—critics like Heather Dubrow, Franco Moretti, Garrett Stewart, Herbert Tucker, Susan Wolfson, and Alex Woloch—were reading aesthetic forms as responses to given social realities. I wanted to know, instead, how both aesthetic *and* social forms acted in the world, and how they interacted and overlapped with each other. Literary critics, who excelled at spotting the difficult overlayings of multiple structures, who understood precisely how complex forms could be, seemed to be missing an opportunity to read social structures—politics—in the same alert, insightful ways.

As I read further about politics and form, I started to notice that literary and cultural studies scholars often assumed that aesthetic forms were tremendously complex, while political forms were comparatively simple. Powerful, even all-encompassing, but simple in themselves. And this, I came to believe, was not altogether wrong. Racism, for example, operates most often as a stark binary, a blunt political instrument rather than a complex formation in itself. But what literary formalists know well is that any simple order gets complicated fast once we start attending to the dense intertwining and overlapping of multiple forms. The best close readers are always attentive to many different forms at different scales operating at once. I began to track the ways that political forms *try* to contain and control us, while often in fact overlapping and colliding with other forms, and sometimes getting in one another's way.

This attention to traveling, colliding forms then brought me full circle, to a critique of the historicism that has become the daily fare of literary studies. From the beginning, the emphasis on local contexts has troubled me. My teachers, colleagues, and interlocutors over the years have insisted that a historical perspective yields irreducible particularity, sheer *difference*, and that it is a grave ethical error to draw too close a likeness between past and present. Presentism, the name for this error, is a charge so serious in literary and cultural studies that it has brought many a conversation to an end. And yet, I have always thought, none of our research *matters* unless it is generalizable, unless we can learn something from it that has implications beyond its own time. Even if the most important lesson we learn is the specificity of each historical moment, that too is a general conclusion—one, ironically, that generalizes specificity itself.

But I have never been convinced that the main value of historicism, even for historicists, lies in the distinctiveness of past periods. The most historically minded scholars choose to study gender norms in ancient Rome or eighteenth-century global commodity routes precisely because comparable arrangements of power operate now: because gender and commodity forms still organize us, carrying their pain and injustice with them; because distributions of authority and goods continue to restrict life and labor; and because we can reflect on the contingency of our own ordering principles when we know that they have at other times been organized otherwise. The past shows us what is possible—and we return, again and again, to its arrangements: the ordering of bodies and spaces, hierarchies and narratives, containments and exclusions. All of these have mattered to us because these configurations are the stuff of injustice, and also because structures like these travel and persist, continuing to organize our lives.

This book, like many others in the humanities, is an attempt to think about how we might make our world more just. One of the places where humans have some agency is in the orders that we ourselves impose: our spatial and temporal arrangements, our hierarchies of value and distributions of wealth—our *forms*. I am not persuaded that smashing or evading these forms has ever been the only or the most effective means to advance the cause of social justice. Arrangements and structurings are too pervasive, and some of them—like a fair redistribution of resources—too valuable, to reject out of hand. Nor am I convinced that it will ever be effective to focus all of our attention on any one form, singling it out as the cause or basis of all the others. It is by no means clear that capitalism always produces sexism, for example, or the other way around. Some forms dominate others at some moments and then falter or recede. But why? Why do gender norms organize the workplace at certain points while at others a workplace hierarchy unsettles gender norms? These questions have led me to recognize the aleatory possibilities that lie in the encounters among forms. The instabilities generated by formal collisions are a major focus of the chapters that follow.

What this book proposes, first and foremost, is a method. I aim to show that paying attention to subtle and complex formal patterns allows us to rethink the historical workings of political power and the relations between politics and aesthetics. Foucault was right to focus on the shapes and arrangements that structure everyday experience. But I have come to believe that he was wrong to imagine that these forms converge in massive regimes of coordinated power. The world is much more chaotic and contingent, formally speaking, than Foucault imagined, and therefore much more interesting—and just a little bit more hopeful as well. Literary formalists have precisely the tools to grasp this formal complexity and, with them, to begin to imagine workable, progressive, thoughtful relations among forms—including containing wholes, rhythms of labor, economic, racial and sexual hierarchies, and sprawling, connective networks of capital. For those who care passionately about unjust arrangements of power, this book argues that formalism offers a promising way forward.

ACKNOWLEDGMENTS

As I come to the end of this book I feel both happily and hopelessly in-debted. So many interlocutors have guided, challenged, supported, and changed me along the way. The first glimmerings of this project date back to undergraduate seminars taught by Claudia Brodsky, who so effectively startled me out of my previous habits of thought that I believe my brain chemistry itself underwent some basic alteration. My colleague Susan Stan-ford Friedman has modeled for me a life of searching, ethical, rigorous, sometimes acutely painful inquiry, never resting content with conventional answers, and endlessly willing to open her mind to new objects and meth-ods if her questions demand it. I strive to be like her. My students have turned the world upside down for me in the best possible way, since they have been my most stimulating teachers. I think particularly gratefully of Mary Mullen and Megan Massino, who prompted me to reshape the initial round of the argument; Cathy DeRose, who sharpened my understanding of networks; David Aitchison, who asked me many searching questions about politics and form; and Jessie Reeder and Virginia Piper, who are now pushing formalism to exciting new places. Virginia had some exceptionally helpful ideas for reorganizing the manuscript of this book.

A long line of generous, luminously intelligent friends and colleagues read and responded to this book as it evolved. Bruce Robbins and Henry S. Turner astonishingly took the time to read the whole manuscript and chal-lenged me to reexamine my claims. Rachel Ablow, Heather Dubrow, Lauren Goodlad, Virginia Jackson, Emily Ogden, Sharon Marcus, Meredith Mar-tin, Andrew H. Miller, and Carolyn Williams are among those who offered invaluable feedback. I count myself lucky indeed to have benefited again and again from conversations with close intellectual friends, who combine sharp intelligence with a warmth and affection that make me immeasur-ably happy: Jan Caldwell, Lew Friedland, Jane Gallop, Rachel Harmon, Anna Kornbluh, Venkat Mani, Nancy Rose Marshall, Martin Puchner, Lisa Sternlieb, Mark W. Turner, and Rebecca Walkowitz. Susan David Bernstein has been an especially responsive and sympathetic companion through the toughest times, and I thank her for dozens of hours of restorative conversation. I am immensely grateful, too, for assorted discussions of forms and formalism with many other treasured colleagues at the University of Wisconsin, including Russ Castronovo, Terry Kelley, Mario Ortiz-Robles, Teju Olaniyan, and David Zimmerman. The University generously supported this work with a sabbatical and two research awards: the Romnes Faculty Fellowship and the Vilas Associates Award.

Three pieces of chapter 3 have appeared in earlier forms. One part of the argument, "Infrastructuralism, or the Tempo of Institutions," was published in *On Periodization: Selected Essays from the English Institute*, ed. Virginia Jackson. I am grateful to the ACLS Humanities E-Book project for allowing me to reprint it here. Another part appeared in an earlier version in my book *Provoking Democracy: Why We Need the Arts* (Oxford: Wiley-Blackwell, 2007). My thanks to Wiley-Blackwell and also to West Virginia University Press for allowing me to reprint part of "Rhythms, Poetic and Political" from *Victorian Poetry* 49, no. 2 (summer 2011): 235–52. Duke University Press and Indiana University Press kindly granted permission to use parts of chapter 5, which appeared as "Narrative Networks: *Bleak House* and the Affordances of Form," *Novel* 42, no. 3 (fall 2009): 517–23 and "From Nation to Network," *Victorian Studies* (forthcoming, 2014).

Family members have been wonderfully supportive: my thanks to Deedee Levine, Peter Levine, Laura Broach, and Ina Jo McKenzie. I am deeply grateful for the work on this book made possible by Alannah De Barra, who spent many hours skillfully and lovingly caring for my children, and Aurora Quinonez, who spent many hours expertly caring for my house.

At Princeton University Press, Alison MacKeen gave me helpful advice all along the way and sent my manuscript to two of my favorite intellectuals on the planet. Nicholas Dames's remarkable thinking about form had already influenced the book in uncountable ways when I received his extraordinary reader's report. As for Amanda Claybaugh, she has always been my best reader: absurdly smart and perceptive, bracing and probing, patient and compassionate. I will spend the rest of my life trying to figure out how to thank her properly.

I still can't believe my luck in sharing a house with the brilliant, visionary Jon McKenzie and our two funny, inquisitive, kind-hearted sons, Eli and Joe. I never expected to lead a life so filled with love and laughter. Jon's exhilarating explosions of thought have often burst open my own, and he has surely been right to urge me to grapple with force as well as form. I dedicate this book to him with the full force of my love.

FORMS

I

INTRODUCTION

The Affordances of Form

If a literary critic today set out to do a formalist reading of Charlotte Brontë's *Jane Eyre*, she would know just where to begin: with literary techniques both large and small, including the marriage plot, first-person narration, description, free indirect speech, suspense, metaphor, and syntax. Thanks to rich recent work on the history of the book, she might also consider the novel's material shape—its size, binding, volume breaks, margins, and typeface. But unlike formalists of a couple of generations before, she would be unlikely to rest content with an analysis of these forms alone. Traditional formalist analysis—close reading—meant interpreting all of the formal techniques of a text as contributing to an overarching artistic whole. A contemporary critic, informed by several decades of historical approaches, would want instead to take stock of the social and political conditions that surrounded the work's production, and she would work to connect the novel's forms to its social world. She would seek to show how literary techniques reinforced or undermined specific institutions and political relationships, such as imperial power, global capital, or racism. Along the way, our critic would most likely keep her formalism and her historicism analytically separate, drawing from close reading methods to understand the literary forms, while using historical research methods to analyze sociopolitical experience. These would seem to her to belong to separate realms and to call for different methods.

But would our critic be right to distinguish between the *formal* and the *social*? Consider the early scenes in *Jane Eyre*, where Brontë first introduces Lowood School. In the morning, a bell rings loudly to wake the girls. When it rings a second time, "all formed in file, two and two, and in that order descended the stairs." On hearing a verbal command, the children move into "four semicircles, before four chairs, placed at the four tables; all held books in their hands." When the bell rings yet again, three teachers enter and begin an hour of Bible reading before the girls march in to breakfast.

Although this new world feels overwhelming at first, Jane—quick-witted and obedient—soon achieves success. "In time I rose to be the first girl of the first class."[1] Critics are used to reading Lowood's disciplinary order as part of the novel's content and context, interpreting the school experience as indispensable to Jane's maturation, for example, or as characteristic of trends in nineteenth-century education.[2] But what are Lowood's shapes and arrangements—its semicircles, timed durations, and ladders of achievement—if not themselves kinds of *form*?

This book makes a case for expanding our usual definition of form in literary studies to include patterns of sociopolitical experience like those of Lowood School. Broadening our definition of form to include social arrangements has, as we will see, immediate methodological consequences. The traditionally troubling gap between the form of the literary text and its content and context dissolves. Formalist analysis turns out to be as valuable to understanding sociopolitical institutions as it is to reading literature. Forms are at work everywhere.

One might object, of course, that it is a category mistake to use the aesthetic term *form* to describe the daily routines of a nineteenth-century school. Surely the relation between literary and social forms is just an analogy, or an identity working at too a high level of abstraction—an expansion of the word *form* so broad as to make it meaningless. But a brief look at the history of the term suggests otherwise. Over many centuries, *form* has gestured to a series of conflicting, sometimes even paradoxical meanings. Form can mean immaterial idea, as in Plato, or material shape, as in Aristotle. It can indicate essence, but it can also mean superficial trappings, such as conventions—*mere forms*. Form can be generalizing and abstract, or highly particular (as in the form of *this* thing is what makes it what it is, and if it were reorganized it would not be the same thing). Form can be cast as historical, emerging out of particular cultural and political circumstances, or it can be understood as ahistorical, transcending the specificities of history.[3] In disciplinary terms, form can point us to visual art, music, and literature, but it belongs equally to philosophy, law, mathematics, military science, and crystallography. Even within literary studies, the vocabulary of formalism has always been a surprising kind of hodge-podge, put together from rhetoric, prosody, genre theory, structural anthropology, philology, linguistics, folklore, narratology, and semiotics.

Chaotic though it seems, this brief conceptual history does make two things quite clear. First, form has never belonged only to the discourse of aesthetics. It does not originate in the aesthetic, and the arts cannot lay claim to either the longest or the most far-reaching history of the term. To bring the disciplinary techniques of Lowood together with the literary techniques of the novel is not then an arbitrary expansion of the notion of form, nor does it draw from outside the history of formalist thinking. Instead, an attention to both aesthetic and social forms returns us to the very heterogeneity at the heart of form's conceptual history. Second, all of the historical uses of the term, despite their richness and variety, do share a common definition: "form" always indicates *an arrangement of elements—an ordering, patterning, or shaping*. Here, then, is where my own argument begins: with a definition of form that is much broader than its ordinary usage in literary studies. Form, for our purposes, will mean all shapes and configurations, all ordering principles, all patterns of repetition and difference.

Why adopt such a broad definition? The stakes, I want to suggest, are high. It is the work of form to make order. And this means that forms are the stuff of politics. Drawing on the work of Jacques Rancière, I define politics as a matter of distributions and arrangements.[4] Political struggles include ongoing contests over the proper places for bodies, goods, and capacities. Do working-class crowds belong in the public square? Do women belong in voting booths? Does earned income belong to individuals? What land belongs to Native Americans? Sorting out what goes where, the work of political power often involves enforcing restrictive containers and boundaries— such as nation-states, bounded subjects, and domestic walls. But politics is not only about imposing order on space. It also involves organizing time: determining prison and presidential terms, naturalization periods, and the legal age for voting, military service, and sexual consent. Crucially, politics also means enforcing hierarchies of high and low, white and black, masculine and feminine, straight and queer, have and have-not. In other words, politics involves activities of ordering, patterning, and shaping. And if the political is a matter of imposing and enforcing boundaries, temporal patterns, and hierarchies on experience, then there is no politics without form.

Literary and cultural studies scholarship has focused a great deal of attention on these various political ordering principles. We have typically treated aesthetic and political arrangements as separate, and we have not generally used the language of form for both, but we have routinely drawn on social scientific accounts of "structure"; we have certainly paid attention to national boundaries and hierarchies of race and gender. And it is a commonplace practice in literary studies to read literary forms in relation to social structures. So: the field already knows a great deal about forms. But it is a knowledge that is currently scattered across schools of thought and approaches. This book proposes to bring together the field's dispersed insights into social and aesthetic forms to produce a new formalist method.

Let me start by articulating five influential ideas about how forms work. These are ideas that have guided literary and cultural studies scholars over the past few decades, but they have remained largely implicit—and disconnected from one another:

1   *Forms constrain*. According to a long tradition of thinkers, form is disturbing because it imposes powerful controls and containments. For some, this means that literary form itself exercises a kind of political power. In 1674, John Milton justified his use of blank verse as a reclaiming of "ancient liberty" against the "troublesome and modern bondage of rhyming."[5] Avant-garde poet Richard Aldington made a similar claim in 1915: "We do not insist upon 'free-verse' as the only method of writing poetry. We fight for it as for a principle of liberty."[6] In our own time, critics—especially those in the Marxist tradition—have often read literary forms as attempts to contain social clashes and contradictions.[7]

2   *Forms differ*. One of the great achievements of literary formalism has been the development of rich vocabularies and highly refined skills for differentiating among forms. Starting with ancient studies of prosody, theorists of poetic form around the world have debated the most precise terms for distinct patterns of rhyme and meter, and over the past hundred years theorists of narrative have developed a careful language for describing formal differences among stories, including frequency, duration, focalization, description, and suspense.[8]

3   *Various forms overlap and intersect*. Surprisingly, perhaps, schools of thought as profoundly different from one another as the New Criticism and intersectional analysis have developed methods for analyzing the operation of several distinct forms operating at once. The New Critics, who introduced the close reading method that dominated English departments in the middle decades of the twentieth century, deliberately traced the intricacies of overlapping literary patterns operating on different scales, as large as genre and as small as syntax. Intersectional analysis, which emerged in the social sciences and cultural studies in the late 1980s, focused our attention on how different social hierarchies overlap, sometimes powerfully reinforcing one another—how for example race and class and gender work together to keep many African-American women in a discouraging cycle of poverty.[9]

4   *Forms travel*. Critics have pointed to two important ways that forms move. First, a range of recent literary theorists, including Wai-Chee

Dimock, Frances Ferguson, and Franco Moretti, have noted that certain literary forms—epic, free indirect discourse, rhythm, plot—can survive across cultures and time periods, sometimes enduring through vast distances of time and space.[10] Something similar is true, though less often acknowledged, for social forms. Michel Foucault draws our attention to the daily timetable, for example, which begins by organizing life in the medieval monastery, but then gets picked up by the modern prison, factory, and school.[11]

The second way in which forms travel, critics suggest, is by moving back and forth across aesthetic and social materials. Structuralism, a school of thought that grew influential across the social sciences in the first half of the twentieth century, made the case that human communities were organized by certain universal structures. The most important of these were binary oppositions—masculine and feminine, light and dark—which imposed a recognizable order across social and aesthetic experiences, from domestic spaces to tragic dramas. Structuralism later came under fire for assuming that these patterns were natural and therefore inexorable, but one does not have to be a structuralist to agree that binary oppositions are a pervasive and portable form, capable of imposing their arrangements on both social life and literary texts. Some critics have also worried that aesthetic forms can exert political power by imposing their artificial order on political life. Frankfurt School theorist Walter Benjamin argued against an embrace of totality in aesthetics, because it he believed it led to an embrace of totality in political communities.[12] More recent critics have often followed forms in the opposite direction: showing, for example, how a social form like a racial hierarchy moves from the political world into a novel, where it structures aesthetic experience.[13]

5   *Forms do political work in particular historical contexts.* In recent years, scholars interested in reviving an interest in form (sometimes called the "new formalists") have sought to join formalism to historical approaches by showing how literary forms emerge out of political situations dominated by specific contests or debates. Since the late 1990s, literary critics like Susan Wolfson and Heather Dubrow have argued that literary forms reflect or respond to contemporary political conditions.[14] Forms matter, in these accounts, because they shape what it is possible to think, say, and do in a given context.

Forms: *containing, plural, overlapping, portable,* and *situated.* None of these ideas about form are themselves new, but putting them together will bring us to a new theory of form.

Affordances

How can form do so many different, even contradictory things? How can it be both political and aesthetic, both containing and plural, both situated and portable? To capture the complex operations of social and literary forms, I borrow the concept of *affordance* from design theory. *Affordance* is a term used to describe the potential uses or actions latent in materials and designs.[15] Glass affords transparency and brittleness. Steel affords strength, smoothness, hardness, and durability. Cotton affords fluffiness, but also breathable cloth when it is spun into yarn and thread. Specific designs, which organize these materials, then lay claim to their own range of affordances. A fork affords stabbing and scooping. A doorknob affords not only hardness and durability, but also turning, pushing, and pulling. Designed things may also have unexpected affordances generated by imaginative users: we may hang signs or clothes on a doorknob, for example, or use a fork to pry open a lid, and so expand the intended affordances of an object.

Let's now use affordances to think about form. The advantage of this perspective is that it allows us to grasp both the specificity and the generality of forms—both the particular constraints and possibilities that different forms afford, and the fact that those patterns and arrangements carry their affordances with them as they move across time and space. What is a walled enclosure or a rhyming couplet *capable* of doing? Each shape or pattern, social or literary, lays claim to a limited range of potentialities. Enclosures afford containment and security, inclusion as well as exclusion. Rhyme affords repetition, anticipation, and memorization. Networks afford connection and circulation, and narratives afford the connection of events over time. The sonnet, brief and condensed, best affords a single idea or experience, "a moment's monument,"[16] while the triple-decker novel affords elaborate processes of character development in multiplot social contexts. Forms are limiting and containing, yes, but in crucially different ways. Each form can only do so much.

To be sure, a specific form can be put to use in unexpected ways that expand our general sense of that form's affordances. Rather than asking what artists intend or even what forms *do,* we can ask instead what potentialities lie latent—though not always obvious—in aesthetic and social arrangements. An imaginative user, such as William Butler Yeats, deliberately pushes at the limits of formal constraints in "Leda and the Swan," a sonnet that captures the single moment that launches the epic story of the Trojan War—at once gesturing to the sweep of epic while remaining powerfully constrained by the sonnet's compact form.

Although each form lays claim to different affordances, all forms do share one affordance. Precisely because they are abstract organizing principles, shapes and patterns are iterable—portable. They can be picked up and moved to new contexts. A school borrows the idea of spectators in rows from ancient theater. A novelist takes from epic poetry the narrative structure of the quest. Forms also afford movement across varied materials. A rhythm can impose its powerful order on laboring bodies as well as odes. Binary oppositions can structure gendered workspaces as well as creation myths. While its meanings and values may change, the pattern or shape itself can remain surprisingly stable across contexts. But as they move, forms bring their limited range of affordances with them. No matter how different their historical and cultural circumstances, that is, bounded enclosures will always exclude, and rhyme will always repeat.

If forms lay claim to a limited range of potentialities and constraints, if they afford the same limited range of actions wherever they travel, and if they are the stuff of politics, then attending to the affordances of form opens up *a generalizable understanding of political power*. A panoptic arrangement of space, wherever it takes shape, will always afford a certain kind of disciplinary power; a hierarchy will always afford inequality.

But specific contexts also matter. In any given circumstance, no form operates in isolation. The idea of affordances is valuable for understanding the aesthetic object as imposing its order among a vast array of designed things, from prison cells to doorknobs. Literary form does not operate outside of the social but works among many organizing principles, all circulating in a world jam-packed with other arrangements. Each constraint will encounter many other, different organizing principles, and its power to impose order will itself be constrained, and at times unsettled, by other forms. Rhyme and narrative may structure the same text; the gender binary and the bureaucratic hierarchy may coincide in a single workplace. Which will organize the other? It is not always predictable. New encounters may activate latent affordances or foreclose otherwise dominant ones. Forms will often fail to impose their order when they run up against other forms that disrupt their logic and frustrate their organizing ends, producing aleatory and sometimes contradictory effects. We can understand forms as abstract and portable organizing principles, then, but we also need to attend to the specificity of particular historical situations to understand the range of ways in which forms overlap and collide.

In many cases, when forms meet, their collision produces unexpected consequences, results that cannot always be traced back to deliberate intentions or dominant ideologies. In a brief but familiar example, most women in academia experience a powerful tension between the biological "clock"—the years when the female body is capable of biological reproduction—and the tenure clock—the university's timetable for evaluating probationary faculty. This is one reason why a disproportionately high number of women opt for academic jobs as adjuncts and part-timers.[17] Since the tenure system predates the entry of women in any substantial numbers into the academy, these consequences do not flow from any particular patriarchal intention or ideology other than the assumption of an uninterrupted adult life.[18] In other words, this clash of temporal forms does not result from an intention to keep women in their places; it is an unplanned collision between two temporal forms, one biological and the other institutional.

Even a prison cell, the grimmest of social forms, does not enforce its simple, single order in isolation. The cell itself is a straightforward enough form: it encloses bodies within surrounding walls. But the prison always activates other forms as well: prisoners are subjected to temporal patterns, including enforced daily rhythms of food, sleep, and exercise; educational trajectories; and the length of the prison term itself. They take part in networks that operate not only within a given prison, but also reach outside the confines of prison walls, including illegal smuggling rings, gangs, and correspondence networks. The latter—from Amnesty International to personal notes to the "Letter from Birmingham Jail"—have long been crucial forms in prisoners' lives. And at the same time as prisoners are contained in cells, patterned in time, and linked to various networks, they are also subjected to numerous painful hierarchies, ranked according to the status of their crimes and their gender and sexual identities. As these forms overlap, some may disrupt the prison cell's containing power. The enclosure of the cell itself does not readily afford expansion or breakdown, but the temporal form of the prison sentence affords shortening or lengthening. And one surprisingly literary form has occasionally cut short the time of a prison term: a story of remorse or redemption can sometimes prompt a pardon.[19] Thus the arc of a narrative can in its own way pry open a cell's enclosing walls.

This analysis of forms—constraining in different ways, bringing their affordances with them as they cross contexts, and colliding to sometimes unpredictable effect—points to a new understanding of how power works. And yet, one might object, if so many things count as forms, from sonnets to prison cells to tenure clocks, then the category is just too capacious. What in this account is *not* form? Is there any way outside or beyond form? My own answer is yes—there are many events and experiences that do not count as forms—and we could certainly pay close attention to these: fissures and interstices, vagueness and indeterminacy, boundary-crossing and dissolution. But I want to make the case here that these formless or antiformal experiences have actually drawn *too much* attention from literary and cultural critics in the past few decades.

That is, the field has been so concerned with breaking forms apart that we have neglected to analyze the major work that forms do in our world. We have tended to assume that political forms are powerful, all-encompassing, and usually simple in themselves: a sexist or racist regime, for example, splits the world into a crude and comprehensive binary, its stark simplicity— black and white, masculine and feminine—contributing to the regime's painful power. We have therefore learned to look for places where the binary breaks down or dissolves, generating possibilities that turn the form into something more ambiguous and ill-defined—formless. Scholars in recent years have written a great deal about indeterminate spaces and identities, employing such key terms as liminality, borders, migration, hybridity, and passing.[20] This work has been compelling and politically important, without any doubt, and it will surely continue to be productive to analyze formal failures, incompletion, and indefinability. But while it may be possible to rid ourselves of particular unjust totalities or binaries, it is impossible to imagine a society altogether free of organizing principles. And too strong an emphasis on forms' dissolution has prevented us from attending to the complex ways that power operates in a world dense with functioning forms.

Perhaps this account of form still seems too abstract, too divorced from material conditions and the ways that power operates on and through embodied experience. A continued focus on affordances will help us here. The term *affordance* crosses back and forth between materiality and design. It certainly helps us to understand the capacities and limitations of materials. Wood affords hard, durable structures. It does not afford fluid streams or spongy softness. A wire affords connection and transmission, and chocolate affords structured shapes as well as a certain gooey viscosity. With affordances, then, we can begin to grasp the constraints on form that are imposed by materiality itself. One cannot make a poem out of soup or a panopticon out of wool. In this sense, form and materiality are inextricable, and materiality is determinant.

But patterns and arrangements also shape matter, imposing order on stone and flesh, sounds and spaces. Constraint moves in both directions.

Things take forms, and forms organize things. The prison cell cannot do its work without the hard materiality of metal or stone, but it also operates as an iterable way of organizing experience, a model of enclosure that can and does travel across many contexts. It is both a thing and a form. Henry S. Turner suggests that we can discover forms from two opposite starting-points: we can begin with the immaterial, abstract organizing principles that shape material realities, or we can begin with the concrete, particular material thing and abstract from it to general, iterable patterns and shapes.[21] From either perspective, forms travel across time and space in and through situated material objects.[22]

The relationship between materiality and form has long been of interest in literary studies. Critics have often assumed that the materiality of a text's content lends itself to certain literary forms: patterns of labor or rhythms of the body yielding certain repetitions in poetry, for example. In one recent essay, Stephanie Markovits argues that nineteenth-century literary writers in different genres often chose to write about diamonds because these objects are suited both to the "containment of lyric" thanks to their perfectly chiseled shapes, and to the motion of narrative, thanks to their extraordinary durability over time.[23] Or to put this in terms of affordances, the materiality of diamonds affords specific experiences of time, including stillness and durability, which the critic then reads as shaping the literary forms that incorporate them. There is a rich suggestiveness in this kind of analysis, but it is important to note that the materials described or evoked by literary texts do not determine their forms in the same way that stone determines durability. Literature is not made of the material world it describes or invokes but of language, which lays claims to its own forms—syntactical, narrative, rhythmic, rhetorical—and its own materiality—the spoken word, the printed page. And indeed, each of these forms and materials lays claim to its own affordances—its own range of capabilities. Every literary form thus generates its own, separate logic. The most common literary formalist reading method involves binding literary forms to their contents, seeking out the ways that each reflects the other, as Markovits does with diamonds. But a typical novel or poem will touch on so many different objects—diamonds and hair, chocolate and the ocean—that it could not possibly adjust its own forms to every material it incorporates. Thus a reading practice that follows the affordances of both literary forms and material objects imagines these as mutually shaping potentialities, but does not fold one into the other, as if the materiality of the extratextual world were the ultimate determinant.

Affordances point us both to what all forms are capable of—to the range of uses each could be put to, even if no one has yet taken advantage of those possibilities—and also to their limits, the restrictions intrinsic to particular materials and organizing principles. Ballot boxes, biological clocks, and lyric poems all take organizing forms. Each of these forms can be repeated elsewhere, and each carries with it a certain limited range of affordances as it travels. But a form does its work only in contexts where other political and aesthetic forms also are operating. A variety of forms are in motion around us, constraining materials in a range of ways and imposing their order in situated contexts where they constantly overlap other forms. Form emerges from this perspective as transhistorical, portable, and abstract, on the one hand, and material, situated, and political, on the other.

Rethinking Formalisms

With affordances in mind, we can see how forms can be at once containing, plural, overlapping, portable, and situated. But every major formalist tradition has limited its definition of form in a way that has missed or excluded one or more of these affordances. For example, we have long known that the New Critics missed something important when they understood literary forms as entirely separate from a situated and material social world. They overlooked the ways in which formal constraints might matter politically; they did not care that forms took shape in specific historical circumstances. But the New Criticism was also interested in some of the affordances of form that have been missing from other theories. In literary and cultural studies, we have a much less refined vocabulary for the differences between social forms than we have for aesthetic ones. Certainly we know that racial hierarchies and walled enclosures organize social groups in different ways, but we have not developed a language for those differences. The New Criticism, with its interest in the differences between forms, can actually point the way forward here, inviting us to develop a richer and more precise terminology for the work of social forms. The New Critics also showed that it is difficult—if not impossible—to exhaust the dense interweaving of formal elements in a short lyric poem. And if it is a challenge to identify and analyze the shaping elements of a single sonnet, then it is certainly impossible to capture the patterns constitutive of an entire society with a handful of categories, such as race, class, gender, nationality, sexuality, and disability. Thus the New Critics' focus on the extraordinary plurality of overlapping forms could prompt us to expand the logic of intersectional analysis dramatically, continuing to take the structures of race, class, and gender extremely seriously, but tracking the encounters of these with many other kinds of forms, from enclosures to networks to narrative resolutions.

The politically minded "new formalisms" that have emerged in literary studies recently have also overlooked one of form's crucial affordances. These critics have insisted on situating literary forms in particular political contexts. Mostly, they have followed one of two paths. Some have read literary forms as legible reflections of social structures. Herbert F. Tucker, for example, reads the meter of Elizabeth Barrett Browning's poem, "The Cry of the Children," as revealing the uncomfortable disjuncture between the embodied time of human life and the jolting experience of factory labor. Barrett Browning's "stop-and-start versification mimics the strain and clatter of steam-driven machinery."[24] A second group casts literary form less as a reflection of a specific social context than as a deliberate *intervention*. Susan Wolfson argues, for example, that the Romantic poets were hardly unknowing purveyors of a "romantic ideology" that masked political struggle in unified "organic forms," as has often been charged: instead, she argues, they were fully aware of the constructedness of literary unities and purposefully deployed formal strategies to investigate problems of ideology, subjectivity, and social conditions.[25] Both groups of new formalists read literary form as epiphenomenal, growing out of specific social conditions that it mimics or opposes. Thus, neither camp takes account of one of forms' affordances: the capacity to endure across time and space. From the gender binary to rhyme and from prison cells to narrative prose, aesthetic and social forms outlive the specific conditions that gave birth to them: the scroll does not altogether disappear with the codex but in fact reemerges with surprising pervasiveness in the age of the Internet; the quest structure of ancient epic remains available to the contemporary novelist. None of these forms spring up anew in response to particular social facts but instead hang around, available for reuse. In this sense, forms are not outgrowths of social conditions; they do not belong to certain times and places.

And indeed, as sociologist Marc Schneiberg argues, it is precisely the endurance of "holdover" forms that can make a society promisingly plural, scattered with alternative ways of organizing resources and goods that could at any moment give rise to more hopeful arrangements. For example, in the 1950s when large, private, for-profit corporations started to dominate the US economic landscape, electricity—crucial to the whole economy— was delivered in significant quantities by local, state-owned enterprises and cooperatives. Every day, when corporate moguls turned on the lights, they remobilized the form of cooperative ownership. The story of US capitalism is therefore not only a deep-rooted dialectical struggle between capital and labor, but also "a path littered with elements or fragments of more or less developed systems of alternatives—a path ripe for exploitation, institutional revitalization and assembly, and containing within it structural possibilities for alternatives."[26] What would enrich and deepen the "new formalism," then, is attention to the *longues durées* of different forms, their portability across time and space.

Genre theory, too, could benefit from more attention to the portability of forms. For many critics, the terms *form* and *genre* are synonymous or near-synonymous.[27] But this book argues that they can be differentiated precisely by the different ways in which they traverse time and space. Genre involves acts of classifying texts. An ensemble of characteristics, including styles, themes, and marketing conventions, allows both producers and audiences to group texts into certain kinds. Innovations can alter those expectations: an experimental epic might invite readers to expand their sense of the genre's themes, while the introduction of print extends and transforms a folktale's audience. Thus any attempt to recognize a work's genre is a historically specific and interpretive act: one might not be able to tell the difference between a traditional folktale and a story recently composed for children or to recognize a satire from a distant historical moment.[28]

Forms, defined as patternings, shapes, and arrangements, have a different relation to context: they can organize both social and literary objects, and they can remain stable over time. One has to agree to read for shapes and patterns, of course, and this is itself a conventional approach. But as Frances Ferguson argues, once we recognize the organizing principles of different literary forms—such as syntax, free indirect speech, and the sonnet—they are themselves no longer matters of interpretive activity or debate: "Even if you failed to notice that the sonnet that Romeo and Juliet speak between them was a sonnet the first time you read Shakespeare's play, you would be able to recognize it as such from the moment that someone pointed it out to you. . . . It could be regularly found, pointed out, or returned to, and the sense of its availability would not rest on agreements about its meaning."[29] Similarly, it is difficult not to agree on the shape of the classroom or the schedule of the prisoner's day, the hierarchy of a bureaucratic organization or the structure of a kinship system. There is certainly some abstraction entailed here, but once we have agreed to look for principles of organization, we will probably not spend much time disputing the idea that racial apartheid organizes social life into a hierarchical binary, or that nation-states enforce territorial boundaries. More stable than genre, configurations and arrangements organize materials in distinct and iterable ways no matter what their context or audience. Forms thus migrate across contexts in a way that genres cannot. They also work on different scales, as small as punctuation marks and as vast as multiplot narratives or national boundaries. Genres, then, can be defined as customary constellations of elements into historically recognizable groupings of artistic objects, bringing together forms with themes, styles, and situations of reception, while forms are organizations or arrangements that afford repetition and portability across materials and contexts.

So far, then, we have seen that the New Criticism missed the political power and the situatedness of constraining forms, intersectional analysis has overlooked the extraordinary plurality of forms at work in social situations, and the new formalists and genre theorists have too often neglected the capacity of forms to endure across time and space. Let us think finally about what has been missing from the Marxist tradition, the most complex and robust school of formalist thinking in literary and cultural studies.

Many Marxist thinkers, from Georg Lukács and Pierre Macherey to Fredric Jameson and Franco Moretti, have cast literary form as an ideological artifice, a neat structuring of representation that soothes us into a false sense of order, preventing us from coming to terms with a reality that always exceeds form. Hayden White, for example, argues that narrative form teaches people to live in "an unreal but meaningful relation to the social formations in which they are indentured to live out their lives and realize their destinies as social subjects."[30] White contrasts reality—which he calls "social formations"—with the unreal coherence of narrative form. But if we understand social formations—such as the gender binary and the prison timetable—as themselves organizing forms, then we can see that White's real-unreal distinction does not hold. Literary forms and social formations are equally real in their capacity to organize materials, and equally *un*real in being artificial, contingent constraints. Instead of seeking to reveal the reality suppressed by literary forms, we can understand sociopolitical life as itself composed of a plurality of different forms, from narrative to marriage and from bureaucracy to racism.

The Marxist emphasis on aesthetic form as epiphenomenal—as secondary—has some distorting effects. First, it prevents us from understanding politics as a matter of form, and second, it assumes that one kind of form—the political—is always the root or ground of the other—the aesthetic. Let me offer an example of what it would mean to read literary forms not as epiphenomenal responses to social realities but as forms encountering other forms.

The gender binary is a form that can impose its order on the home, the laboratory, the prison, dress, and many other facts of social life. Now let's consider an encounter between the gender binary and a narrative, Thomas Hughes's best-selling novel *Tom Brown's Schooldays* (1857). The narrative begins by establishing a fiercely masculine world: the all-boy Rugby School, which is a training-ground for Christian colonial power.[31] Tom, the protagonist, undergoes a series of adventures: a race, a football match, a fight with bullies. In every case, he succeeds by standing firm, and as a result the first half of the novel becomes remarkably repetitive, testing the hero in the same way over and over again. He meets each challenge, like "all real boys," by refusing to give ground.[32] But the narrative form of *Tom Brown's Schooldays* takes an odd turn halfway through. It becomes more narratively interesting, and also, strangely, suddenly feminine. The wise headmaster Thomas Arnold decides that Tom and his friends must become more mature. He assigns Tom a new boy to look after, "a slight pale boy, with large blue eyes and light fair hair, who seemed ready to shrink through the floor . . . would be afraid of wet feet, and always getting laughed at, and called Molly, or Jenny, or some derogatory feminine nickname" (217–18). Saddled with responsibility for another, Tom becomes anxious and learns to submit to God. He is so careful of the younger boy's welfare that he becomes feminine himself, "like a hen with one chick" (231). If the hero is victorious in the first half because he manfully withstands a series of assaults, the second half turns him into a pliable, recognizably feminine character: yielding, submissive, and open to alterity. The narrative suddenly becomes a *Bildungsroman*, a novel of development, filled with lessons learned and changes in the protagonist's outlook and values.

What is going on here? One could say that Thomas Hughes wanted a narratively rich resource like the *Bildungsroman* to transform his repetitive, static story of boyish adventures into a more satisfying arc. The gender binary would have come in handy for this purpose, since the opposite of the brave, unyielding masculine character was the anxious, feminine one, open to change in precisely the way required for *Bildung*. According to this account, Hughes would have incorporated femininity into the text as an aftereffect of his narrative desires. Conversely, we could argue that because he valued a submissive Christianity, Hughes gravitated to the yielding character of the *Bildungsroman*, tractable in a way that fell on the feminine side of the gender binary, and adopted the narrative form of the pliable character as an aftereffect of his religious convictions. We don't know which came first. What we do know is that both the literary and the social form—*Bildung* and the gender binary—preexist the text in question. Both move from other sites into this text, carrying their own ways of organizing experience with them. While we might speculate about which form is primary, or about Hughes's own motivations, the text itself shows us something interesting about what happens when narrative form encounters the gender binary and the two begin to operate together. In fact, a predictable, generalizable hypothesis about form unfolds from this collision, regardless of the author's intentions or the origins of either form. As long as pliability—the susceptibility to development—falls on the feminine side of the gender binary, the *Bildungsroman* will have to be a feminine genre, even when its protagonists are male.

Most Marxist formalist critics would approach the narrative form of *Tom Brown's Schooldays* as the working out of an ideological position or as an "abstract of social relationships."[33] Most politically minded new formalists would read the text as a response to the immediate social world around it. The formalism that emerges here is different: I read narrative and gender as two distinct forms, each striving to impose its own order, both traveling from other places to the text in question, and neither automatically prior or dominant. One might say that I am flipping White's terms upside down: rather than hunting for the buried *content of the form*, I propose here to track *the forms of the content*, the many organizing principles that encounter one another inside as well as outside of the literary text. Instead of assuming that social forms are the grounds or causes of literary forms, and instead of imagining that a literary text has *a* form, this book asks two unfamiliar questions: what does each form afford, and what happens when forms meet?

From Causation to Collision

The first major goal of this book is to show that forms are everywhere structuring and patterning experience, and that this carries serious implications for understanding political communities. This starting-point entails a *Gestalt* shift for literary studies. It calls for a new account of politics and of the relations between politics and literature. In theory, political forms impose their order on our lives, putting us in our places. But in practice, we encounter so many forms that even in the most ordinary daily experience they add up to a complex environment composed of multiple and conflicting modes of organization—forms arranging and containing us, yes, but also competing and colliding and rerouting one another. I will make the case here that no form, however seemingly powerful, causes, dominates, or organizes all others. This means that literary forms can lay claim to an efficacy of their own. They do not simply reflect or contain prior political realities. As different forms struggle to impose their order on our experience, working at different scales of our experience, aesthetic and political forms emerge as comparable patterns that operate on a common plane. I will show in this book that aesthetic and political forms may be nested inside one another, and that each is capable of disturbing the other's organizing power.

This is not to say, however, that the world of forms is a happy free-for-all. The second major goal of the book is to think about the ways that, together, the multiple forms of the world come into conflict and disorganize experience in ways that call for unconventional political strategies. Critics and theorists have tended to assume that powerful social institutions integrate and homogenize experience; they put into practice coherent ideologies that organize and constrain experience. This book puts an emphasis on social *dis*organization, exploring the many ways in which multiple forms of order, sometimes the results of the same powerful ideological formation, may unsettle one another. And yet, disorganization is not always better than order, and we will see how competing forms can sometimes produce pain and injustice as troubling as any consolidation of power.

Approaching form in this pluralizing way to include both social and aesthetic forms, and arguing that no single form dominates or organizes all of the others, moves us away from one of the deepest political convictions in the field: that ultimately, it is deep structural forces such as capitalism, nationalism, and racism that are the truly powerful shapers of our lives. Critics are not wrong to hold on to such explanations: our lives are certainly organized by powerful structuring principles, and it would be a grave mistake to overlook them. But at the same time I would argue that an exclusive focus on ultimate causality has not necessarily benefited leftist politics. It has distracted us from thinking strategically about how best to deploy multiple forms for political ends.

My work has been influenced here by Brazilian legal theorist and politician Roberto Mangabeira Unger, who makes the case that too strong an analytic emphasis on deep structures is disabling for radical politics. It limits our attention and our targets to a small number of the most intractable factors, factors so difficult to unsettle that most people abandon the attempt altogether. What if we were to see social life instead as composed of "loosely and unevenly collected" arrangements, "a makeshift, pasted-together" order rather than a coherent system that can be traced to back to a single cause? Unger argues that such an approach would draw attention to the artificiality and contingency of social arrangements and so open up a new set of opportunities for real change by way of feasible rearrangements.[34] Like Unger, Jacques Rancière too draws attention to the radical potential that lies in acts of rearrangement.[35]

The formalism I propose here draws from Unger and Rancière to shift attention away from deep causes to a recognition of the many different shapes and patterns that constitute political, cultural, and social experience.

I draw attention in particular to the ways that different arrangements can collide to strange effect, with minor forms sometimes disrupting or rerouting major ones. In a context of many overlapping forms, the most significant challenge for political actors is the fact that complicating any single form one might advocate are multiple organizing principles always already at work, often clashing and interrupting and rerouting one another. These overlaps open up unfamiliar opportunities for political action and show why the most effective route to social change might not be traditional ideology critique, which aims to expose the false and seductive discourses and cultural practices that prevent us from recognizing human unfreedom, that universalize and naturalize the oppressive social structures that stand in the way of emancipation. If forms always contain and confine, and if it is impossible to imagine societies without forms, then the most strategic political action will not come from revealing or exposing illusion, but rather from a careful, nuanced understanding of the many different and often disconnected arrangements that govern social experience.

Carolyn Lesjak has recently argued against the version of formalism I articulate here, because she sees it as a recipe for political quietism.[36] But in fact the primary goal of this formalism is radical social change. All politics, including revolutionary political action, will succeed only if it is canny about deploying multiple forms. Revolutions must mobilize certain arrangements, certain organized forms of resistance—the takeover of the public square, the strike, the boycott, the coalition. And any redistribution of the world's wealth, which I strongly favor, must follow some kind of organizing principle. Marx's classic slogan, "From each according to one's ability; to each according to one's need," is a careful balancing of inputs and outputs, a structural parallelism that might well govern the organization of energies and distributions in a radical and just new order. Which forms do we wish to see governing social life, then, and which forms of protest or resistance actually succeed at dismantling unjust, entrenched arrangements?

My focus on the movement and assembly of forms prompts me to rely on a kind of event I call the "collision"—the strange encounter between two or more forms that sometimes reroutes intention and ideology. I offer many examples of such collisions, in part to unsettle the power of another explanatory form in literary and cultural studies: the dialectic. Literary and cultural studies has of course long been influenced by Marx's dialectical materialism, and the structuralists, by identifying binary oppositions as a basic structure of social life, broadened dialectical thinking beyond Marxism within the field. Indeed, since the structuralist moment, it has been easy to spot dialectical structures at work everywhere, their dynamic oppositional energies providing the animating force behind historical change: "the dialectic of good and evil, but also that of subject and object; the dialectic of rich and poor and also that of male and female or black and white; the dialectic of Right and Left, but also of poetry and prose, high culture and mass culture, science and ideology, materialism and idealism, harmony and counterpoint, color and line, self and other, and so on. . . ."[37] But while it is no doubt true that much painful historical experience has emerged out of deep social contradictions, I argue in this book that the binary opposition is just one of a number of powerfully organizing forms, and that many outcomes follow from other forms, as well as from more mundane, more minor, and more contingent formal encounters, where different forms are not necessarily related, opposed, or deeply expressive, but simply happen to cross paths at a particular site. Suspending the usual models of causality thus produces new insight into the work of forms, both social and aesthetic.

Narrative

The form that best captures the experience of colliding forms is narrative. It is by no means the only form I will use or examine in this book, but it is a particularly helpful one for the analysis of forms at work. What narrative form affords is a careful attention to the ways in which forms come together, and to what happens when and after they meet. Narratives are especially appealing for a skeptical formalist reader because they tend to present causality metonymically, through sequences of events, rather than by positing some originary cause. They afford "conjoining," to use David Hume's words, rather than "necessary connexion."[38] Narratives are valuable heuristic forms, then, because they can set in motion multiple social forms and track them as they cooperate, come into conflict, and overlap, without positing an ultimate cause.

Since social forms can move across contexts, taking their range of affordances with them, they can reveal their potentialities in fiction as well as nonfiction. We saw gender at work in *Tom Brown's Schooldays*. As a formalist reader, I put my stress not on the fact that gender is a social fact being conveyed or registered by the literary text, but that it is a binary form that *carries its affordances with it into the novel*. Bruno Latour mentions in passing that fiction writers often do better than sociologists at capturing social relations because they are free to experiment, offering "a vast playground to rehearse accounts of what makes us act."[39] Like Latour, I treat fictional narratives as productive thought experiments that allow us to imagine the subtle unfolding activity of multiple social forms.

I

My interest in the collision and unfolding of forms prompts me to pay an unusually serious kind of attention to plot. Not all plots are equally interesting, and I focus most of my attention here on a few extraordinary ones. Sophocles's *Antigone*, Charles Dickens's *Bleak House*, and David Simon's *The Wire* present the movement of forms in exceptionally shrewd and unconventional ways that expand a conventional sense of how social worlds work. I spend time in this book describing narrative unfolding in each of these works.

This may seem like a surprising approach for a formalist reader. Following the plot has rarely been considered a sophisticated or valuable interpretive practice by any literary school, and describing the movement of narrative events might risk what New Critic Cleanth Brooks most strongly decried as the "heresy of paraphrase." For Brooks, literary objects are unlike other texts because they are organized by a "principle of unity" that ultimately harmonizes unlike and sometimes conflicting elements—rhythms, images, connotations—into a balanced whole. The problem with paraphrase, in his view, is that simple statements or propositions about the world always fail to capture the poem's subtle interactions among various parts.[40] In the next chapter of this book, I will subject Brooks's insistence on unity to critique. But in the meanwhile, I want to suggest that my enthusiastic embrace of plot paraphrase does take up his New Critical project in one specific way: plot is difficult to reduce to a single message or statement, and as a form it too mobilizes the subtle interrelations of multiple elements. Unlike a taxonomic chart that organizes forms into separate categories, narrative privileges the interaction of forms over time. Paraphrasing plotted narrative thus yields an irreducible complexity that is ironically consonant with the aims and values of the New Critics.

To return to *Jane Eyre*, for example, we can read the section that deals with Lowood School as a thoughtful investigation of how disciplinary forms can unfold in intricate interrelation, their patterning of experience capable of crossing back and forth between fiction and the social world. Sometimes the school's forms work perfectly together: a timed bell signals a shift in spatial order; a student who obediently follows both spatial and temporal arrangements successfully climbs the ranks. But not always: an unjust punishment by the top of the school's patriarchal hierarchy gives rise to a dissident, nonpatriarchal network as Miss Temple, Helen Burns, and Jane Eyre come together to create a new social form, a triadic "counter-family."[41] In the sheltered privacy of Miss Temple's room, other forms then come into play. Miss Temple invites Jane to defend herself against the accusations of Mr Brocklehurst according to the rules set forth by courts of law. Jane gives her own testimony "coherently" and in a "restrained and simplified" manner that convinces her audience of her innocence and allows her to be publicly cleared (83). Thus a clandestine network of women, a closed room, the rules of the courtroom, and a newly organized and controlled kind of storytelling come together to resist Mr Brocklehurst's authority.

This interaction of forms also brings with it some strange side effects. It throws into an odd kind of disarray another form—the binary division between public and private—as the secret courtroom, which joins intimate storytelling with the adoption of impersonal, public rules, permits a public exoneration of Jane. The hierarchy of the school, too, becomes oddly double, emerging as both enabling and tyrannical, since Jane's exoneration gives her the confidence to climb Lowood's ladder, while at the same time refusing Mr Brocklehurst the power that is supposed to derive from his place at the top of the same ladder. Meanwhile, the model of the courtroom teaches Jane how to tell stories that work for her own ends—carefully arranged and simplified to win over audiences. Thus the plotted form of the narrative itself takes shape at the intersection of a number of other forms—a hierarchy, an enclosed space, a network, and a set of legal rules.

This is an example of a reading practice that does not fit any familiar formalism. But it draws from all of them.

Whole, Rhythm, Hierarchy, Network

Organizing this book are four major forms. These are by no means the only forms, but they are particularly common, pervasive—and also significant. Though we have not always called them forms, they are the political structures that have most concerned literary and cultural studies scholars: bounded *wholes*, from domestic walls to national boundaries; temporal *rhythms*, from the repetitions of industrial labor to the enduring patterns of institutions over time; powerful *hierarchies*, including gender, race, class, and bureaucracy; and *networks* that link people and objects, including multinational trade, terrorism, and transportation. All of these have resonant corollaries in literature and literary studies: the bounded whole has long been a model for lyric poetry and narrative closure; rhythmic tempos organize poetic meter and sometimes literary history itself; hierarchies organize literary texts' investments in certain values and characters over others; and networks link national cultures, writers, and characters.

Each chapter takes up one of these forms as it organizes literary works, social institutions, and our knowledge of both literature and the social—

that is, scholarly conversations in the field. For each of the major forms we will encounter in this book, I will ask four sets of questions:

1 What specific order does each form impose? The chapters that follow make the case that simply attending carefully to the affordances of each form produces some surprising new conclusions: for example, that what we call narrative closure does not in fact enclose, and that one of the most famous of the supposedly formalist New Critics paid not too much but too little attention to lyric form.

2 How has scholarly knowledge itself depended on certain organizing forms to establish its own claims, and how might a self-consciousness about scholarly forms shift the arguments that literary and cultural studies scholars make? I spend time here showing how some of the most determinedly antiformalist scholars have necessarily depended on organizing forms in their own arguments.

3 How should we understand the relationship between literary and political forms? Moving beyond the practice of reading aesthetic forms as indexes of social life, I consider ways in which literary and social forms come into contact and affect one another, without presuming that one is the ground or cause of the other.

4 Finally, what political strategies—what tactics for change—will work most effectively if what we are facing is not a single hegemonic system or dominant ideology but many forms, all trying to organize us at once? If politics operates through different kinds of forms—spatial containers, repetitions and durations over time, vertical arrangements of high and low, networks of interconnection—then resistance to one of these may not emancipate us from the others. It might even establish or reinforce the power of another form. The most significant and challenging claim of this book is that many, many forms are organizing us at all times. Where exactly, then, can we locate the best opportunities for social change in a world of overlapping forms? Can we set one form against another or introduce a new form that would reroute a racial hierarchy or disturb exclusionary boundaries? I argue that we need a fine-grained formalist reading practice to address the extraordinary density of forms that is a fact of our most ordinary daily experience.

A great variety of formal examples will make their appearances in this book: theme parks and management hierarchies, classical tragedies and well-wrought urns, literary history and gender theory. This wide-ranging array establishes the portability of the method, showing that this approach can productively cross sites and institutions, from medieval convents to modernist sculpture, from the early American postal system to postcolonial criticism. Though I will draw many examples from Victorian Britain because this is the field I know best, this is a project that necessarily carries us far from any given period of literary or cultural study.

A final chapter will offer a surprising, even counterintuitive, paradigm for bringing all four major forms together. HBO's remarkable recent television series, *The Wire* (2002–2008), conceptualizes social life as both structured and rendered radically unpredictable by large numbers of colliding social forms, including bounded wholes, rhythms, hierarchies, and networks. Dependent on a narrative logic that traces the effects of each formal encounter on the next, it refuses to posit a deep, prior, metaphysical model of causality to explain its world. By tracking vast numbers of social patterns as they meet, reroute, and disrupt one another, *The Wire* examines the world that results from a plurality of forms at work. I argue that this series could provide a new model for literary and cultural studies scholarship.

Intended to act as a methodological starting-point, this book proposes a way to understand the relations among forms—forms aesthetic and social, spatial and temporal, ancient and modern, major and minor, like and unlike, punitive and narrative, material and metrical. Its method of tracking shapes and arrangements is not confined to the literary text or to the aesthetic, but it does involve a kind of close reading, a careful attention to the forms that organize texts, bodies, and institutions. "Close but not deep," to borrow Heather Love's elegant formulation, this is a practice that seeks out pattern over meaning, the intricacy of relations over interpretive depth.[42] And yet, at the same time, this is also a method that builds on what literary critics have traditionally done best—reading for complex interrelationships and multiple, overlapping arrangements. I argue that it is time to *export* those practices, to take our traditional skills to new objects—the social structures and institutions that are among the most crucial sites of political efficacy. I seek to show that there is a great deal to be learned about power by observing different forms of order as they operate in the world. And I want to persuade those who are interested in politics to become formalists, so that we can begin to intervene in the conflicting formal logics that turn out to organize and disorganize our lives, constantly producing not only painful dispossessions but also surprising opportunities.

WHOLE

Totality. Unity. Containment. Wholeness. For many critics, these words are synonymous with form itself. To speak of *the* form of a work of art is to gesture to its unifying power, its capacity to hold together disparate parts. For Aristotle, the work of literature must be "whole and complete," coming to "resemble a living organism in all its unity." In 1818, Samuel Taylor Coleridge argued that the art work "holds in unity" the "variety of parts." In the twentieth century, both Marxists and New Critics understood form as a closed whole. This long tradition of conceiving literary form as unifying and containing persisted across multiple strands of literary criticism, from Peter Brooks's psychoanalytic reading of narrative form as "totalizing" to Fredric Jameson's Marxist analysis of the "synchronic unity of structurally contradictory or heterogeneous elements." It continues into our own time with Alex Woloch's new formalist reading of the novel as a "unified symbolic and structural system" and Eric Hayot's work on world literature, which invites us to compare the "diegetic totality" of literary works from around the world.[1]

The emphasis on artistic wholeness is in large part what brought both forms and formalist reading practices into disrepute in the 1970s and 1980s. Theorists advanced two major critiques. The first line of argument was that literary and aesthetic forms never actually achieve a bounded wholeness. Readers and writers, embodied and located in time and space, bring specific knowledge and experience to any aesthetic object, activating and reshaping its meanings in ways that shift over time and across cultures. Art cannot then have meaning outside of the social contexts in which it is circulated and consumed: interpretations change according to the material form of the text as book or oral performance, its actual and intended audiences, and contemporary debates, such as arguments about gender norms or changing definitions of art. There is simply no such thing as an aesthetic whole that can be separated from the social worlds of its creation and reception.[2]

The second and related critique is that the celebration of wholeness is pernicious on political grounds. Critics in the past three decades have worked hard to resist and unsettle social unities and totalities, celebrating instead difference and diversity. Take poststructuralist feminist Luce Irigaray, for example, who argues strenuously against "the discrimination and individualization of form." She decries this as the "phallomorphism" of the West, the "value granted to the only definable form . . . the *one* of form, of the individual, of the (male) sexual organ, of the proper name, of the proper meaning." While the masculine West understands the world through and as constraining singular form, she argues, women's sexuality offers an emancipatory alternative because it is diffuse and plural.[3] For Irigaray and many others, the trouble with form is precisely its embrace of unified wholeness: its willingness to impose boundaries, to imprison, to create inclusions and exclusions. The valuing of aesthetic unity implies a broader desire to regulate and control—to dominate the plurality and heterogeneity of experience.[4]

Theorists who are concerned about the political implications of unity and totality tend to be antiformalists: that is, they resist the containing power of form. But in the process they maintain the traditional formalist premise that forms totalize and unify. Indeed, I want to suggest here that formalist and antiformalist critics have shared a specific presumption about the politics of literary form that has endured and flourished, virtually unchanged, since the era of the New Critics: the assumption that literary forms can be easily mapped onto political communities—that there is an effective homology between the bounded wholeness of the lyric poem, for example, and the bounded wholeness of a nation. As Marc Redfield puts it, "The polished sides of the well-wrought urn mirror the providential order of the political itself."[5]

The two strands of critique I have been describing come together in the work of deconstruction. Jacques Derrida argued famously that no work of literature can ever achieve a closed unity, since each word takes on its identity in and through its relation to other traces or marks that are not in fact contained in any given object but unfold in the unending process he called *différance*. This matters a great deal, in Derrida's work, because the desire for bounded wholeness has grave political consequences. He painstakingly shows how the relation between inside and outside—between what properly belongs and what can be expelled or abjected—grounds the whole project of Western philosophy, and that this foundational struggle to distinguish the closed, essential inside from the unnecessary outside also generates the worst kinds of political injury.

Derrida's reading of the scapegoat in ancient Athens, for example, exposes the violent desire to impose clear boundaries as well as the inevitability of the city's failure to work as a closed system. After sacrificing the scapegoat, the city reconstitutes its unity, closes around the security of its inner courts, gives back to itself the word that links it with itself within the confines of the agora, by violently excluding from its territory the representative of an external threat or aggression. That representative represents the otherness of the evil that comes to affect or infect the inside by unpredictably breaking into it. Yet the representative of the outside is nonetheless *constituted*, regularly granted its place by the community, chosen, kept, fed, etc., in the very heart of the inside.[6]

Here as elsewhere, Derrida shows how there can be no belonging—no inside—without a "constitutive outside." The political costs of an enclosing wholeness are urgent. From ancient sacrifices to fascism and the anti-immigration policies that will concern Derrida in his work on hospitality, totalities depend for their own coherence on violent acts of expulsion and abjection.

Since this early moment of deconstruction, it has become commonplace for literary and cultural studies scholars to launch critiques of bounded wholes. Some scholars have continued Derrida's exploration of the constitutive outside—Judith Butler most prominently, drawing our attention to queerness as an abjected category that allows heteronormative political communities to operate, powerfully and punitively.[7] Other critics have celebrated resistance to imprisoning political enclosures and boundaries, including nation-states, domestic walls, prison cells, and bounded subjects.[8] Still others have drawn attention to the failures of artificial political boundaries to contain the complexity of social experience.[9]

Despite their differences, all of these scholars agree that the possibility of justice or emancipation lies in refusing the power of containing wholes, whether by deconstructing the opposition between inside and outside, by rupturing or resisting constraints, or by arguing that they have never successfully contained in the first place. Our preferred literary texts these days have not been well-wrought unities but texts that stage discontinuities and disruptions to resist containing form.[10] Even Susan Wolfson, perhaps the most influential of new formalist readers, argues that Romantic poets purposefully questioned and disrupted organic form, refusing mythical wholeness in favor of "fissures," "discontinuities," and "dissonances."[11] Thus the new formalist repeats the old formalist presumption that wholes are there to contain, while continuing the deconstructive tradition of celebrating resistance and rupture.

I strongly endorse the critical tradition that warns against the power of unities to imprison and expel. It is true that bounded containers have been among the most disturbing of all political forms, organizing the violence of fascism, apartheid, and the abjection of the queer, as well as the serious environmental and ethical consequences of limiting our understanding of political community to human subjects.[12] But I will contend here that deconstructive methods, while powerful, are not the only effective responses to these models of unified wholeness.

This chapter takes its lead from the long traditions of thought that seek to link aesthetic, philosophical, and political domains by way of the bounded whole. I will explore the claim that aesthetic objects share the formal property of unity with exclusive political communities and grounding philosophical concepts, but along the way, I will pose a question that is not familiar in this tradition, a question about the affordances of bounded wholes. Most critics have attended to one crucial set of affordances, focusing their attention on the fact that totalities exclude and imprison. In the process, they have not stopped to ask whether they might lay claim to other, more progressive affordances as well. Paying attention to the full range of affordances of literary and political wholes will challenge the assumption that all totalities must be disrupted or broken. In fact, I will argue, we cannot do without bounded wholes: their power to hold things together is what makes some of the most valuable kinds of political action possible at all.

I begin by focusing on two influential literary scholars—Cleanth Brooks and Mary Poovey—selected here to represent two influential schools of thought in literary studies, New Criticism and New Historicism. Though it would be reductive to group many subtly different thinkers together, Brooks effectively stands for most of the New Critics in one respect: his presumption that good poetry achieves a taut unity out of complex materials. The New Critics almost universally shared this understanding of poetry: we might think of William Wimsatt's "total structure," Ronald S. Crane's "concrete whole," and William Empson's "the thing as a whole."[13] Even René Wellek and Austin Warren, who insisted on a more historical approach to literary texts than many of the New Critics, differentiated poetry from ordinary language on the grounds that "every work of art imposes an order, an organization, a unity on materials."[14] Brooks is the thinker who most explicitly and famously associates literary form with a bounded container, returning again and again to the well-wrought urn, a clear shape with spatial contours that distinguish inside from outside.

Poovey is a fair representative of historicists who came to prominence in the 1980s and 1990s in her critique of this New Critical presumption. Poovey and others forcefully refused to read literary texts as unified and autonomous, isolated from social experience. Stephen Greenblatt, one of the most influential of this school, drew insights and models from anthropology to argue that literary texts were embedded in historically specific social worlds, shaped by particular cultural codes and conditions and able to act on them in turn.[15] Poovey goes even farther than most of her contemporaries in rejecting canonical art works altogether, instead seeking to understand broad historical discourses through distinctly nonaesthetic objects like double-entry bookkeeping. Perhaps the field's staunchest antiformalist, she is explicit in her rejection of New Critical approaches to reading on political grounds.

Brooks and Poovey thus stand not only for influential schools of thought, but also for opposite ends of the formalist spectrum. And their approaches to form reflect their opposing political and social values. Brooks uses the figure of enclosed wholeness to celebrate unity in art and in life, while Poovey is committed to resisting the imposition of containing forms on social experience. So far, predictable enough. But as we will see, what is surprising is that Brooks, despite himself, undermines his own figure for poetic form: the well-wrought urn is not in the end a particularly fitting figure for the lyric poem. He opens up a serious question about the homology between literary form and containing unity that is at the heart of his own aesthetic-political project. I will make the case that Poovey, also despite herself, actually points us to a more rigorous formalist analysis of containing wholes, attentive to differences and interactions among forms, than does Brooks.

Growing out of my reading of Poovey is my claim that literary and cultural studies scholars—even those most suspicious of political boundaries—rely on bounded wholes in our own scholarly work as much or more than we resist and challenge them. This is because these forms afford certain kinds of valuable thinking. Following in a Platonic tradition, I will connect wholeness to the very possibility of conceptualization. Scholars routinely draw boundaries around their objects of analysis, delimiting concepts, deciding what to include and what to exclude, with the result that many progressively minded scholars, even those most resistant to formal totalities, are in fact dependent on the very shapes they critique. Bounded wholes enable certain kinds of political possibilities that we might choose to embrace, even while we remain wary of their oppressions and constraints. I suggest here that we will want to draw on the containing and unifying power of concepts, despite their dangers, in the interests of genuinely emancipatory and transformative political work.

How might that work look? My final intervention here is to offer a newly strategic solution to the power of unifying containers. If we imagine that our only option is to critique, shatter, or resist them, we reinforce the idea that bounded wholes are always and necessarily dangerous and successful, on their own terms, at organizing experience. I will offer a methodological alternative to breaking forms apart. I will turn to a number of historical and literary encounters among bounded wholes, including medieval church spaces, narrative closure, and the division of Victorian life into gendered "separate spheres," to ask what exactly bounded wholes afford and what happens when they cross paths with other forms in the world. This is a rejection of the constraining power of totalities and unities that at once refuses a powerful strand of the formalist tradition and constitutes a strong formalism in its own right.

The Well Wrought Urn

No theoretical text has done more to sediment the field's sense of form as bounded unity than Cleanth Brooks's *The Well Wrought Urn* (1947). Widely read and taught, it went through multiple editions in 1947 alone and continued to be used as a textbook for decades after its first publication. At first, Brooks's notion of form sounds far from imprisoning: working by "contradiction and qualification," the poet is "forced into paradoxes by the nature of his instrument."[16] Evoking irony and wonder, poetry reconciles discordant attributes in ways that "violate science and common sense" (17). All of this would seem to celebrate the slipperiness of language, its refusals to settle and stabilize. But there is another impulse at work in *The Well Wrought Urn*. While the constant shifts and subtle contradictions in poetic language are valuable, Brooks says that they ought to be "directed and controlled" (8). Indeed, such paradoxes are valuable, ultimately, because they point us to a new, transcendent oneness: the poet offers up "an insight which preserves the unity of experience and which, at its higher and more serious levels, triumphs over the apparently contradictory and conflicting elements of experience by unifying them into a new pattern" (195).

The figure Brooks most often uses for this ultimate unity is a material container.[17] The well-wrought urn is now so familiar as to seem like an obvious model for poetry, but I want to pause for a moment here to think through the implications of this figure. Brooks tells us absolutely straightforwardly, again and again, that the poem *is* the urn.[18] And it is true enough that Shakespeare, Donne, Gray, and Keats all suggest a likeness between their poems and the urns they describe. But words laid out on a page cannot be said to "contain" the way that urns do. Thanks to the unfolding structures of language, we read poems—including brief, lyric ones—as temporally unfolding sequences, even if we hypostatize them in the end. And quite different from the durable urn's enclosure of a pile of ashes, the poem's capacity to control and unify linguistic materials happens in and through those materials themselves.

Brooks himself seems to grasp the limitations of the urn as a figure for poetry and so introduces another formal paradigm. "The structure of a poem," he writes, "resembles that of a play . . . something that builds conflict into its very being" (186–87). There are two forms, then, that convey poetic structure: one a container that imprisons and controls, the other a dynamic process that brings together conflicting elements. Ultimately, Brooks always opts for the satisfying enclosure of the urn: he never imagines unending and uncontained plurality—sheer difference. But by tacking back and forth between two other art forms as his figures for poetry, Brooks offers up an irresolution—even a vagueness—at the heart of his understanding of poetic form. Is the poem an urn or a play? Is the aesthetic form of drama, too, an ultimately containing form, resolving its conflicts into a final whole? Or is the poem a form that mediates *between* urn and play, that has qualities of both spatial form and dramatic conflict? That *The Well Wrought Urn* never answers—or indeed explicitly raises—these questions suggests a troubling mystification of form at the heart of Brooks's famous formalism.

There is one clear value that emerges from this formal confusion. What Brooks emphasizes over and over again is a dialectic of lively energy and strict control that always ends in containment. Thus scholars have repeatedly argued that a certain politics implicitly drives Brooks's work.[19] Flourishing in the Cold War US academy, poetry takes on the contours of a triumphantly democratic society. The poet "must perforce dramatize the oneness of the experience, all the while paying tribute to its diversity," Brooks writes, endorsing a poetic *e pluribus unum* against the implied shadow of enforced Stalinist unity (195). The poem, like the liberal state, encourages plurality while also ultimately containing it.

Such a homology between aesthetic and political unity is by no means limited to liberal democracy. We could cite a range of examples—such as the cultural nationalist William Butler Yeats, the fascist Léon Daudet, and the Marxist Georg Lukács—all of whom imagined literary form as the proper corollary, and even the vehicle, of a politically integrated wholeness.[20] To bring all of these together may risk simplifying or overlooking their very real differences, but I link them here for two reasons. First, the neat homology between political and aesthetic traditions of totality has tempted many thinkers to assume a ready connection between the unifying work of literary forms and the unifying work of political community—an assumption that embraces a similarity between forms as the only significant or effective kind of formal relationship. The politics that results is also dangerous. Indeed, my second reason for bringing these different schools of thought together is to underscore the poststructuralist argument that what all of these models share is one of the crucial affordances of bounded wholeness: as a unity joins disparate elements into one, it always depends on a "constitutive outside." It is created and maintained by acts of exclusion. Recent theorists have been right to insist that this is the political danger that always haunts the embrace of unified form.

What I want to suggest about Brooks's particular legacy for those critics interested in practicing formalism today, however, is a counterintuitive conclusion: that there is no need to throw out the baby of Brooks's formalism with the bathwater of his politics, because far from being too much of a formalist, Brooks is actually *not formalist enough*. He shows surprisingly little interest in the conspicuous differences among the forms he invokes—poetic, plastic, theatrical—and the formal problem that his chapters really seem to care about, ultimately, is the act of containing, unifying, or controlling. His valuing of containment allows Brooks to obscure formal differences and relationships, the embrace of control in the end overshadowing any specific attention to the intricacies of form.

It is in part this embrace of unity as an objective that has prompted the field to squirm at the political implications of New Critical reading. When we think of form, we think of a containing wholeness, which in turn calls up frightening models of political control and totality, ranging from fascist wholeness to liberal assimilation. And the consequence is that we may have lost opportunities to think about intricate relations between the forms that Brooks suggests but never investigates. Does a formalist reading practice always and necessarily entail a valuing of containment and exclusion? In what specific ways are poetic forms like and unlike political communities? How do literary forms encounter or reflect or enact political ones?

A Social Body

It is the consummate antiformalist, Mary Poovey, who begins to point us to an answer. By her own account, Poovey could not be farther from the New Criticism, methodologically or politically. As one of the leaders of the widespread shift toward historically situated and politically conscious reading practices, she has argued against formalism as a method throughout her career. In *Uneven Developments* (1987), she claimed that she did "not respect the boundaries of the texts . . . as formalist critics of all persuasions do."[21] In 2001, she accused the poststructuralists of remaining tied to the model of the organic whole despite their rejections of totalizing form.[22] And in *Genres of the Credit Economy* (2008), Poovey extended the same line of argument by revealing the implicit formalism of two of her fellow historicists, Claudia Klaver and Catherine Gallagher. She made the case that Klaver and Gallagher hinge their readings on contradictions and discrepancies, which they presume are legible to readers both past and present. But they in fact begin from the premise of organic wholeness: after all, it is only against a backdrop of formal unity that contradictions become perceptible.[23] Rejecting this premise, Poovey advocated forgoing literary interpretation altogether in favor of "historical description," uncovering the categories and generic expectations that guided the text's composition and first reception rather than imposing anachronistic ideals of wholeness on audiences who might not have shared these values.

It is intriguing, in this context, to note the crucial importance of bounded shapes to Poovey's rigorously historical *Making a Social Body* (1995), a scholarly account of the rise of mass culture in Britain in the nineteenth century. "The image of the social body . . . was used in two quite different ways," she writes: "it referred either to the poor in isolation from the rest of the population or to British (or English) society as an organic whole."[24] This double meaning had some disturbing consequences:

> it allowed social analysts to treat one segment of the population as a special problem at the same time that they could gesture toward the mutual interests that (theoretically) united all parts of the social whole. The phrase *social body* therefore promised full membership in the whole (and held out the image *of* the whole) to a part identified as needing both discipline and care. (8)

Here Poovey refers explicitly to the "organic whole," evoking the formalist tradition that dates back to Aristotle. *Making a Social Body* can in fact be read as a critical response to those who conceive of society in formal terms, as a bounded and unified whole. Poovey is deeply interested in the dangerous power of unities to organize experience, and she is as alert to fissures and fractures in those wholes as she is to their aspirations to impermeable unity and integration. This attentiveness is precisely what allows her to see the implicit unities at work in Klaver and Gallagher, just as it draws her to track powerful new conceptualizations of the single, bounded society of Victorian Britain.

In sharp contrast to Cleanth Brooks, who finds solace and value in the image of an ultimate unity, Poovey worries that such visions of wholeness created massive new political, social, and economic effects. The illusion of unity, realized in institutions, effected an actual "process of homogenization," the consequences of which can still be felt in today's repetitive mass culture. No wonder, then, that Poovey so strongly resists formalist reading practices: the most important target of her own critique would seem to be precisely the unified wholeness that Brooks celebrates in *The Well Wrought Urn*.

But this conclusion actually points to a crucial link between Poovey and her New Critical forebear. Brooks and Poovey agree that formalist literary criticism offers the perfect corollary to a unified political community, fostering a delicate and artful unity out of contradiction and difference. To be sure, Brooks celebrates the power of unity, while Poovey struggles against it. But both of these markedly dissimilar critics write criticism that absolutely depends on the structuring principle of the bounded whole. In this way, Poovey's work continues the central organizing logic of *The Well Wrought Urn*.

Let me now take the argument a step farther. It is important to note that Poovey's book is itself organized by the single containing form that she criticizes: the concept of the social body. It is this idea that allows her to gather particular historical evidence and to arrange it so that we can grasp her argument. This definition of the concept is close to what Plato called the *eidos*, usually translated as *form*. In common Greek usage, *eidos* meant "figure" or "shape," and evoked visual experience.[25] For Plato it was that mental operation that established stable categories amid the chaotic evidence of experience. While few critics in our own time would join Plato in imagining that our concepts inhabit an ideal and timeless sphere, we might take account of the fact that even in the most historically rigorous scholarship *concepts* continue to do the work for us of imposing order on disparate materials: including and excluding, gathering specific examples while separating these from other categories of particulars.

Poovey puts a careful emphasis on the "dynamics" of "*formation* as an active concept—not on *culture* or *formation* as nouns of stasis or realization" (1), but she also explicitly restricts her focus to a field strictly bounded in time and space: Great Britain in the period 1830–1864. These boundaries carefully contain the materials of her analysis within a scholarly whole unified in time and space. Meanwhile, her central terms—cultural formation, body, domain, economy—are *also* containers, unifying concepts that can gather together disparate objects and traverse historical periods and

II

contexts. Even as Poovey pursues the limits and ambiguities of these concepts, it is their function as ordering principles that allows us to understand
her thesis about the emergence of British mass culture.

Poovey's reliance on bounded forms to organize her own arguments is,
moreover, like that of many other historicists. Take, for example, two other,
quite different, recent works of criticism: Meredith McGill's *American Literature and the Culture of Reprinting, 1834–1853* (2003) and Donald E. Pease's
New American Exceptionalism (2009). Both scholars are, like Poovey, interested in false and seductive fantasies of social wholeness, and both place
clear temporal and spatial boundaries around their evidence. McGill begins
with the 1834 US case of *Wheaton v. Peters*, the first Supreme Court ruling
on constitutional copyright, which permitted US publishers to reprint British and other foreign texts without penalty. She then uses this frame to
contest classic readings of antebellum US writers as voices of an emerging
unified nation, inviting us to see them instead as operating within a "culture
of reprinting" saturated with inexpensive reprints of foreign texts.[26] Pease
analyzes the struggle to produce unifying "state fantasies" in the period between the end of the Cold War and the start of the Global War on Terror.[27]
Both scholars focus their arguments on a distinct set of concepts, and both
set temporal and spatial boundaries around their evidence. These are powerfully argued, field-transforming books, and the tight focus of these two
scholars is usefully clarifying: after all, unless we have clear conceptual organizing principles and some starting and ending points, temporal and spatial, we might never begin the task of sociohistorical understanding at all.

But this means that historicists like Poovey, McGill, and Pease actually
continue the tradition of unifying and containing form in the making of
their own arguments: isolating the problem of wholeness or unity, drawing
temporal and spatial boundaries around evidence, and deciding what belongs and what does not. Uncannily like Brooks, these historicists pursue
complexities and fissures—disruptions, paradoxes, and contradictions—but
they also show how these work together to create unifying containers—the
social body, the state fantasy—which are precisely what hold their books
together. Indeed, the bounded, unified social body is actually a much more
persuasive model of a tense and bounded unity than Brooks's lyric poem.
And while the New Critic might well have been able to do without the
urn, the historicist scholar would be ill-equipped to perform her scholarly
work without the concepts—those bounded and containing wholes—that
organize her critical thinking and argument.

In a wonderful thought experiment, Jorge Luis Borges suggests that
even the ordinary operations of thought are impossible without this work

34

of conceptual abstraction. In the short story, "Funes the Memorious," the title character is knocked on the head, and his brain begins to work in an unusual way. His perception and memory are now "perfect"—filled with endless, particular detail. "He knew by heart the forms of the southern clouds at dawn on the 30th of April, 1882, and could compare them in his memory with the mottled streaks on a book in Spanish binding he had only seen once and with the outlines of the foam raised by an oar in the Río Negro the night before the Quebracho uprising." To Funes, all the rest of humanity looks "addlebrained, absent-minded," but he himself cannot think. Why not? Because "To think is to forget differences, generalize, make abstractions." Since he cannot abstract from experience, nouns themselves fail him: "Not only was it difficult for him to comprehend that the generic symbol *dog* embraces so many unlike individuals of diverse size and form; it bothered him that the dog at three fourteen (seen from the side) should have the same name as the dog at three fifteen (seen from the front)."[28] Incapable of "ideas of a general, Platonic sort," the character of Funes invites us to ask if it is possible to refuse formalist abstractions in favor of particularities. How particular can we be? And how can we make arguments at all without abstract concepts to contain the potentially endless diversity of experience?

To return to Poovey via Borges's story, we can see how containing form works in three crucial ways in *Making a Social Body*. First, bounded wholeness is the target of Poovey's political critique—the oppressive, imaginary unity of the social body. Second, specific temporal and spatial markers contain and limit Poovey's own evidence. And third, a set of conceptual containers brings together her historical material. I deeply appreciate the rigorous ways in which Poovey traces the historical emergence of a single, alarmingly homogenizing concept with significant material consequences. But I also want to make clear that despite her antiformalist rhetoric, her argument rests on a necessary formalism.

My reading of Brooks and Poovey here in fact invites a reversal of the usual story: where the New Critical Brooks is too little a formalist, the historicizing Poovey is far more a formalist than she is willing to recognize. She does not delight in the transcendent and unifying power of containing boundaries, but she does show a profound interest in the power of forms to organize and contain. Her work insists on a constant and vigilant attention to the ways in which political-epistemological forms take shape and seek to dominate and transcend the manifold materials of experience. And at the same time her own concepts order her historical materials, imposing boundaries around what counts as evidence and putting forward abstractions that allow us to group particular details together. What her work powerfully suggests, then, is that while some containing wholes—like the social body—may confine and restrict us in homogenizing, oppressive, and violent ways, others—like the critical concept—can be used against them. Conceptual wholes are in fact indispensable containers for scholars seeking to make arguments about particular historical formations that they identify, define, and describe. Indeed, Poovey's work shows how bounded wholes can enable critique, allowing the progressive scholar herself to organize her own historical materials through compelling and coherent concepts. She cannot show us the dangers of containing wholes without relying on containing wholes.

Poovey imagines doing away with wholeness and containment altogether to embrace a purposefully deforming shapelessness, a kind of historically descriptive reading that does not depend on wholes. Like many others, she suggests that it is possible and desirable to opt for formlessness over form. I am skeptical: I cannot imagine what it would mean to rid ourselves of bounded enclosures altogether. They are simply too common, too pervasive, too *constitutive* of social relations, thought, and material structures across cultures and time periods to be disregarded or left behind. Aside from urns, nations, and concepts, we find bounded wholes and enclosures all over the place: the huge walled enclosure of "Great Zimbabwe," begun in southern Africa in the fourteenth century, probably encircled the houses of families with the highest status, marking them off from others. In 1516, the Venetian Senate voted to segregate Jews in the *ghetto*, the gates of which were locked each night. For many centuries, Cherokee hunters used solid natural boundaries, such as cliffs and banks, to create enclosures where they could capture and kill tough-skinned buffalo. These are arbitrary examples, connected only by their dispersal in place and time: they do not serve the same purpose or have comparable sources, values, or implications. But since they lay claim to no common root, together they suggest that the bounded container that separates inside from outside is not a distinctive but an *ordinary* form, reinvented here and there, now and then. This pervasiveness does not mean, however, that we are doomed to acquiesce to the power of containers. Instead, we can draw from Poovey's critical use of conceptual unities against political unities to see how forms can disrupt one another's power.

Indeed, my central question is one that too often remains unarticulated at the heart of formalist and antiformalist criticism alike: I want to consider clearly the relations among forms—discursive, aesthetic, conceptual, material, political. Where Brooks moves easily, too easily, between the lyric poem and the political community, Poovey implicitly separates her own unifying concepts from the political unities she investigates and critiques. Thus it is Poovey who hints at a serious new contribution to the theorization of form: she does not start from the premise that wholes always mirror, enact, or reflect one another, each reinforcing the other's values and ends, but suggests that these forms may come into productive conflict. The goal, then, is to think about how one might put bounded wholes to work for strategic ends.

Contending Wholes

Let me introduce two specific sociohistorical examples that show how different bounded wholes might collide to generate ideologically intriguing results. The first comes from medieval Europe. In 1298, in a doctrine known as *clausura*, Pope Boniface VIII decreed that religious women should be strictly cloistered. For the first time the enclosures of monks and nuns were officially distinguished, and nuns were sharply divided from the growing variety of religious women's groups and sects. Double-barred and gated windows, locked doors, curtains, and walls increasingly separated nuns from the secular world. This decree drastically restricted these women's movements and their access to donors and influence, while striving to limit sexual temptations and scandals.[29] Justified as a way to protect women, *clausura* also very clearly worked to disempower them.

But the cloister was not the only bounded spatial container that organized the lives of European nuns. The sacred space of the church or chapel was also a walled, containing shape. Its innermost and restricted places were often considered its holiest, such as "a chapel with an inner cloister" or "an altar behind a rood screen."[30] A hierarchy of spaces within the church privileged the sites that were most enclosed and protected. The result, according to June Mecham's work on the convent at Wienhausen in Lower Saxony, was that cloistered women could cast themselves as especially holy—indeed, as more capable than their male counterparts of gaining access to miraculous experience. The Wienhausen nuns began to practice a devotion that enacted the Stations of the Cross within the convent, each literally walking "in the footsteps of Christ" (153). They even characterized their convent *as* Jerusalem, its nuns and abbesses claiming special access to unity with Christ. Paradoxically, then, the boundaries of the cloister, which afforded deliberate and powerful constraints on women, afforded something different too: centrality. Since the Church favored restricted and inaccessible places, the forcibly enclosed nuns could make persuasive claims to unique spiritual power and a feminine religious superiority. To be precise, the boundaries of the convent afforded imprisonment *and* centrality. They enacted both affordances at once. If we have tended to assume that bounded shapes always contain in the same oppressive ways and must therefore always be shattered, here we see how two bounded shapes, so similar that they could share the same literal form, did not reinforce or consolidate each other, but rather overlapped in a way that yielded an unsettling political effect.

Another more recent example shows how the complex relations between political containers might collide in oppressive ways and then be rearranged to create a new and more progressive model of community. In the United States in the 1930s, the Methodist Episcopal Church, the Methodist Episcopal Church–South, and the Methodist Protestant Church sought to reunite for the first time since the Civil War. Newly combined into a single whole, the Methodists also split into six official jurisdictions, five of them organized by geography and the sixth, called the "Central Jurisdiction"— made up of 367,000 African-Americans from across the nation—by race. Thus several bounded unities overlapped. There was the newly united Church—coterminous with the territorial boundaries of the nation. A split between North and South remained operative, as these two containers vied to impose their separate principles on the whole. The organizing principle that motivated the South, however, was not only its geographical unity but also an altogether different spatial form: racial segregation. Long divided in practice into black and white church buildings, each a container for a racially homogeneous congregation, the Northern Methodist Church joined with Southerners who wanted black members altogether excluded. Segregation was the enactment of a logic of inside and outside that sat uneasily beside the aspiration to national unity.

In the 1950s, progressive activists launched a series of attacks on the racializing logic of the national church by demanding formal harmony and totality—citing the principle of global human brotherhood:

> In Christ there is no east or west,
> In him no south or north;
> But one great fellowship of love
> Throughout the whole wide earth.[31]

Was Methodism divided by race or united by nation or joined into "one great fellowship of love"? Did it exclude black worshippers or make them "central" to the unification of the national church? The answer, of course, was that it was all of these. A surprisingly complicated heaping of spatial containers—the world, the nation, the North, the South, and racial segregation—each following a different logic of inclusion and exclusion, overlapped to produce a profoundly unstable state of affairs. Although what has most often worried theorists is the imposition of a single bounded whole, or a series of coordinated shapes that reinforce one another's power, the most progressive activists in this example were those who resisted internal divisiveness and the plurality of different forms in favor of a single, overarching unity. Ultimately, they succeeded, persuading the Methodists to desegregate. Rejecting the dividing form of race and the split between North and South as organizing principles, the church eventually claimed a single, harmonious and inclusive wholeness.

There are three points that these historical examples make clear. The first is that containers do not afford only imprisonment, exclusion, and the quelling of difference; they also afford centrality and inclusiveness. The second point is that no single ideological or political whole successfully dominates or organizes our social world. In fact there are so many of them operating at all times that strange collisions are ordinary—more routine than concerted alignments. The third conclusion is that the nuns who embraced *clausura* and the Methodist activists who invoked the organizing principle of a global Christian fellowship were canny formalists, using unifying shapes to disconcerting and novel ends. The Wienhausen nuns used one spatial container to unsettle another, while the Methodists exposed the conflict among the containing forms that constituted their church and urged a new formal harmony. In this, both groups were better formalists than Cleanth Brooks, who paid too much attention to controlled unity and too little to the specificities of form.

The circumstances behind these examples are not new, or unique: multiple sacred and profane spaces have overlapped in many societies over many centuries, and Methodist activists were taking part in a large-scale debate about the proper relations among containing forms—regional, national, global, and racial—that had been raging for more than a century and continues into our own time. Indeed, the fact that forms repeat, and bring a limited range of affordances with them, means that we can learn from medieval nuns and Methodist activists: their strategic uses of form can be replicated precisely, because forms are not so historically specific that their operations change radically from place to place.

Closure, Enclosure

For literary critics, an attention to the multiple bounded wholes at work in social situations helps us to rethink the historical contexts for literature as social conditions organized not by single, powerful ideologies, but by numerous contending and colliding forms. And this approach has another use as well: it can prompt a recognition that literary forms have a power quite different from the one they have traditionally been assigned—not the power to unify and contain like an urn, but rather a power more like that of the Wienhausen nuns and Methodist activists, to set forms against one another in disruptive and aleatory as well as rigidly containing ways. This analysis will push us beyond the model of literary form as containment, and invite us to reconsider the relations between literary forms and social containers as something other than reflective homologies.

Let us consider first the literary technique known as *closure*, the ending of narrative, which has been of particular interest to Marxists and other schools of ideology critique. Closure is typically read as bringing the competing values and interests of the narrative's middle into a stable containing order. "By the device of an ending," Terry Eagleton writes, "bourgeois initiative and genteel settlement, sober rationality and romantic passion, spiritual equality and social distinction, the actively affirmative and the patiently deferential self, can be merged into mythical unity."[32] Closure is not only the ending of a story, but the enclosing of discordant energies and possibilities into a single ideological whole. We are not far from Brooks here: the containing form of the text mirrors a model of social unity.

But let us pause for a moment to think in a more formally precise way about closure. To say that narratives *enclose* or *contain* social material is to use a spatial figure to describe stories. This implies that narratives hold their materials together in the same way as funerary urns, when in fact they are forms organized by their unfolding over time. The term *closure* thus elides the different affordances of narrative and spatial enclosure. I want to spend some time thinking about this elision, and more generally to push beyond the spatializing terms that have so often dominated arguments about literary form. Critics habitually use literary form in two competing ways: first, as an overarching textual unity (such as the marriage plot or epic), but also as the many, smaller and more varied techniques that go into shaping and structuring a text (such as metaphor, the couplet, peripeteia, the cliffhanger, monologue). What if we understood literary texts not as unified but as inevitably plural in their forms—bringing together multiple ordering principles, both social and literary, in ways that do not and cannot repress their differences?[33] From this perspective, could one formal element of a text ever manage to contain and control the others?

A specific narrative example will show how a plurality of forms offers a more accurate account even of a text's ending than the figure of closure. I have chosen the ending of Elizabeth Gaskell's *North and South* (1854–55) because it seems consummately ideological: it brings together the queenly, loving woman and the powerful, self-made man, England's industrial north and its agricultural south, bourgeois manufacturing and aristocratic wealth, and it throws in a concession to the working class in the form of regular meetings between management and labor, to complete its image of a harmonious national whole. This is a classic example of an ending that seeks to quell social contradictions in favor of a transcendent unity. But we might notice that even so, the usual terms of literary formalism actually occlude rather than reveal the workings of narrative form. That is, although we regularly call the formal phenomenon of a novel's ending its closure, what the novel imagines in its conclusion is really not an enclosure at all, but a *beginning*—the launching of a series of social and political relationships (a marriage, a set of alliances, investments, and meetings between management and labor) that have significance as a model for the nation precisely *because* they will endure beyond the narrative's end. The ending's political force depends not on resolution and finality, but on repetitions that will extend past the time represented in the text. To call this closure and containment is to overlook the future implied by the text, a deliberately uncontained temporal process.

If closure is too spatializing a term for narrative endings, I want to draw attention to the fact that there *are* some crucial spatial social forms that vie to impose order on the ending of this text. *North and South* is a novel that organizes itself in large part around a split national space: the agricultural South where Margaret Hale begins, and the industrial North that she comes to value. The South is associated with rural beauty, economic and social sluggishness, and an accepted gap between peasantry and gentry. The North values hard work, haste, and the possibility of upward mobility as well as sudden economic decline. Numerous critics, from W. A. Craik and Susan Johnston to Catherine Gallagher and Barbara Leah Harman, have considered the ways in which the novel organizes itself spatially, not only around a divided nation, but also around public and private and urban and rural spaces.[34] In a fascinating recent argument, Julia Sun-Joo Lee has made the case that Gaskell was troubled by another geographical division, too, the split between the US North and South that was having a significant economic impact on the Lancashire textile industry described in the novel. The ups and downs of the novel's Northern protagonists depended on the flow of slave-picked cotton from the US, and although Gaskell herself was an abolitionist, the North of England, where she lived, overwhelmingly sided with the South in the brewing US unrest. Geographical divisions were turned upside down, Lee suggests, with "the British North generally aligning itself with the American South and the British South aligning itself with the Union."[35] In this transnational context, two spatial organizations collided, and Gaskell could not reconcile her own desires for abolition on the one hand and a strongly unified Britain on the other. She found herself drawn to but also troubled by conflicting desires for national unity— Southern secession for the sake of British unity, or an abolitionist demand for US reconciliation that would depend on division within Britain. The joining of the British North and South that marks the end of the novel, then, comes at the expense of a reconciliation of the US North and South, and this bothered Gaskell, who could not make the forms she valued work together. The result, as Lee puts it, was "ontological distress," a distress, I would argue, that is precisely formal. It grows out of the impossibility of resolving multiple political forms into a single containing unity.

This reading of *North and South* looks not for a fit between literary forms and social facts—the container of the novel's closure and the container of national unity, for example—but rather for the ways in which social forms bring their logics with them into the novel, working both with and against literary forms and producing unexpected political conclusions out of their encounters. There are at least three forms at work in this example: the form of the novel's ending, which offers a set of contracts and agreements that are intended to organize relationships into the future, and the forms of two split nations, each seeking to create unity across differences. In theory, these should all be enclosed, homologous forms. But there is no way for Gaskell to resolve the bounded shapes of *North and South* into a satisfying conclusion—much as she wants to—as long as two different Norths and two different Souths and two different national unities contend for formal dominance. In the end, she opts for the unity of her own nation, but she is distressed to find that she has necessarily sacrificed both her own abolitionist commitments and her desire for another nation's unity along the way. Here, as in the Methodist Church, the fractures and dissonances are not liberating, but in fact more troubling than any single containing whole. The irreconcilable spatial forms Gaskell invites into her text push her to a political position she does not want, and the end of the novel remains necessarily haunted by the discordant forms of the two national wholes, the unity of each contributing to the division of the other.

This example might seem to represent just one unhappy compromise for a particular writer, thwarted in her particular intentions, but a second text from the same period, John Ruskin's *Sesame and Lilies* (1864), allows us to see how bounded wholes can collide in ways that exceed individual intentions and carry ramifications beyond the single text. In nineteenth-century Britain, as elsewhere, gender was often conceptualized spatially, as the "separate spheres" that divided the masculine, public world of politics and business from the protected, sanctified, feminine world of the private home. Many thinkers brought the nation and the feminine sphere close together, or merged them: both were "domestic" spaces, bounded wholes that needed protection.[36] Scholars interested in ideology have long argued that domestic ideology underwrote the power of the state, each shape reinforcing and consolidating the power of the other. Anne McClintock writes that "the image of the natural, patriarchal family . . . came to constitute the organizing trope for marshaling a bewildering array of cultures into a single, global narrative ordered and managed by Europeans."[37] In this influential account, domesticity functioned as a powerful organizing figure, containing the internal contradictions of the social while reinforcing the racism of imperial expansion.

At first, *Sesame and Lilies* seems a classic exemplar of this domestic ideology. Ruskin writes: "The man, in his rough work in the open world, must encounter all peril and trial . . . But he guards the woman from all this; within his house, as ruled by her . . . need enter no danger, no temptation, no cause of error or offense."[38] The walls of the private home emerge as a containing form that traps women, much like the doctrine of *clausura*. But although Ruskin confines women to the home, he also moves easily back and forth between the household and the nation as a whole, thinking of both bounded shapes as "home." In the process, rather than supporting or consolidating one another, the shape of the nation begins to transform the containment of femininity: that is, Ruskin imagines women's proper duties within the family expanding to involve a vast range of caretaking social activities, including looking after the poor and protecting the environment. And as the home stretches to reach the borders of the nation, it undermines the very separation of spheres that organized the gendered logic of domesticity in the first place:

> the man's work for his own home is, as has been said, to secure its maintenance, progress, and defence; the woman's to secure its order, comfort, and loveliness. Expand both these functions. The man's duty, as a member of a commonwealth, is to assist in the maintenance, in the advance, in the defence of the state. The woman's duty, as a member of the commonwealth, is to assist in the ordering, in the comforting, and in the beautiful adornment of the state. What the man is at his own gate, defending it, if need be, against insult and spoil, that also, not in a less, but in a more devoted measure, he is to be at the gate of his country, leaving

his home, if need be, even to the spoiler, to do his more incumbent work there. And, in like manner, what the woman is to be within her gates, as the centre of order, the balm of distress, and the mirror of beauty: that she is also to be without her gates, where order is more difficult, distress more imminent, loveliness more rare. (109)

If political power has often meant putting bodies, things, and ideas in their proper places, we can see here the strange political consequences that can ensue when two containing shapes—the private home and the nation as home—overlap and converge. Women's proper place might be within the home, but when the home expands to become the nation, women are not contained within domestic walls after all. There turns out to be no single proper place for women, thanks to a collision of forms that multiplies and expands the number of their proper places. The bounded space of the home echoes or mirrors the bounded space of the nation, but the formal equivalence of the two containing shapes itself undermines rather than reinforces the social power of gendered spheres.

The result is not an intention we can limit to Ruskin the writer, arguing that he deliberately crafted a powerfully subversive text. The same blending of home and nation crops up across Anglophone cultural contexts, because in English the two containers can always be implied by the single word *home*. Amy Kaplan's research shows us that a strikingly similar logic held sway in the United States in the nineteenth century, for example, where white American women could be at once victims of a disabling separate-spheres ideology and powerful players in the production of racism and imperialist expansion: "If domesticity plays a key role in imagining the nation as a home, then women, positioned at the center of the home, play a major role in defining the contours of the nation and its shifting borders with the foreign."[39] Whenever the nation is cast as home, feminine confinement to the domestic sphere can be transformed into national political agency. To put this another way: the *content* of the concept domesticity is always and necessarily *two forms*: the containing shape of the home and the containing shape of the nation. By bringing together two different shapes, the composite, internally divided form of domesticity does not reflect a single intention or ideology but is capable of generating a set of social, political, and cultural possibilities of its own. This is a collision that arises out of the two implied forms of domesticity, and as such it can travel, performing the same conflicting work wherever it appears.

Sesame and Lilies won a broad and enthusiastic audience. By 1905 it had sold 160,000 copies in multiple editions, published in London, Manchester,

Toronto, Philadelphia, New York, Boston, and Grahamstown, South Africa. Within a few decades it had been translated into Spanish, German, Italian, and most famously into French by Marcel Proust.[40] Since its strange formal logic allows it to shift easily between a submissive confinement to the home that serves the interests of patriarchy and a civically minded caretaking that offers powerful alternatives to the status quo, it is perhaps not surprising that Ruskin's readership divided into two almost completely antithetical groups. On the one hand, the book was widely distributed to young girls, often as a school prize, in order to encourage in women an obedient domesticity. George Gissing's novel, *The Odd Women*, represents this group of readers through the repressive husband, Widdowson, who urges his young wife to read Ruskin so that she will appreciate the benefits of confinement within the home:

> Everything he said presupposed his own supremacy; he took for granted that it was his to direct, hers to be guided. . . . 'Woman's sphere is the home, Monica. Unfortunately, girls are often obliged to go out and earn their living, but this is unnatural, a necessity which advanced civilization will altogether abolish. You shall read John Ruskin; every word he says about women is good and precious.'[41]

But despotic husbands were not Ruskin's only admiring readers. Dozens of progressive and independent New Women—many of them unmarried— also used *Sesame and Lilies* to justify their radical work in the public sphere. Seth Koven has shown how late-century feminists and activists found inspiration in Ruskin's lectures. Carrie May of the Cheltenham Ladies' College invoked Ruskin when she urged her students to "help in the formation of new unions, by undertaking some of the work of organisation which [laboring] women themselves can hardly be expected to carry out unaided," while Margaret Sewell, founder of the first women's settlement house, quoted Ruskin when she sought to differentiate her own serious work from the more sentimental model of women's philanthropy.[42]

Thus Ruskin, like Poovey, the Wienhausen nuns, the Methodist activists, and Elizabeth Gaskell, prompts a new set of formalist conclusions about the social operations of bounded wholes. While it is true that boundaries, such as those around nations and convents, do indeed confine and imprison, expel and exclude, they can also be put to use to disrupt the controlling power of other bounded shapes, the encounters themselves providing opportunities for new and emancipatory social formations. While we might want to resist the dominance of unified wholes by crushing them, or by rupturing their boundaries, a productive alternative involves not the destruction of form but its multiplication. That is, an effective strategy for curtailing the power of harmfully totalizing and unifying wholes is nothing other than to introduce *more wholes*.

Conclusion

Let me conclude by turning to a final example, one that seeks to create a meaningful unity out of multiplicity. This is not Cleanth Brooks's lyric poem, or Mary Poovey's social body, though it shares many of their characteristics. Often shot through with dramatic tensions, it is a unifying container marked by material boundaries and exclusions. But this enclosed unity, unlike the ones we associated with New Criticism or with homogenizing nationalism, is one that we literary and cultural critics tend to like: the seminar room.

The seminar emerged in Germany in the eighteenth century. Though various in its first incarnations, it soon took on a recognizable shape: a professor chose a small body of talented students and shifted them away from the usual tasks of mastering a prescribed body of materials toward the active production of original knowledge through the use of specific disciplinary methods. Enclosed in a room—sometimes even behind locked doors[43]—charismatic individual historians, philologists, and philosophers introduced intimate cohorts of students to source materials and research questions, and expected them to arrive at new truths through interpretation and discussion, collaboration and competition. Writing became the new test of success, displacing older modes of oral examination.[44] Some Americans who had studied in Germany became enthusiastic proponents of seminar methods, and by the 1880s these had become a staple of US colleges and universities.[45]

Early advocates saw the seminar as a way to foster originality and independence of mind by asserting a new kind of equality between teacher and student.[46] New spatial arrangements were understood to produce students capable of a kind of independent subjectivity. In 1893, James Canfield of the University of Nebraska described his own shift from lectures to seminars this way:

> I came down from my high desk and put a long table in the middle of the room and put the students about it and we called it the council table. I remember the thrill of pride felt by a young man when he walked in one day and floored me on a proposition I had made a few days before. I thought then I had begun to make men.[47]

Canfield's account of course sounds remarkably disciplinary—in the Foucauldian sense—involving the molding of "free," self-governing subjects through strategies of selection, examination, and panoptic spatial arrangements, as the students and teacher sit around a long table and observe one another.

Contemporary colleges and universities have inherited these elements of the seminar, almost entirely intact, from the late nineteenth century. Because it is expensive to run such faculty-intensive classes, and because they must be restricted in size, seminars continue to be exclusive bodies—whether they are reserved for first-year or graduate students.[48] They also continue to foster disciplinary norms: containing their members within an enclosed space, they promote a sense of individuation and independence through mutual observation and normalizing patterns of competition and comparison. But by and large academics strongly value seminars. Why is this? Given our skepticism about disciplinary techniques and our habits of vigilance when it comes to unifying shapes—the lyric poem, national totality, the domestic sphere—why do we not train our skeptical, critical eyes on this particular form as well?

We have seen how the unifying concept in historicist scholarship shapes material and imposes limits, but we have noted that even as it constrains, it also makes thinking possible. We have seen, too, how the struggle to avoid or rupture confining shapes is not the only response to their potential power: multiple forms can also interrupt and reroute one another. From this perspective, the seminar room may exclude, unify, and contain, but it accomplishes another, more congenial task as well. Ideally small enough to allow everyone to participate, and organized around thought-provoking questions, the seminar room affords acts of collective, open-ended thinking that then have the potential to unsettle conventional, rigid social and conceptual forms. In 1892, Columbia professor E.R.A. Seligman called the seminar "the real center of the life-giving, the stimulating, the creative forces of the modern university."[49] The *Boston Daily Globe* described Harvard's new freshman seminar program in 1959 as advancing "experimentation," "probing into the unknown with discipline and daring."[50] And this tradition of understanding the seminar as fostering original, critical, creative, and experimental thinking clearly continues into our own time. At St. John's College, seminars demand "openness to new ideas" and encourage students to "embrace unfamiliar territory." At Georgetown, the seminar is uniquely "challenging," and resistant to conventional fields of research. Wheaton College organizes each first-year seminar around a topic that has "generated controversy among the scholars, policy makers and others who have grappled with

47

it" in order to foster "critical engagement with controversial ideas."[51] Not least of the seminar's controversial, critical targets has been the bounded unity of the nation-state. Patricia Hill Collins teaches a seminar at the University of Maryland on complex intersections of race, gender, and nation.[52] And Mary Poovey's *Making a Social Body* has certainly found its way onto the reading list of many a graduate seminar.[53]

Capable of crossing disciplinary boundaries, encouraging critique and innovation, and prompting deliberately open-ended discussion about such confining wholes as convents and nation-states, the seminar room is a bounded, enclosed shape that sets out to disrupt other bounded, enclosed shapes. Can it succeed? Most of us literary and cultural studies scholars behave daily as if it can and does.

RHYTHM

Unlike the constraints of artful unities and rigid boundaries, rhythmic forms have often seemed natural, arising from the lived time of the human body. "Metre begins with the pulse-beat," wrote Ralph Waldo Emerson in 1872."[1] Contemporary poet Clarence Major continues this tradition, writing that "Poetry has its basis in the very beating of our hearts, in the rhythm of our footfalls as we walk, in the pattern of our breathing."[2] Joining poetry and music to the body's own patternings of time, rhythm can seem uninhibited, effortless—conveying "existential freedom" and expressing "presence and pleasure."[3]

And yet, rhythm can also be punishing, the shackles of an imposed metrical or musical form. Martin Munro contrasts the African music that slaves brought with them from Africa—repetitive, cyclical, polyrhythmic, and dialogic, expressing the pleasures of a participatory and embodied collective—with high-culture European music of the eighteenth and nineteenth centuries, which favored "linearity, teleology, and synthesis."[4] Munro then complicates this account: slave masters figured out that slaves would work better if they were singing. As it turned out, "repression had its own rhythms, not least the steady crack of the master's whip" (16–17). Terrifyingly, rhythms reveal opposing affordances: on the one hand, they can produce communal solidarity and bodily pleasure; on the other, they can operate as powerful means of control and subjugation. Whether imposing a temporal order on bodies or labor, sounds or machines, rhythmic form has the potential to do serious political work.

Rhythms, if we define the term broadly, are pervasive. From shift work and travel timetables to religious rituals and the release of each summer's blockbuster movies, repetitive temporal patterns impose constraints across social life. Often these forms are routinized—the predictable rhythms of everyday life, such as clocking in to work or the release of children from school. Sometimes these temporal markers repeat at long intervals: the harvest, the reunion, the centenary celebration. Typically many are overlaid, as a particular person might struggle to balance work and school schedules, remembering when to pay the electric bill, see a probation officer, take communion, and swallow a pill, pausing at regular intervals to accommodate the need for food and sleep and to celebrate significant events on individual, family, national, and religious calendars.

Sociologists have long argued that the coordination of temporal rhythms is a particularly powerful technique of social cohesion. Pierre Bourdieu writes that "the whole social order imposes itself at the deepest level of bodily dispositions through a particular way of regulating the use of time, the temporal distribution of collective and individual activities and the appropriate rhythm with which to perform them."[5] The attempt to impose temporal order has certainly been a hallmark of large-scale modern uses of power. European empires sought to force peoples around the world into a single narrative of progress—from savagery to civilization, or from "developing" to "developed"—while they also imposed a single global clock, with England's Greenwich Meridian marking the time standard. By the early twentieth century, most cities in Europe and the Americas had installed synchronized clocks in public places, "to guarantee punctuality, control of time and the standardization of conduct in relation to time."[6] Eviatar Zerubavel has argued that a modern society develops a sense of solidarity precisely through temporal patterning, as its members share a standardized set of expectations about when events should happen (dances never take place in the morning), how long they should go on (entertainments last about two hours, a doctor's appointment no more than one), and at what intervals (piano lessons happen once a week, presidential elections every four years). Though conventional, these expectations are so entrenched that "determining whether a certain situation or event is 'normal' or not depends, to a large extent, on its temporal profile."[7] Standard repetitions, durations, and arcs of development organize our experiences of everything from sleep and sex to governments and the global economy.

And yet, the story of the standardization of time in modernity itself often follows a remarkably orderly temporal progression—a narrative that tells of a shift from the organically coordinated time of small communities, based in natural cycles, to the artificially, mechanically coordinated time of modern life, ending in homogeneity, the standardization of time around the globe. This orderly narrative is misleading on both ends. The tempos of preindustrial societies do often rely on bodies, seasons, and daylight, but they also include artificial and coercive patterns that impose norms on their members and separate them from outsiders.[8] Conversely, modern societies never altogether leave the tempos of nature behind: shifts in seasons, patterns of breathing and heart rates, the body's frequent need for food and sleep, and the reproductive body continue to structure temporal experience even when these have been mechanized and manipulated. In his classic work, *Time and the Other*, Johannes Fabian argues that Europe's narrative of a progressive modernity itself repeats an ancient temporal model: the divine and providential mission of a chosen people, who claim a sacred relationship to time.[9]

Rather than sharply distinguishing ancient and modern temporalities, then, I want to make the case that the rhythms of social experience, both modern and premodern, are multiple and heterogeneous, drawing their patterns from such disparate sources as seasonal changes, religious ritual, kinship norms, the demands of labor, reproduction, war, and changing technologies. In modernity the superimposition of rhythms becomes much more complex than it once was, to be sure, and it would be a mistake to argue that there is no difference between the accelerated time of industrial-technological change and the regular cycles of traditional plantings and harvests. But if we are to understand the ways in which social experience is powerfully constrained and organized according to temporal forms, whether modern or not, we would do well to adopt a keen attentiveness to multiple patternings of time.

Reading the rhythms of the world in a formalist fashion, alert to the temporal organizing principles that govern social organizations and institutions, we find a social world where temporal structures often thwart or compete with one another.[10] This is the case even within a single institution: consider what happens, for example, when the standard three-year grant to scientists runs up against the struggle to understand long-term processes such as climate change.[11] In order to understand the political and social power that temporal forms exert—their capacity to regulate and organize our lives—we need a kind of analysis capable of revealing how temporal patterns collide.

In theory, literary criticism should be able to contribute to this analysis of social time in valuable ways, because critics have had to develop a range of subtle practices for thinking about temporal patterning, addressing such forms as meter, seriality, and plot. And yet, spatial form, as we saw in the previous chapter, tends to dominate critical analyses of form, obscuring the workings even of time-bound forms like the novel. Nicholas Dames has made the argument that it was not always so: critics today have inherited our ideas of novelistic form from the early twentieth-century theorists Henry James and Percy Lubbock, who wanted to resist the headlong, unthinking absorption in plotted narrative that was associated with a growing mass readership. In order to develop a detached, distancing attention to the novel, they started to treat it as a synchronic unity. Borrowing a new vocabulary from the visual arts, they adopted such terms as *point of view* and *perspective,* now standard terms in novel criticism.[12] What got lost in this new critical paradigm, Dames argues, was an older theory of the novel that had borrowed its terms from music rather than painting. Putting an emphasis on the temporality of the reading experience—sequence, flow, repetition, and duration—nineteenth-century critics had once focused on the novel's form as a rhythmic experience. In refusing this interest in rhythm, twentieth-century criticism grasped even the most time-bound of literary forms—poetic meter and novelistic plot—as ultimately stilled and contained, as in the well-wrought urn and narrative closure. And although the past hundred years have seen many excellent scholars of plotted dynamism and poetic meter, whose work has powerfully informed my own reading practices,[13] the field has by and large inherited a dominant definition of literary form as spatially unifying, which has too often distracted us from the specificity of temporally unfolding forms.[14]

I make a threefold argument here for paying a richer and more detailed attention to rhythms, both social and aesthetic. I start with the importance of attending to the temporal forms that structure historicist literary and cultural studies scholarship. Since the 1980s, historicist accounts of cultural experience have tended to spatialize time, understanding history in terms of periods, which function for scholarship more like bounded containers than unfolding patterns. To think about periodization critically, I take up the question of institutional time. Historicist scholars routinely attribute the beginnings and ends of periods to the working of social institutions. Building on the work of theorists in the social sciences who call themselves "new institutionalists," I will make the formalist argument that institutions themselves are composed of overlapping repetitions and durations, which routinely violate the frame of periodization that typically organizes historicist scholarship. The heterogeneity and endurance of social rhythms thus invites a new kind of sociocultural analysis, asking us to reimagine the social landscape as characterized by contending rhythms that extend forward and backward in time.

In the second part of the chapter, I will ask how we might put this kind of analysis to use. I focus on one example from the late 1920s, when avant-garde artists managed to alter US law by cannily recognizing the work of multiple social rhythms. Here, I make the case that despite their power to coerce and organize, rhythms, like bounded wholes, can be put to strategic ends and have the potential to work with and against other forms to surprisingly transformative political effect.

Finally, I will ask how a new approach to rhythm might help us to re-think the relations between literary forms and social arrangements. I turn to prosody to argue that literary critics have often made the limiting assumption that aesthetic tempos must reflect the time of social institutions. In considering a poem about Queen Victoria by Elizabeth Barrett Browning, I will point to an alternative reading practice that takes poetic meter as its own organizing principle, one that competes, struggles, and sometimes even interferes with other organizations of social time.

Along the way, my own objects will often stray far from literature, music, and the other arts, as I look at the temporal patterning of universities, economies, governments, and theme parks. I need to say a word, therefore, about why I have chosen "rhythm" as my organizing concept for this chapter. The term *rhythm* moves easily back and forth between aesthetic and nonaesthetic uses. It is conventional to say that there are work rhythms and social rhythms.[15] The traditional claim that poetic and musical rhythms arise in the body suggests an easy crossover between artistic and nonartistic realms. Rhythm is therefore a category that always already refuses the distinction between aesthetic form and other forms of lived experience. At the same time, an attention to aesthetic rhythms can also help us here. A set of reading practices drawn from the analysis of plotted dynamics and prosody can provide a new kind of training for thinking seriously about the tempos of social experience, focusing our attention on the complex and overlapping rhythms that structure even a single institution. We can use our understanding of the affordances of aesthetic rhythms—repetition and difference, memory and anticipation—to understand social rhythms. An inattention to temporal patterning has obscured some crucial insights into the operations of historical change and the exercise of power, but the skills of a literary formalist, meticulous about the different operations of specific forms, can afford a convincing new understanding of the time-bound workings of political power.[16]

Periods as Forms

The past three decades in literary and cultural studies have witnessed the emergence of numerous and rigorous methods for understanding the relations between aesthetic objects and the social contexts of their production and reception. And yet, this turn to history has tended, surprisingly often, to depend on notions of cultural wholeness, as though historical contexts were spatial containers—"self-contained wholes."[17] Consider, for example, the influential theorization of context put forward by Catherine Gallagher and Stephen Greenblatt, who write that each culture is "a whole life-world" that can be regarded as one "text," with "a shape, a complex individuality by which we come to identify the peoples who live together in a particular time and place."[18]

Of course, many scholars, especially recently, have opted for more open conceptions of culture, focusing on transnational currents and the rupture of borders, and few critics have absolute faith in orderly temporal boundaries. And yet, the vast majority of literary and cultural studies scholars do continue to rely on historical periods, however provisional, to establish boundaries around their work. Wai-Chee Dimock claims that historicists have borrowed models of temporality from Newton, for whom "time functions in exactly the same way as a spatial coordinate. It is a place, a location, a sequence of units on a calibrated line—and, for all those reasons, a container to which any event can be assigned."[19]

We can see how historical periods work as bounded containers in two recent, field-transforming, dazzling works of historicist literary criticism. The first, Sharon Marcus's *Between Women* (2007), explores the startling range of ways in which Victorian women engaged in relationships with other women—including objectification, infatuation, egalitarian friendship, voyeurism, and stable marriage. This plasticity and variability of relations, Marcus argues, radically unsettles the two entrenched models that have dominated scholarship on the histories of gender and sexuality: the notion of gender as an opposition between masculine and feminine, and the conception of sexuality as a continuum.[20] My second example, Denise Gigante's *Life: Organic Form and Romanticism* (2009), makes the case that scientific thinkers during the Romantic period developed a new concept of unpredictable, *lively* life that crossed from natural science to aesthetics.[21]

As they trouble well-established accounts of literary and cultural history, these two critics explicitly depend on the period to draw boundaries around their materials. Marcus begins her argument in 1830, about the time when companionate marriage and the notion of men and women as opposite sexes had become the norm for all classes in Britain, and she ends in 1880 with the claim that new discourses of eugenics and sexology had begun to undermine the models of sex and marriage that had dominated the mid-Victorian period. Gigante starts her story in 1740, when scientific publications across Europe began to return to a notion of "vital power" to challenge the theory of "preformation" dominant during the Enlightenment, and she ends it in the 1840s with the "epistemic break" represented by the beginnings of cell theory.

To be sure, both critics resist any absolute notion of the period. Marcus is quite willing to "recognize that much of what we consider Victorian can be traced back to the eighteenth century and persisted long after 1880" (7), and Gigante writes that she does not mean to say "that all natural philosophers of the Romantic period embraced the concept of vital or formative power" (21). But they nonetheless turn to period markers to assemble their materials into effective cultural arguments, and both ultimately justify conventional periodization.[22]

On the one hand, then, these historically minded critics recognize and appreciate the artifices of periodization; on the other, they not only depend on conventional period categories but also explicitly reinforce them. The period is an artificial unity, perhaps, but it is one that allows meaningful understandings of cultural experience to emerge. In this respect, the most sophisticated historicist criticism starts to sound uncannily like the antiquated, ahistorical practice it supposedly replaced: the New Criticism. Like the tidy art works beloved of the New Critics, historical periods operate as constructed wholes that give intelligible shape to complex cultural materials, enabling us to grasp significant interrelationships among their parts. Since form defined in this way is often aligned with ahistorical transcendence, the form of the historical period emerges as paradoxical indeed. Periodization is an abstract, transhistorical organizing principle that is used to reveal rooted and local historical specificity. Or, to put this another way: the period is the strange form that antiformalism often takes.

This conclusion might prompt an immediate objection: namely, that far from *privileging* such unifying forms, historicist and cultural studies scholars have persistently drawn attention to faultlines, fissures, and boundary-crossings. David Perkins writes that "we require the concept of a unified period in order to deny it, and thus make apparent the particularity, local difference, heterogeneity, fluctuation, discontinuity, and strife that are now our preferred categories for understanding any moment of the past."[23] In this account, periodization allows us to posit a wholeness, which we put forward only long enough to violate its boundaries. And yet, formalism might still be a help here, since the ruptures themselves follow an insistent pattern: containment and subversion, law and transgression, and boundaries and boundary-crossing, all of these sharing a repetitive, organizing structure.[24] And although the dynamic of subversion and containment might now seem dated compared to more recent explorations of cultural plurality and plasticity—such as Marcus's—the continuing reliance of today's most sophisticated critics on the period as an organizing principle for scholarship suggests that we are not out of the formalist woods quite yet. The container endures as a structure for thinking about historical time.

One reason why the period continues to work as a powerful organizing principle in literary studies is that, according to many scholars' accounts, the beginnings and endings of periods are coterminous with the social life of institutions. Marcus, for example, maintains that the institution of companionate marriage organizes the period she has chosen, while Gigante turns to a pan-European network of scientific research that offers a new hypothesis about epigenesis in the 1740s. Marcus and Gigante are like many other recent scholars in focusing their attention on the work that institutions do to give shape to social experience. For these thinkers, institutions come *first*, and this in two senses: they come before cultural phenomena, and they stimulate or shape cultural production.

But institutions, so crucial to the work of historicizing literary texts, rarely form the focus of literary scholars' analytic attention. Critics who address the power of particular institutions frequently leave the term *institution* undefined and unexamined.[25] The few who have engaged institutions directly have pointed to a tension in the meaning of the term. On the one hand, as Homer Brown explains, institutions imply endurance: "From the Latin *instituare*, to institute means literally to cause to stand or stand up, to move something to standing or at least the illusion of standing in one place—that is to say, something that *stays*."[26] On the other hand, the act of instituting implies the introduction of something new, a break with the past. This tension suggests a reason why institutions may be so useful to periodization: they mark starting-points—moments of inception—followed by significant durations.[27] In other words, they give form to temporal experience.

So: what exactly *is* an institution? How do institutions shape the tempos of social experience? What kind of interruption does the act of instituting entail? And how and why do institutions endure?

Since institutions organize not only the objects that we study, but our own scholarly practices, staying within conventional practices of historical argumentation risks failing to address the fundamental problem of how institutions actually impose order on historical time. And it is here, I hope, that a new formalism can prove useful. Both institutions and periods can be seen as forms in the sense that both are ways of organizing heterogeneous materials. Both afford certain kinds of constraints and opportunities, bringing bodies, meanings, and objects into a political order. But the constraints and opportunities they afford are not the same, because their forms are not the same. If periods act like bounded wholes, institutions are crucially composed of rhythms—patterns of duration and repetition over time.

The Strange Patterns of Institutional Time

While English studies scholars have most often turned to Marx, Foucault, and Bourdieu for understandings of the power wielded by particular social institutions, a group of social scientists largely unknown to literary critics have been investigating precisely the questions that lie at the intersection of institutions and periodization: the ways that institutions both introduce change and maintain stability. The "new institutionalists" are a large and various crowd, mostly sociologists, political scientists, and economists, who share an interest in the ways that institutions maintain norms, expectations, and hierarchies over time, as well as the ways that they stimulate, accommodate, and respond to change. These scholars vary not only in their disciplinary strategies, intellectual trajectories, and objectives, but also in their political perspectives, and they cannot consequently be viewed as a coherent group, either disciplinarily or ideologically.[28] But their focus on the ways that institutions organize social time provides promising new starting-points for a formalist literary and cultural studies.

First of all, the new institutionalists have worked to define the term *institution* in precise and productive ways. Conventionally, the word refers to governments, churches, prisons, and other official organizations, but it also carries a broader sense that encompasses all regulative practices, all orderly and established customs or usages. The new institutionalists bring these two meanings together to argue that institutions operate at a wide variety of levels: from official and highly complex organizations (such as the state, the law, or the university) to organized practices and patterns of behavior (such as the family or a game) to powerful conventions that shape experience (such as gender norms or patriotic values). New institutionalism is thus in part a way to address differences of scale. These scholars suggest that between the macro-level of markets or nations and the micro-level of individual actors we find the many institutions that actually organize the great bulk of our social experience—marriage, insurance policies, the weekly soccer game, church hierarchies, the department meeting, the codex, shipping routes, liberal democracy, racism, and the supermarket, to name only a few familiar institutions that operate on different scales and with different kinds of constraints, values, rules, and expectations.

When it comes to time, institutions are most notable for their stability. Brown suggests that the term *institution*, with its implications of endurance, has given rise in literary studies to an almost exclusive focus on edifices—a conflation of institutional power and duration with literal buildings.[29] But this is misleading: institutions are as much or more constituted by patterns as they are by bounded spaces, as much organized by rules and practices that need to be repeatedly reenacted as they are by containing walls.[30] Political scientists James March and Johan Olsen define institutions as "relatively enduring collection[s] of rules and organized practices, embedded in structures of meaning and resources that are relatively invariant in the face of turnover of individuals and relatively resilient to the idiosyncratic preferences and expectations of individuals and changing external circumstances."[31] Institutions endure, then, only because participants actively reproduce their rules and practices.[32] Whether acting as administrators or parents, macho men or diligent students, poker players or welfare recipients, we play parts set out for us by institutions, and, as we do so, we reproduce the institution itself.[33] To maintain stability, institutions depend less on buildings than on what Joseph Roach calls *surrogation*—the process of filling places and stepping into roles of departed others.[34]

One of the crucial affordances of temporal rhythms—repetition—is thus essential to the endurance of institutions. But the initial act of instituting also disrupts entrenched routines. New institutionalists argue that at the moment when each institution comes into being, it is likely to break with old patterns in order to reflect the agendas of a particular, powerful group. But because institutions are defined in part by their repetitions over time, they also last well beyond such official agendas.

Let me offer an example close to home for literary critics, which is the curriculum of English literary study. According to Gauri Viswanathan, English studies became a discipline of study in India before it was institutionalized in Britain. The British colonial administration needed a way to persuade Indian subjects to adopt colonial power willingly, embracing the superiority of the colonizers. This was no easy task: it seemed to many British thinkers that their superiority had everything to do with their Christianity, but another, equally crucial British value was freedom of religion, and the British were particularly reluctant to impose Christianity on Indians, because they expected outright resistance to attempts at conversion. The solution, Viswanathan argues, was English literature: officially secular, literary works could transmit Christian morality and the superiority of the imperial social order without explicitly imposing an alien religion.[35] The curriculum was then brought back home as a way of socializing English readers into an enthusiasm for national and colonial rule. Later, US literature entered the curriculum for similarly nationalist ends: in the 1920s, scholars concerned about the marginality of American literature began to celebrate the work of US writers. By the 1950s, American literature had become a weapon in the cultural armory of the Cold War.[36]

It is perhaps not surprising to learn that the particular agendas of powerful institution-builders led to a nationalist organization of literary studies. But what is intriguing is that we have continued to repeat those agendas as the institutionalized study of literature has lasted into our own time. Although scholars in the past few decades have succeeded in exposing the ideological roots and narrow confines of national literatures, the curricula of English departments typically remain organized around nations. Indeed, despite the fact that many—if not most—of us practicing literary criticism have a distaste for nationalist and imperialist agendas, and understand literatures as transnational formations that include multiple languages and geographies, the institutional patterns of nineteenth- and early twentieth-century English departments persist.

Why is this? The new institutionalists describe a phenomenon they call "path dependency." Once an institution has "started down a track, the costs of reversal are very high."[37] These costs make it impractical and sometimes unfair to make major institutional changes. For example, faculty might hold on to the model of national literatures in the classroom because they have concerns about undergraduates studying for the GREs, or because they feel anxious about graduate students in a job market organized around national fields. They might feel constrained by their own limited knowledge, which has been shaped by training organized around national literatures. They might struggle against bureaucratic structures that make it difficult to work across languages and university departments. And they might rely on the convenience of being able to assume a shared set of texts that allow them to talk to one another in national fields about the act of reading literature. So: institutional patterns become increasingly entrenched, allowing reliance on the form of the nation as an institutional organizing principle to endure surprisingly vigorously in English studies, despite the fact that many of us have lost faith in it.

Path dependency explains the staying power of periodization, too, as an institutional form in literary and cultural studies. Even when the New Criticism was in its heyday, the vast majority of courses in English departments continued to be organized around historical periods inherited from generations before. An entrenched curriculum allowed the old historicist forms to persist so long, in fact, that when new historicism came into fashion it fit readily into the old period containers, and there was no need to rearrange English departments in any comprehensive way.[38] These days, although scholars can generate forceful critiques of period boundaries, we largely continue to make hires, teach, and organize scholarship in most of the same period categories that the field employed more than half a century ago. Ironically, periodization has lasted across periods. And it has lasted specifically through repetition and recurrence, a containing form that has again and again imposed its order on courses, curricula, conferences, and scholarship across decades.

What this example shows, most importantly, is that *institutions preserve forms*. Their repetitive rhythms over time afford stability. Indeed, the recurrence of the same forms over time is essential to the work of institutional organization. Without those repetitions, institutions would cease to be recognizable as such, and without forms, institutions would not be able to impose order on bodies, discourses, and objects. But this conclusion unsettles conventional ideas about periodization. If multiple institutions structure our experience, if these various institutions have emerged out of different cultural circumstances, and if their forms remain relatively stable through repetition over time, then the different values that produced those ways of organizing people and ideas actually *persist in the forms of the institutions themselves*.

Far from organizing social time into discrete periods, institutions effectively compel us to live in multiple periods at once. For example, we who work in English departments live in nineteenth-century imperial time and twentieth-century Cold War time when we teach national literatures. We live in medieval monastic time when we follow a daily class schedule. In fact, we live in both the medieval period and the eighteenth century, since as Foucault argues, eighteenth-century factories, prisons, and schools borrowed schedules from medieval monasteries so that ordinary people might learn to regulate themselves for the efficient ends of a disciplinary society. The winter break is older than any of these, a cyclical ritual that reaches back before the early Christians to pagan celebrations of the winter solstice.

And it is not only the academic timetable that registers the endurance of multiple institutional pasts. When we collect our pay stubs, we are working in a late nineteenth-century bureaucracy; when we petition the dean and then the provost, we are calling up an eighth-century model of monastic administration; when we attend conferences and symposia, we are drawing on institutional traditions that range from ancient drinking parties to assemblies of dissenting church delegates; when we open up our computer desktops, we are using a twenty-first-century technology, but one that itself swallows up and incorporates a whole range of technologies used by earlier generations—the writing desk, the file cabinet, the typewriter, the calculator, the balance sheet, the messenger boy, the postal system, and the photography lab, among others.

When we think of academic life, then, are we living in ancient times, or in the eighth, fifteenth, eighteenth, nineteenth, twentieth, or twenty-first century? Add to this mix that none of us live *solely* in the academic institution, but are likely to have daily experiences of such institutions as the marketplace, kinship, religion, media culture, and the state—all of which are constituted by their own multiple and conflicting temporalities stretching backward and forward in time—and it begins to look as if attempting to grasp our own historical situatedness in terms of the containing form of the period makes no sense at all.

One might conclude quite simply, of course, by observing that these temporal patterns make clear that the present is shot through with traces of the past, which is a compelling reason to study history. Or one might claim that our own, specifically postmodern era is characterized by precisely this mix of cultural and historical anachronisms. But I want to make three quite different claims about the temporality of institutions.

My first claim is that no cultural period could ever be temporally discrete or coherent. By definition, as we have seen, institutional rhythms afford stability, preserving forms. And if the initial, particular, local circumstances that give rise to each institutional form endure with the very repetition and survival of that institution's forms, then they really cannot be so particular or local after all. They travel through time precisely by virtue of the fact that they are institutionalized—repeated in and through institutions. Paradoxically, that is, institutions both preserve *and* violate the specificity of cultural situations. Moreover, since multiple institutions coexist, their local, particular points of origin also coexist. And so a society is best characterized as a mixing together of different points of origin that coexist as enduring institutional forms.

My second claim is that since institutions are not static structures but rather relatively consistent reiterations of norms and practices, they necessarily follow temporal rhythms. Patterns of institutional time involve repetitive rituals—from religious observances to patterns of clocking in and clocking out to final exams. Each institution follows its own tempo or set of tempos—repetitive patterns of reenactment that themselves reconstitute the institution in and through each iteration. It is in fact precisely repetition that preserves the legitimacy, stability, and autonomy of institutions. Thus institutions are literally brought into being by marking time—by reviving past forms and preserving them for the future in patterns spaced closely enough to enact continuity. And yet, since institutions also coexist with other institutions, an institutional environment ends up overlaying numerous tempos. And so, in their constant overlapping and juxtaposition,

III

institutions necessarily both reinforce and unsettle temporal patterning: they mark time in the form of repeated practices that make them recognizable as institutions, but together they jumble and superimpose multiple and incommensurable rhythms.

My third point is that since institutions persist and survive through repetition—through the citation of rules and the performance of practices— they are never present as such. They are materialized *across* time, through performative processes that cite prior events in every moment of their instantiation. Two kinds of time operate here: not only do institutions constantly cite earlier institutionalized patterns, but they also themselves exist *as* shuddering, flickering repetitive performances. The university depends on routines of performance and evaluation; the state takes on its force and identity by enacting and enforcing laws; gender norms are mobilized and remobilized every day through practices of labor, dress, speech, and movement. These institutions cannot thus ever be grasped as *present*—they cannot be tied to any particular present, and they take place in processes of repetition and citation such that no moment finds them fully present. The strange tempo of institutions invites us, in other words, to focus on recurrence over time, on repetitive tempos of experience that endure well beyond local moments.

This interest in uneven and overlapping temporalities might remind us of Raymond Williams, who made an influential case against classic "epochal" Marxist models of time by introducing the idea of dominant, residual, and emergent elements. Williams argued that while some formations, like industrial capitalism, are effective and powerful at a given time—and therefore "dominant"—others provide dynamic alternatives and possibilities for change and resistance. "Residual" elements are leftovers of a past moment that survive into the present, still active and effective, but at some remove from the dominant social forms, which often seek to incorporate them and put them to use to dominant ends. The rural village, for example, stands at a distance from industrial modernity, representing an alternative, but is also incorporated into the dominant mode as a fantasy or escape. Meanwhile, "new meanings and values, new practices, new relationships and kinds of relationship are continually being created," and some of these provide genuine alternatives to the dominant social formations. These are "emergent" practices that will eventually come to displace the dominant.[39]

Williams's model is indeed a productive one, and it helps to move us away from the understanding of historical time as a sequence of bounded containers. But I want to point to three ways in which it might be adjusted and elaborated to take account of the complexity of institutions, all of which

62

have to do with temporal form. First of all, Williams implicitly relies on a single form to organize the relations between dominant, residual, and emergent, and that form is a narrative of linear unfolding. The residual and the emergent are always marked as either "past" or "future" in relation to the dominant. Williams claims, for example, that organized religion is residual, a definition that assumes the exorable march forward of secularization, a path that has begun to look markedly uncertain around the world in recent years.

Second, Williams's broad-brush account of social institutions—industrial capitalism, organized religion—imagines such vast and monumental social forces that it does not, at least in the grain of this description, capture the formal heterogeneity that characterizes even dominant institutions, the complex superimposition of schedules, practices, routines, and repetitions that organize our daily experience. Indeed, each institution lays claim to many residual and emergent elements. We saw this in the example of the university, where temporal moments are so jumbled as to suggest that institutions simultaneously incorporate dominant, residual, and emergent forms.

And third, repetition as a form is so crucial to the endurance of institutions that it helps us to understand how apparently residual elements can last into distant futures, thus collapsing distinctions between dominant, residual, and emergent. That is, if we understand institutions as taking shape every day through the reenactment of norms and practices, this means that they always depend on citations borrowed from the past. There is thus nothing in the dominant that is not in some sense residual.

And yet, one might object, even if institutions last, surely they begin in particular places and times. Just as the form of the nation starts to organize English studies in the nineteenth century, so the form of companionate marriage comes to dominate domestic arrangements in Britain around 1830. Both of these organizing principles last well beyond the time of their origin, but, according to this claim, their moments of institutionalization can be isolated as clear and important beginnings. I want to suggest, however, that this notion of a break is often misleading. I draw from Derrida's claims about the iterability of the sign—necessarily repeated across time, without origin, and capable of breaking with any single context[40]—to suggest that institutional forms such as enclosures or rituals or kinship relations, repeated across different contexts, do not begin anywhere in particular, their sites of origin receding into ever more distant pasts.

We can see this logic at work in one of the most influential texts for historicist scholars: Michel Foucault's *Discipline and Punish*. Foucault has not only been an extraordinarily influential thinker on the question of institutions in literary and cultural studies; in his insistence on locating specific institutions in particular historical moments, he has also been called the field's "most notorious periodizer."[41] But a look at *Discipline and Punish* suggests that the great periodizer was also fascinated by processes of diffusion across time, processes by which institutional forms spread beyond their initial contexts. The text concentrates significant attention on the ways in which institutions borrow and adopt strategies from other times and places and put them to new ends. The minute and highly specified practices of comparing and judging that are so crucial to disciplinary institutions, for example, borrow from judiciary mechanisms that go back at least as far as ancient Rome: "drawing on a series of very ancient procedures," Foucault writes, to "create . . . a new functioning of punishment."[42] Even more memorably, the enclosed, segmented space of Bentham's panopticon draws on seventeenth-century plans for partitioning a city caught in the grip of a plague epidemic. "On almost every occasion," Foucault explains, disciplinary strategies "were adopted in response to particular needs: an industrial innovation, a renewed outbreak of certain epidemic diseases, the invention of the rifle or the victories of Prussia" (138). But far from remaining local and particular, they soon circulate from army to school to factory to prison.

Why do small, local techniques of discipline, begun in one institution, spread to others, often with startling speed? To use my own terms rather than Foucault's, I want to suggest that it is because these forms afford portability. That is, techniques of organizing bodies or objects spread quickly because they are simple, iterable, efficient ways of imposing order on heterogeneous materials. Timetables, repetitive exercises, rows, circles, the shape of the dormitory or the rhythm of the monastery—all of these travel from one institution to another, from one time to another, precisely because they can break with any single context; they are useful ways of imposing order that can crop up wherever and whenever they are needed. This transhistorical power is what makes form seem suspicious to those critics committed to particularity: it is its capacity to cross contexts that testifies to form's abstraction. But paradoxically, according to Foucault, it is also exactly the generalizability—the portability—of forms that particular institutions depend on as they respond to specific and local pressures, borrowing shapes and rhythms from other institutions to solve immediate problems.

What is most alarming about Foucault's understanding of these forms in *Discipline and Punish* is his sense that they are capable of spreading so widely that they can come to dominate a whole society. That is, they work together: the prison "is not alone, but linked to a whole series of 'carceral' mechanisms which seem distinct enough—since they are intended to alleviate pain, to cure, to comfort—but which all tend, like the prison, to exercise a power of normalization" (308). Yet, while the capacity of forms to work toward common ends allows them to seem frighteningly powerful en masse, and while there is certainly truth to the claim that techniques of normalization have so successfully permeated the social body as to organize the daily work of schools, hospitals, bureaucracies, families, and prisons, it is my argument that an attentiveness to the operations of institutional forms suggests quite the reverse of Foucault's conclusions: occasionally an institution's repetitive patterns align, but more often they work across and athwart one another, generating a landscape of power that is nothing if not messy and uncoordinated.

Paradoxically, in fact, Foucault gives us the very tools we need to grasp the impossibility of his own nightmarish era of the total coordination of "carceral" forms. He points us to the remobilization of old forms for modern uses, such as monastic time for prison discipline, and although he focuses only on those forms that are put to use for newly powerful ends, his logic implies that lots of other old forms might also be waiting around, available for reuse. Thus Foucault's interest in enduring forms might prompt us to begin noticing an array of archaic institutional forms that linger long through patterns of repetition and reenactment—among them the historical period, the seminar, and the electricity cooperative—which provide ongoing alternatives to any single, coordinated and monolithic regime of power.

Colliding Rhythms

If any given institution can bring multiple forms from different historical moments into play, and remobilize them over time through citation and repetition, then a society organized by multiple institutions will be shaped not only by multiple points of origin but also by plural and conflicting rhythms. Let me offer an example that shows how social tempos can overlap, both coordinating and conflicting.

My example is deliberately mundane and familiar: public school schedules in the United States and Europe, which typically include a long summer break. Although there is a common myth that the summer holiday is a holdover from an agrarian calendar, historians of education have argued that in fact in the nineteenth century, attendance in school was *highest* for rural children in the summer, since bad weather did not prevent them from making the journey, and since their labor was most urgently needed for the spring planting and fall harvest. It was actually urban schools that repeatedly lengthened the summer break, citing "hot and unhealthy summer months due to epidemics, vacations, and a general truancy of students."[43]

As middle-class families began to organize their lives around escapes from crowded urban centers to summer retreats, new leisure industries— camps and resorts—followed suit, arranging their schedules, too, around an annual summer rhythm, in many cases depending on youth labor as well as the profits made from vacationing families. Other rhythms then began to be synchronized with the academic calendar, including the launch of new television seasons each fall. Social tempos were deliberately aligned.

But in recent years, as national pressures to improve test scores have mounted and working parents have struggled to find affordable summer care for their children, some schools have sought to shorten the summer holiday. This has in turn provoked a backlash. The State of Virginia, for example, passed a law that no public school could begin classes before Labor Day. This rule is called the King's Dominion Law, after the popular theme park that lobbied for it.[44] Since its implementation, some schools have successfully petitioned for waivers, many of them claiming that school closings on harsh winter days will threaten test scores by shortening the academic year.[45] Thus the annual tempo of public schools largely continues down a familiar, repetitive temporal path, but encounters conflicting pressures from the tourist industry, family incomes, winter weather, and (in the United States) from the testing required by federal law.

This example points to three aspects of institutional social rhythms that help to deepen and modify the social models of institutional time we see in Bourdieu, Williams, and Foucault. First, one of the affordances of rhythms is portability: institutions can borrow temporal forms from one another, as businesses and media took on the rhythms of the school year, which itself followed the rhythms of the leisured urban middle class, which was responding in part to an annual cycle of summer illness and hot weather. Foucault would agree so far. But unlike models drawn from Foucault and Bourdieu, we can see from this example how institutions also compete for authority over the management of temporal rhythms, sometimes working against one another. Thus theme parks, which borrowed their annual tempo from urban schools, now resist changes to that pattern urged on them by those very schools, as well as the state, progressive organizations, and working parents. Second, no single institution dominates or causes all of the tempos at work here. They cannot all be traced back to the nation-state, the Church, the economy, or nature. Rhythms drawn from all of these sources continue to organize us, often at the same time. Third, even the most dominant and entrenched rhythms are vulnerable. We can see how institutions are on the one hand strongly path dependent—it is difficult to change the school year once it has hardened into a familiar rhythm—and on the other hand encounter constant pressures both from within and without to shift their tempos. And the fact that the temporal forms of institutions involve patterns of practice that must be repeatedly reenacted for an institution to endure creates a certain weakness—a repeated opportunity for breaks and transformations. The rhythms of institutions afford not only portability, then, but also interruption and transformation. Their affordances include pauses and stoppages, lengthening and shortening.

This emphasis on rhythm and repetition allows us to return to the problem of historicism, and to reject the spatial container once and for all as the best form of historical time in literary and cultural studies. Historicist scholars have gotten into the habit of looking for a homology between period-containers and historical institutions, seeking out correspondences between the temporal boundaries of periods and the beginnings and endings of institutions. The crucial methodological point here is that the match will rarely, if ever, be a good one: the containing form of the period does not work particularly well to convey the messy tempos of institutions. Their forms are different. The insights of the new institutionalism thus point us to a considerably different starting-point from that of the new historicists—away from the notion of a single "shape" or "individuality" to describe a delimited context or institution, and toward the superimposition of iterable processes over time, sometimes over very long stretches. The *longue durée* can structure the scholar's analysis alongside the formation of a specific institution, and ideally, these different temporalities must be seen to function together and differently, overlapping and colliding, to produce a diachronic complexity as subtle and finely grained as any careful, scholarly grasp of cultural particularity. Indeed, since this kind of diachronic analysis unsettles the very notion of a historically specific time period, it suggests that the act of historicizing should mean, quite precisely, *refusing* any enclosed, bounded notion of cultural experience in favor of intricately intertwined transhistorical processes of transmission and citation across time. This means that social institutions are not nearly as successful at imposing a clear shape on social time as historicist scholarship so often presumes, and that we need a different model from the familiar container of the historical context to organize the work of cultural analysis.

It is a version of formalism that provides the tools we need to distinguish the ways in which different tempos shape, reinforce, unsettle, or alter one another. The fact that we are not in the habit of such close attentiveness when it comes to social formations points to a sorely missed opportunity: it has become routine to take the forms of institutions for granted as singular, coordinated, and monolithic, while carefully exploring the most elusive and subtle structures that organize literary texts. It is time to acknowledge that social experience, too, is composed of subtle and conflicting temporal organizing patterns, and to address directly the relations between aesthetic and social tempos.

Strategic Time: Originality and Precedent

For politically inclined readers, a formalist's understanding of social tempos will matter only to the extent that it can help us to effect social change. I want to suggest that a new attention to rhythm has this potential. So far, I have focused on institutional endurance and repetition over long periods. In this section of the chapter, I will focus on another affordance—one that we saw briefly in the school calendar example: the capacity for rhythmic repetitions to be broken, for institutional routines to be interrupted. In the example that follows, a small group of artists understood institutional rhythms so well, so cannily, that they were able introduce a change in the law. Specifically, the artists in this case understood something subtle about the specific affordances of institutional rhythms. They saw that the rhythms of the law, like those of poetry and music, depend not only on repetition but also on difference—variations and departures that repeat past patterns, but never perfectly. Ingeniously emphasizing institutional affinities between the rhythms of the art world and the rhythms of common law, rebellious artists of the historical avant-garde won a victory that surprised just about everyone. Nested in the overlaps and encounters of rhythms, they realized, lay politically strategic opportunities.

In October of 1926, the Romanian sculptor Constantin Brancusi shipped a new sculpture in bronze from Paris to New York. Now known as *Bird in Space*, the work was heading to photographer and art collector Edward Steichen, one of the foremost supporters of the European avant-garde in the United States. At the harbor, Steichen's purchase encountered an unexpected difficulty. Customs officials refused to allow the object to be categorized as a work of art, asserting that it belonged instead to the same import category as "table, household, kitchen, and hospital supplies." It was to be taxed at 40 percent of its value.[46]

To many in the art world, the whole affair was an affront, but the classification of the *Bird* as a kitchen utensil seemed particularly outrageous. Marcel Duchamp, then living in New York, was one of the few who tried to take advantage of the law's categories, pointing out that if the object was really a "potato masher" then it could not possibly be worth the $600 that Brancusi had charged for it. It would surely bring something more like $35 or $40 on the open market. If it was art, it would be tax free, and if it was a kitchen utensil the tax would be less than $20. The *Chicago Post* responded that Brancusi could charge what he liked for a kitchen utensil, and perhaps the *Bird* was simply an extremely expensive potato masher.[47]

There was as much antagonism raging against Brancusi in the mainstream press as there was support for him in the art world. The *New York City Sun* insisted that customs' refusal to recognize the *Bird* as art was "a good thing," representing "a healthy independence of French opinion."[48] Trying to foster a national culture, this article tapped into American anxiety about the innovative new art coming out of Europe. A common objection targeted the industrial material of the work. It is "a tall, slender, highly polished object, which looks like nothing so much as, say, half an airplane propeller," claimed the *New York American*,[49] and the *Providence Journal* complained that the *Bird* was "nothing more than an oval spindle of bronze," rightly classified by customs officials as "mere junk."[50] Breaking with familiar traditions of representation and national standards of taste, Brancusi's work was too strange to qualify as art.

One might assume that in the legal battle of *C. Brancusi v. United States* (1928), the force of nationalist popular feeling or traditional institutions of high art would prevail over the rebellious avant-garde. But the unfolding of events does not fit the standard narrative of the lone artist quashed by popular taste, a corporate-driven mass media, conservative institutions, or the state. There were two major legal questions that had to be answered in the courtroom. The 1922 Tariff Act, which defined the kind of sculpture that could qualify as duty-free art under the law, stipulated that to qualify as art a work must be "original." This would not seem to be much of a problem for the deliberately strange, challenging work of the European avant-garde, which defined itself by its departures from tradition. But the demand for originality in this case ran up against a second question set by recent legal precedent. *United States v. Olivotti* (1916) had defined sculpture as an art that carves or models "imitations of natural objects in their true proportions of length, breadth, and thickness, or of length and breadth only."[51] To qualify as art, a work did not only have to be original; it had to be mimetic as well.

Implicitly, two models of temporal process—two temporal forms—vied for priority in the trial. Originality entails a break, a refusal to repeat the past. In the moment of the historical avant-garde, the rejection of mimesis was of course a crucial sign of this break. Mimesis, by contrast, entails a

III

double repetition: on the one hand, art that aims to be realistic deliberately seeks to repeat the experience of the object in the world, doubling the real; and on the other hand, by the 1920s, this kind of realism felt so familiar, so conventional, that it seemed utterly exhausting in its repetitiveness.

In a sense, then, it was the very question of repetition itself that was on trial. The lawyers for the government were eager to show that Brancusi's art was too extreme, startling, and new-fangled too meet the law's definition of sculpture as representational. They spent much of the trial grilling witnesses about his failure to represent a bird in a straightforwardly realistic way. One judge famously asked a witness: "If you saw it in the forest, you would not take a shot at it?" (20). Jacob Epstein—himself a noted avant-garde sculptor—argued in his testimony that the title *Bird* was not the equivalent of the object, but rather a cue to a new way of reading. He said: "If the artist called it a bird, I would take it seriously if I have any respect for the artist whatever. It would be my first endeavor to see whether it was like a bird" (30). Epstein put his emphasis not on the object's likeness to the world, but on the artist's conception. And he imagined that the artist's title was there to shape the viewer's understanding of the work. Epstein offered the court a theory of art as that which would not repeat but would transform the perceptions and assumptions of the audience: the title would teach the viewer to perceive the object in a new and instructive way, and the object, in turn, would prompt a new perception of the world. This was a path not of substitutions but of development, as each step built on the one before: first the title, then the art work, then the world, each calling for an unfamiliar experience of the next.

The notion of art as an engine of social change was in keeping with a certain understanding of art's capacity for development that was already at work in customs law. "Free art by multiplying the art objects of the country will develop an artistic taste among the people, which will in turn create a demand for artistic products, and so call into existence new domestic industries which will give employment at high wages to skilled laborers."[52] As art transformed people, it would stimulate further creativity, triggering both economic development and homegrown artistic production. On economic grounds, as well as artistic ones, it was more important to establish the artwork's power to create and transform than to enforce the replication of any established model or style. This similarity suggested that Epstein's account of art as transformative and future-oriented might be more compelling than the rhythm of endless, circular repetition envisioned by *Olivotti*.

And yet, this is not quite the end of the story. Brancusi's legal team soon found that they had to reckon with the opposite problem. Was it possible

70

that the work could be *too* original? If it was completely unlike other art objects, it might represent such a radical break from the past that it would cease to count as art altogether. Institutionally speaking, an art object has to repeat the norms of art in some recognizable way in order to belong to the art world at all. Institutions, as we have seen, ensure their own stability by way of repetition. As the trial went on, the opposing counsel took up this line of attack, exaggerating rather than undermining Brancusi's originality. William Henry Fox, Director of the Brooklyn Museum, was asked whether the museum contained any work that looked like Brancusi's *Bird*. When he agreed that it was "distinct," the lawyer pounced: "different from all other sculptures by artists, it is isolated from what we call art?" (42). Epstein was asked if he "had made anything like the Exhibit 1 ... in all your thirty years?" Epstein replied that he had not, and this response opened the door to further skepticism about Brancusi's work. "So he stands practically isolated and alone in this particular class of art?" (30).

The next moment in the trial was to prove decisive. Epstein produced a precedent. Brancusi's work, he said,

> is related to a very ancient form of sculpture, I should say even to the Egyptian. He does not stand absolutely alone. He is related to the fine ancient sculpture, like the early Egyptian, three thousand years old. If you would like to bring into the court a piece of sculpture, ancient sculpture, which I happen to have, I can illustrate. (30)

The sculptor was permitted to leave the stand in order to fetch the object, a three-thousand-year old Egyptian image of a hawk. Judge Waite, comparing it to Brancusi's *Bird*, asked Epstein to articulate the similarity. Epstein claimed that the likeness lay primarily in the fact that the ancient work was, like the *Bird*, abstract but evocative. The judge was convinced: "The wings and feet are not shown, still you get the impression it is a hawk" (31). Egyptian sculpture, like Brancusi's *Bird in Space*, lacked details associated with real birds. It was not anatomically complete, but its simplified contours nonetheless produced an "impression." The ancient sculpture could therefore act as a precursor to modern abstract art.

At this moment, then, the tempo of avant-garde originality started to look startlingly similar to the rhythms of common law. Anglo-American law seeks to relate each new case to its precedents, setting each in a tradition, but also striving to acknowledge the specificity of the new, the potential for each example to demand a departure from tradition. New precedents are set when the particularities of the case call for a shift or expansion of definitions. Thus common law always tries to balance its fidelity to the past with an acknowledgment of the unpredictable newness of the future.[53] In theory, avant-garde art does the opposite, representing the effort to make a decisive break with tradition and the weight of the past. The tempos of the law and the avant-garde should find themselves fundamentally at odds.[54] But Epstein astutely refused the usual rhetorical argument that the avant-garde deliberately ruptures its connections with the past. If the *Bird* was to be recognized as an original artwork, it must be shown to be new, yes—but not so new that it would cease to belong to the category of art. Connecting abstraction to an ancient precedent, Epstein affirmed that what had seemed like the shocking art of the avant-garde actually repeated elements drawn from a venerable history.

Perhaps it is not surprising, then, that the final decision in *Brancusi v. United States* showed respect for the art world's innovations:

> [*United States v. Olivotti*] was handed down in 1916. In the meanwhile there has been developing a so-called new school of art, whose exponents attempt to portray abstract ideas rather than to imitate natural objects. Whether or not we are in sympathy with these newer ideas and the schools which represent them, we think the facts of their existence and their influence upon the art world as recognized by the courts must be considered. (115)

With this decision, customs law added a crucial social element to its long-standing definition of art as the work of individual geniuses; here, whatever spark of creativity there is takes place in "schools" that together form an independent "art world." And indeed, despite the radical strangeness of Brancusi's abstraction, what finally emerged in the courtroom proceedings was a definition of the avant-garde not as a rule-breaker but as a repetitive and self-regulating institution.

As in any legal case, expert witnesses had to demonstrate their qualifications in order to testify. All of the witnesses for and against Brancusi were grilled on their training, their prizes and diplomas, their time spent writing about or creating art, and the galleries and magazines where their work had appeared. The lawyers on both sides worked hard to argue that certain journals, museums, and schools were legitimate sources of expertise on the question of art. In this context, Brancusi's team had little trouble establishing the professional status of the artist. Certified experts attested to his international reputation, his numerous high-profile shows, his portrayal in recognized arts publications, his place in art history classrooms, and his dedication to the exclusive activity of art-making. To hear these witnesses repeatedly invoking awards and guidelines, recognized authorities and international reputations, one might think that the goal of the radical avant-garde was to be conventional, disciplined, and orthodox.

Epstein's precedent and the court's grasp of the art world as a rule-bound institution came together to make Brancusi's work seem to conform to a familiar, sanctioned set of institutional rhythms that balanced tradition and innovation, repetitions and ruptures, in ways that were easily recognizable to the judges. And this was not duplicity or selling out on the part of the art world: Epstein's reliance on precedent revealed a real, though rarely acknowledged, rhythm of the avant-garde. Originality can never be so absolute that it leaves the past altogether behind, since even the most radical of artistic departures in some way acknowledge what they are leaving behind. In the moment of avant-garde rebellion, it was in fact the institution of the art world that most effectively guaranteed artists like Brancusi their connection to tradition. For despite the artists' own fierce resistance to institutionalization, a loose network of journals, galleries, reviewers, and scholars continued to make decisions about what counted and what did not count as part of the unfolding history of art.[55]

In the end, it was a canny grasp of institutional tempos that won Brancusi the battle. By harmonizing what might seem to be the very different tempos of the avant-garde art world and the state, the two came to seem like allies rather than antagonists. When the law granted the art world its freedom to pursue eccentric and innovative techniques, it did not imagine art as a rebellious and hostile force. Instead, the customs court cast the art world as a fellow institution, self-sufficient and coherent, with its own rules and guidelines, its own repetitions and its own authorized ruptures from those patterns. Equally willingly, the art world accepted its own tempo as a pattern of originality and precedent, repetition and difference—innovative but not too innovative, and free but not too free. And so it was that the court could find firmly in favor of the avant-garde sculptor, itself enacting a break in a repetitive rhythm that overturned legal precedent, allowing art to depart from dictionary definitions, national majorities, and commonsensical responses to art.

Prosody

If it is important to understand encounters between social tempos in order to bring about social change, how should we go about understanding the relations between the temporal forms that organize literary texts—meter, rhyme, plot—and the multiple and colliding rhythms that organize and dis-organize the social institutions that surround them? While scholarship on the novel has been meager in this regard, critics of poetry have in recent decades paid rich and substantial attention to rhythm, and this is what draws me to consider prosody here. New Critics like Cleanth Brooks favored the idea of a static lyric whole, but new formalists have been eager to interpret the relationship between metrical forms and social institutions. Most often, they have looked for likenesses or homologies, reading poetic meter as a re-flection of social tempos. Ivan Kreilkamp, for example, argues that Victorian poetry could be read in a newly "super-charged realm of electricity, speed, heat, and light" as offering up metrical experiences of social "shock ... mo-bility, acceleration, discontinuity, the transitory, the elusive and the ephem-eral."[56] Metrical forms here match or mirror lived temporalities.

I want to offer an alternative model for relating the rhythms of poetry to the rhythms of social experience, which, as we have seen, are often messy, complex, and overlaid. What if we consider meter as another of these social rhythms, not an epiphenomenal effect of social realities, but capable itself of exerting or transmitting power? One reason that politically minded crit-ics have felt uncomfortable with reading for form in poetry is that meter has often been likened to imprisonment and containment, its patterns un-derstood as "curbs and shackles."[57] This suggests that metrical forms, like prisons and schools, arrange and control their materials. And to some ex-tent this is true. While poetic rhythms do not carry the same material force, or coerce the same bodies, they do afford the imposition of a temporal order. Here, I will make the case that rhythmic forms and political institu-tions both seek to control time, but they do so in different and sometimes contending ways.

It is Elizabeth Barrett Browning who has most insistently pointed me to this conclusion. A poet who was deeply interested in the compli-cated and often incoherent temporal experience that resulted from the superimposition of social institutions—anticipating the work of the new institutionalists—she is also a poet whose own meter frustrates conven-tional readings. In "The Young Queen" (1837), Barrett Browning investi-gates the different shapings of time at work in the transfer of power that is the royal succession. By no means the best known or the best loved of Barrett Browning's poems (Alethea Hayter in fact calls it "among the worst and most embarrassing"),[58] the poem fails to please readers and critics, I will argue, precisely because it refuses to assimilate literary to social time. It seems mawkish and inelegant because it violates assumptions about for-mal unity and about the coordination of social and poetic time, but it is precisely in this failure that the poem points the way to a new set of protocols for reading the relations between the time of poetry and the time of institutions. I am going to look, first, at the temporalities Barrett Browning describes in the content of the poem, and then I will explore her shaping of temporal experience through meter. For the moment, form and content need to be kept separate because the poet herself does not assimilate one to the other.

An epigraph from the new queen precedes the poem proper. Spoken on the day of the king's death, her words emphasize the abruptness of the event:

This awful responsibility is imposed upon me so suddenly and at so early a period of my life, that I should feel myself utterly oppressed by the burden, were I not sustained by the hope that Divine Providence, which has called me to this work, will give me strength for the performance of it.[59]

With an accession too sudden and too early, the too-youthful queen inspires Barrett Browning to meditate on the organization of temporal experience in this national event. The emphasis on abruptness frames our experience of the poem. The text proper then opens with the dead body of the king:

> The shroud is yet unspread
> To wrap our crowned dead;
> His soul hath scarcely hearkened for the thrilling word of doom;
> And Death, that makes serene,
> Ev'n brows where crowns have been,
> Hath scarcely time to meeten his for silence of the tomb. (1–6)

The whole poem takes place in the brief moment before the king is enshrouded. It is fitting that the word "scarcely" appears twice in this opening stanza: the turnover of royal power is by necessity rapid—any noticeable pause between one reign and the next would risk discontinuity or a power vacuum. Thus Barrett Browning draws our attention to the fact that the event of royal succession must come so quickly that it has to interrupt another momentous ritual: the funeral. Death, unlike succession, demands a pause: in the first stanza death calls on the king to prepare for the next life, while in the third stanza the grieving widow and nation suggest that death also demands a lag for others, who must struggle to assimilate the loss. But the death of a king also requires the sudden succession of a queen, too young and distinctly *un*prepared.[60] Both social institutions follow a temporal logic proper to themselves: the rapidity of succession makes political sense, just as the deliberate and solemn ritual of the funeral allows the dead, the family, and the nation to prepare for life after death, but the two overlap in this uncomfortable moment. The funeral is properly regulated, the succession frighteningly abrupt.

The second stanza explicitly marks the "confusing" overlap between the funeral and the monarchy:

> St. Paul's king-dirging note
> The city's heart hath smote—
> The city's heart is struck with thought more solemn than the tone!
> The shadow sweeps apace
> Before the nation's face,
> Confusing in a shapeless blot both sepulchre and throne. (7–12)

The public announcement of the king's death is described as a dirge—a slow and measured kind of music—while the shadow of the royal death moves quickly. The result is a temporal and spatial disarray: city and nation, church and state, death and succession add up to "a shapeless blot," an inability to separate two powerful institutions, here evoked as spatial containers—"sepulchre and throne"—one moving at a measured pace in the city, and the other hurrying the nation ahead.

Barrett Browning is not satisfied with the overlapping of just two institutional tempos. She adds the time of maturation—the queen's abrupt coming of age in the moment of her succession. Building on the epigraph, the poet reflects on what it feels like to leave childhood behind in such a dramatic way: "Perhaps our youthful queen / Remembers what has been—/ Her childhood's rest by loving heart, and sport on grassy sod—" (37–39). That time is over now, but Barrett Browning suggests that it can be exchanged for an equally joyful future. The poet urges the young queen to "leave such happy days behind, for happy-making years!" (45). In the moment of succession, the young queen abruptly shifts from subject to monarch, a transition offered to us as a single moment rather than a process of slow development. And while the form of this life process is a substitution of maturity for youth, the content of the experience may remain continuous: happiness—for both past and present, subject and sovereign.

The final stanza introduces a crucial political element to this process of substitution. The poet imagines that the queen's joy in the nation will take the place of her mother's joy in her:

> And so the grateful isles
> Will give thee back their smiles,
> And as thy mother joys in thee, in them shalt *thou* rejoice.
> Rejoice to meekly bow
> A somewhat paler brow,
> While the King of kings shall bless thee with the British people's voice.
> (49–54)

Not surprisingly for one of her republican inclinations, Barrett Browning allows God to legitimate the queen by way of the people's voice, and so the succession turns into a moment where God and people unite together to consecrate the bowing and meek young queen. But most importantly for our purposes here, time undergoes a transformation in the process. The event of succession, figured for us first as a transition from childhood to adulthood, now takes shape as a legitimating *political* relationship. In place of the developing time of progression, Barrett Browning offers us the back-and-forth movement of reciprocity. Both are substitutions, but the political exchange does not depend on time moving forward; it is unambiguously a *meanwhile* ("While the King of kings . . ."). And yet Barrett Browning manages to merge these two registers, as in line 51: "And as thy mother joys in thee, in them shalt *thou* rejoice." By allowing "joy" to act as the constant, the poet invites the shift from childhood to adulthood to become one with the mutual happiness that marks the queen's relationship to her people. In other words, Barrett Browning's highly compact language overlays two different ordering principles such that they become indistinguishable—a temporal order wherein the child is replaced by the adult and a legal order wherein the people and the queen assent to one another.

Taken as a whole, the poem describes a surprising layering of temporal registers: the moment of death, the ceremonial time of the funeral, the transition from childhood to adulthood, and the abrupt transfer of state power, acceded to at the same moment by God, the people, and the young queen. The text goes out of its way to cast this national event as organized by varied tempos: the startling suddenness of death, the regularity of the tolling bell, the "childhood's rest" cut short by the king's death, the meanwhile of a reciprocal relationship between queen and people, and the abrupt transfer of state power. Barrett Browning indicates clearly that this kind of heaping can lead to a "confusing," "shapeless" experience, an unwieldy pile of social, political, and even biological rhythms—if we include birth, death, and maturation in the list of elements that shape temporal experience.

To return to prosody, then: what poetic rhythm could do justice to this blurry superimposition of real rhythms in the world? It seems noteworthy that Barrett Browning opts neither for a highly regular, standardized rhythm, such as might celebrate the peaceful transmission of power, nor a jerky and abrupt one, such as might point to the shock of death as an integral part of the institution of the monarchy. Nor does she merge the two, moving back and forth between regular and irregular tempos to reflect stability and change, the necessary transitions entailed by a constitutional monarchy. She does not violate regularity in such a way as to point us to outright revolution; and yet, neither does she try to cover over the anxieties and contradictions that mark a constitutional monarchy. Nor does she give us multiple metrical patterns, heaped upon one another to reflect the confusing shapelessness that results from the blurring of "sepulchre and throne," not to mention the time of maturation, the time of ritual, and the time of legitimation.

Instead, she gives us a relatively—but far from perfectly—regular rhythm in a metrical form that both evokes traditional prosody and also departs from it. "The Young Queen" is structured as two lines of iambic trimeter followed by a fourteener, or 6, 6, 14. This pattern is very close to the "poulter's measure" defined by the sixteenth-century poet George Gascoigne—an alternating pattern of 12 and 14 syllables. After the sixteenth century, these long lines are often broken up: a poulter's measure can become 6, 6, 8, 6—a pattern commonly used in hymns and called "short meter."

We can see Barrett Browning as either dividing the long poulter's measure by chopping the alexandrine in half, or as extending short meter by merging its last two lines into one. Many of her stanzas come close indeed to short meter, since quite a few of her long lines are divided by a clear caesura after 8 syllables ("And leave such happy days behind, for happy making years!" [45]), and yet, the fact remains that the third and sixth lines look strikingly elongated on the page and certainly resist the ordinary appearance—and name—of short meter. Thus Barrett Browning's odd pattern of 6, 6, 14 repeats traditional meters, themselves repetitive patterns, while also unmistakably altering them.

On the one hand, there is no perfectly recognizable, conventional poetic form at work; on the other, there is no outright resistance to convention, either. One could choose to read this pattern as a deliberate manifestation of Barrett Browning's own liberalism—in favor of moderate change rather than stasis or revolution. But this reading would overlook the temporal concerns of the poem, with its emphasis on the heaping of incommensurable temporalities that together constitute both the personal and the national experience of this event. That is, Barrett Browning's meditations on the temporality of state power in this poem do not revolve around questions of proper and improper speeds or rates of transmission; they reflect instead on a piling up of multiple institutional tempos that are *necessarily* superimposed at the moment of royal succession. To say that Barrett Browning's metrical choice expresses the desire for a restrained pace in politics, then, is to miss the fact that in this poem she carefully figures numerous paces operating at once—inextricable and even indistinguishable from one another. We cannot have the peaceful transmission of power without the startling abruptness of death; we cannot bury the dead with measured and respectful ceremony while also waiting for the young queen to feel ready for her new responsibility. Haste and rest do not compete here; nor do they alternate. The social situation simply demands the coexistence of multiple tempos— the simultaneous workings of diverse speeds.

Critics, as we have seen, have often assumed that prosody is political insofar as it mirrors rhythms in the world. But this poem points to a markedly different conclusion. By organizing her text around a meter that does not evoke any of the particular social tempos she describes, Barrett Browning suggests that poetry can impose its own order. Both the poem and the state are composed of rhythmic repetitions and sudden breaks. But poetry does not here simply translate or represent the rhythms of the state; poetic meter affords an organizing of temporal experience in its own way in the moment of reading, just as political power does in the moment of royal succession, which means that the state and the poet are actually at work on one and the same project—the struggle to impose temporal order. In this reading, Barrett Browning's altered poulter's measure adds yet another tempo—another rhythm to pile onto the patterns of state and family, funeral knells, and the sudden loss of childhood. All of the possible tempos of our experience, the poet suggests—social, political, biological, and aesthetic—structure our experience, no one of them dominating or organizing the others. We cannot trace all of them to the same origins: in the state, for example, or in nature.

It seems only right in this context that Barrett Browning should experiment with a prosody that is notably incommensurable with the forms of the social world. This is a poetry that proclaims the independence of prosody, its refusal to be read as merely epiphenomenal. But if this poetic form refuses secondariness, it refuses primacy too: prosody emerges neither as hopefully emancipatory nor as powerfully all-constraining. Rather, like other rhythms, poetry can impose order on time only in a social context constantly organized and reorganized by other tempos, producing a surprisingly "shapeless" temporal experience. And although it might be tempting to read Barrett Browning's insistence on the independence of prosody as a naive or idealist view of poetry as emancipated from the shackles of history or experience, this would be to overlook the overt meditations on power and social institutions that constitute the major focus of this poem. This is not a poetry that seeks detachment from politics, or one that tries to mask the complex institutional pressures that come to bear during symbolic rituals of the nation-state. Rather, I would argue that Barrett Browning's exploration of the independence of prosody in poetry with explicit political content points the way to an understanding of literary form as bound up in political life, without becoming subordinate to it.

And this conclusion calls for a new look at the political force of form. Those who resist form and formalism typically worry about the capacity to impose a powerfully homogenizing, unifying order on the social. Barrett Browning points the way to a different hypothesis: what if the organizing forms of the world do not—cannot—unify experience? If they emerge from different institutions and organize material according to different logics, perhaps they do not work together. In this light, metrical "law" emerges as one law among many others, none capable of subsuming other temporal rhythms, or of being subsumed.

Formalist ways of reading, as we have seen, are famous for prompting us to understand works of art as tightly organized wholes, fusing concepts and linguistic relationships into a single, densely patterned unity. Barrett Browning invites us to envision a more open-ended reading of metrical form that, by focusing on multiple and distinct principles of temporal order, leads not to equilibrium but to collision, superimposition, even mind-boggling disarray. Aesthetically, this is risky indeed, since meditations on shapelessness threaten to look muddled themselves. And such formal openness can also seem illegible, given the usual protocols of reading poetic forms as indices of preexisting social formations. But Barrett Browning's metrical choices in this poem on Queen Victoria do point to a fruitful new conception of the relations between literary and political forms: the idea that the organizing principles of our social world—including poetry—follow different repetitive tempos and durations, all constraining our experience but none dominating it. Forms do organize us, but on a daily basis we are organized at once by multiple social, political, biological, and aesthetic rhythms, each imposing a different order and following a different logic. They do not work together, and so in the end are not able to impose a single coherent order on experience. If Barrett Browning is right—if it is true that many conflicting and overlapping organizing principles merely *try* to impose monolithic laws on experience, while often instead producing confusing and shapeless blots rather than integrated power—then a new formalism will have to take account of the temporal patterns of art and life as organizing and shaping, yes, but also as plural and colliding, jumbled and constantly altered, each, thanks to the others, incapable of imposing its own dominant order.

IV

HIERARCHY

The word *hierarchy* comes from the Greek *hieros*, meaning "sacred," and *arche*, meaning "rule." The term was first used in the sixth century CE, when it referred to levels of angelic choruses, but it soon came to be applied to the governance of the Church, to describe its strictly ordered levels of authority and subordination. Gradually, from the fourteenth to the seventeenth centuries, its meaning widened beyond the religious context to apply to the natural sciences and to society more generally.[1] These days it can refer to organizations, values, and social relationships.

It is not difficult to understand hierarchies, like bounded wholes and rhythms, as forms: hierarchies arrange bodies, things, and ideas according to levels of power or importance. Hierarchies rank—organizing experience into asymmetrical, discriminatory, often deeply unjust arrangements. The most consistent and painful affordance of hierarchical structures is inequality. Hierarchies are in this respect the most troubling of all the forms we will consider in this book.

Across the humanities, hierarchies have drawn a great deal of attention, as scholars have sought to understand why and how such flagrantly unequal structures succeed in imposing their order on the world. Since the 1970s, theorists have paid especially close attention to the binary oppositions that organize a great deal of cultural and political experience: masculinity and femininity, public and private, mind and body, black and white. These had seemed universal and simply neutral to structuralist thinkers like anthropologist Claude Lévi-Strauss in the 1950s and 1960s.[2] But the poststructuralists who followed argued that these binaries were always covertly hierarchical and that their seeming neutrality had justified violence and inequality for centuries.

Since the Greeks, the poststructuralists argued, Western thought had longed to ground transcendent truth in a single, foundational concept, such as reason, mind, man, or the public sphere. Philosophers tried to establish the identity of each fundamental concept through what it was not, defining reason against madness, mind against body, man against woman, public against private. And what poststructuralist thinkers argued was that the second term—the excluded other (madness, body, woman)—always emerged as degraded or abjected. As the philosopher Elizabeth Grosz puts it:

> Dichotomous thinking necessarily hierarchizes and ranks the two polarized terms so that one becomes the privileged term and the other its suppressed, subordinated, negative counterpart. The subordinated term is merely the negation or denial, the absence or privation of the primary term, its fall from grace; the primary term defines itself by expelling its other and in this process establishes its own boundaries and borders to create an identity for itself.[3]

Grosz, like many others, has argued that foundational hierarchical binaries typically work together, coordinating with one another to strengthen whole structures of power. By this account, the privileged term in each binary reinforces the privileged terms in all of the supposedly foundational binaries; thus the rational, masculine, public subject governs the emotional, private, woman object: he is all mind, she body. And as these binaries align, the theory goes, they consolidate power and agency in the hands of white, male subjects.[4]

Many theorists in the humanities since the first wave of poststructuralism have sought to disrupt these painful hierarchical binaries by revealing their instability and conventionality, the necessary contamination of the first, foundational term by the second, abjected one, and hence the impossibility of policing the boundary between the two. Judith Butler, among the most influential of these theorists, writes:

> Gender is the mechanism by which notions of masculine and feminine are produced and naturalized, but gender might very well be the apparatus by which such terms are deconstructed and denaturalized. Indeed, it may be that the very apparatus that seeks to install the norm also works to undermine that installation, that the installation is, as it were, definitionally incomplete. . . . Whether one refers to "gender trouble" or "gender blending," "transgender" or "cross-gender," one is already suggesting that gender has a way of moving beyond that naturalized binary.[5]

Gender, as "mechanism" and "apparatus," is no fact of nature, but an instrument or device that produces hierarchical distinctions. And in generating distinctions it also affords the possibility of undoing them.

Such deconstructive approaches to binaries are now so familiar in literary and cultural studies that they have themselves become something like second nature in the field. While I have learned a great deal from this rich theoretical literature and will draw on it here, I will also depart from it in three specific ways. First of all, I want to separate the form of the binary from the form of the hierarchy. Poststructuralist theory has alerted us to the troubling fact that seemingly neutral binaries can hide hierarchies, but that does not mean that the two forms are always the same. Binary forms divide a field of objects, bodies, or ideas into two domains. The use of two refrigerator compartments, one for vegetables and the other for fruits, imposes a binary—a perfectly humdrum one—that does not mask a worrying hierarchy. Astronomers have identified seventeen pairs of stars that operate as nonhierarchical binaries, a small minority of star systems, but an intriguing phenomenon nonetheless.[6] While it may not be particularly interesting to discuss nonhierarchical binaries in literary and cultural studies, because these are precisely the ones that have few troubling implications, a rigorous formalism keeps these two forms separate for analytical purposes, the better to grasp what each affords and how each works. If it is true that binaries do not always coincide with hierarchies, it is a formalist method that will help us to understand when and how the two forms converge and reinforce one another's organizing power.

While some binaries are not hierarchies, it is also true that some hierarchies are not binaries. My second departure from the poststructuralist approach entails an attention to the sheer variety of hierarchical structures that organize us. Compare the gender binary, a simple structure, to the organizational hierarchy of a transnational corporation, for example. Or consider racism, which both splits the world into a simple binary—white and nonwhite—and also frequently functions as a spectrum, where gradations of skin color organize power and privilege within each category. Class, too, typically takes the shape of a composite, multilayered hierarchical structure. In Europe in the eighteenth and nineteenth centuries, the scale moves up from the lowest ranks of beggars and indigents to factory and farm workers, soldiers, artisans, and petit bourgeois shopkeepers, to bankers, military officers, large landowners, and upper nobility. Within the aristocracy and the military are many minute gradations. To be sure, one could characterize class in terms of simple binaries—bourgeoisie and proletariat, haves and have-nots—but Marx himself was interested in distinguishing levels within these categories, separating the urban proletariat from the rural peasantry and the *Lumpenproletariat*, that ragtag group that allied itself with the monarchy and financial sector in 1848, and so became a major obstacle to working-class revolution.[7] All hierarchies afford gradation, in other words, and their numerous ways of structuring inequality invite a formalist's close consideration.

My third and most important departure from deconstructive methods builds on the first two: as many different hierarchies simultaneously seek to impose their orders on us, they do not always align, and when they do collide, they are capable of generating more disorder than order. This argument will be familiar from other chapters, but it is most surprising when it comes to hierarchies, since these seem like the most straightforward manifestations of brute power. In fact, as they collide with other hierarchies and an array of other forms in social situations, hierarchies often go awry or are rerouted, and they can activate surprising and sometimes even progressive effects. The most strategic approach to the power exerted by hierarchies, then, is not always to dismantle, flatten, or upend them. If we start instead by observing hierarchical forms to see what arrangements they impose and to consider what happens to their organizing power when they intersect with other forms, we can find new ways of disturbing their power. It is the intersections of hierarchies with other forms and the intriguing, often unanticipated consequences that follow that will form the main focus of this chapter.

Social scientists have recently articulated a similar starting-point, arguing that hierarchies turn out to be surprisingly fragile, unpredictable, and vulnerable to breakdown. International relations theorist Alexander Cooley writes: "We have been taught ... that hierarchical polities are relatively functional, ordered, and well-governed entities." But as a result, scholars have failed to notice "the types of control losses and authority slippages in hierarchical organizations and [to ask] why the mere imposition of hierarchical governance does not always lead to the outcomes predicted by a dominant power." The reason we do not pay attention to these slippages, Cooley argues, is that we put too much emphasis on ideology and identity at the expense of understanding the complex work of "organizational forms."[8]

This chapter will develop Cooley's claim, arguing that if we consider closely the workings of hierarchical forms, we will find that they exert a far less orderly and systematic kind of domination than we might expect. I begin with a reading of Sophocles's *Antigone*. In this tragedy, the playwright sets a number powerful hierarchies in motion, almost all of them organized as simple binaries: masculine over feminine, king over subjects, friends over enemies, gods over humans. As these meet and intersect in the course of the dramatic action, a firm insistence on one hierarchy typically ends up reversing or subverting the logic of another, generating a political landscape of radical instability and unpredictability. *Antigone* has had of course an enormous influence on Western philosophy, and in some ways I approach it here more like a philosopher than a conventional literary critic, considering not the play's generic conventions and artful language but rather the relations of power and value that it presents, explores, and questions. But I do not, like many philosophers, conclude by siding with one character over another—Antigone or Creon, for example—or by trying to stake a position that fuses or critiques the implicit values that the tragedy stages. I make the case instead that Sophocles is unusually interested in the ways that dominant terms of hierarchical binaries fail to align and coordinate, and indeed relentlessly get in each other's way, leading to outcomes that elude the intentions of even the most powerful characters. In this way, Sophocles offers a robust answer to Elizabeth Grosz and other theorists who have focused their closest attention on cases where binary structures reinforce one another. Reading this tragedy as a plausible thought experiment, I suggest that Sophocles unfolds a persuasive but unfamiliar account of power, as he carefully works out the repercussions of multiple overlapping hierarchical binaries operating at once.

Sophocles, then, invites us to imagine that hierarchies interfere with one another's capacity to organize the world. The second section of this chapter expands to include other forms: what happens when bounded wholes and rhythms, too, come into the picture, organizing our experience atop or alongside hierarchies? Do these different, nonhomologous forms work with or athwart one another? My main focus here will be gender norms, a problem of longstanding interest in literary and cultural studies, and one we have already encountered in this book. Gender operates as a particularly stark form, a blunt binary that imposes its order not only on bodies, but also on other social forms, such as public and private spaces, divisions of labor, styles of dress and speech, and authority. While Butler is right to point to "cross-gender" and "transgender" as challenges to the binary, we can see how even these terms recognize the boundary line that constitutes the form of gender in the first place. The simplicity of the gender binary makes it an especially portable form, one that organizes materials and values both ancient and modern, across periods and continents.

For Sophocles, gender appears as a binary opposition that divides into higher and lower categories, but in *Antigone* it becomes complex and interesting when it runs up against other very similar binary forms. And indeed, although gender is simple in itself, organizing many realms of experience according to its straightforwardly oppositional logic, the formal story grows knotty and strange because the gender binary crosses paths so consistently with *other* forms—wholes, rhythms, and other hierarchies. As these many overlaps occur, the form of gender ends up producing ideologically strange effects. At times, as we will see, it can even come into conflict with *itself.*

The first two parts of this chapter focus on hierarchies that are also binaries. In the third part of the chapter, I will turn to a far more complex formal pattern: the bureaucratic hierarchy, that quintessentially modern management ladder, with its pecking order of subordinates and superiors. What form does an organizational hierarchy take, and can it impose a clear order on workers and the processes of their labor? Drawing from scholarship in the sociology of organizations, I argue that bureaucratic forms frequently clash and collide with each other, the management hierarchy overlapping with multiple tempos, bounded spaces, and other hierarchies, including—to come full circle—the hierarchical binary of gender.

A formalist analysis of hierarchy has two implications for literary and cultural studies. First, this approach points us to an unfamiliar analysis of power relations, offering a critique of prevailing assumptions about the political contexts of cultural production and reception. Second, as I will argue in the concluding section of this chapter, hierarchies matter to the act of reading, the vertical form of the hierarchy shaping our daily interpretive practices. In fact, I will make the case that political readings of texts both generalize forms and rank them. I turn here to Bruce Robbins, who suggests that hierarchies structure even the most politically progressive writing in literary studies, including postcolonial, Marxist, and feminist criticism. The goal, familiar now from previous chapters, is not always to find a way beyond hierarchies, but to figure out how to work productively with them.

Antigone

Written in fifth-century BCE Athens, *Antigone* has fascinated philosophers and political thinkers into our own time. Deliberately disobeying the formal edicts of the state in favor of ancient customs that honor family ties, Antigone herself has been taken to stand for a variety of values and positions, including a violent legal order that predates the state, the struggle between ethics and politics, mourning, femininity, monstrosity, civil disobedience, and the queering of kinship. Hegel, Schelling, Kierkegaard, Lacan, de Beauvoir, Irigaray, Derrida, Žižek, and Butler are among the many thinkers who have understood the drama as posing crucial questions about proper and improper relations among self, kin, and state. Hegel, most famously of all, argued that the play revolved around a collision between a nonpolitical, feminine devotion to a particular family and a masculine, universalizing commitment to the public good in the form of the state.[9] Two principles, familial piety and citizenship, each vie for ascendency over the other.

And yet, to reduce the play to *two* principles does not quite do it justice. The king, Creon, insists on the superiority of masculinity and upholds the power of the state over kinship, enforcing the legal division between insiders and outsiders as he does so. Antigone, by contrast, sets her loyalty to ancient gods over state power, asserting her feminine right to disobey the state publicly in the name of a familial love that she argues should take precedence over the law. Both claim to hold the good of the people higher than their own private interests. In other words, Sophocles gives us not two but at least six major organizing principles: public and private, gods and humans, king and people, man and woman, obedience and disobedience, and friend and enemy. All of the characters understand these binaries as hierarchies, with one term in the pair higher than the other.

From the very beginning, both major and minor characters struggle to make choices in the face of these contending hierarchies. In the first scene, Antigone tells her sister Ismene that Creon, the new king of Thebes, has denied their brother Polyneices a customary burial, which, she says, dishonors the laws of the gods. When Antigone urges Ismene to help her bury Polyneices, to honor the sacred ties of kinship rather than the king's unjust orders, her sister is horrified:

> [T]hink how we will die, most miserably of all, if in defiance of the law we transgress the power of the king. We must remember that we were born women, not to fight against men. . . . I, at least, will beg those beneath the ground to forgive me, since I am coerced in this; I will obey those who are in power. [10]

Ismene invokes two hierarchical binaries—king and subjects, and men and women. Antigone insists that a third—gods and humans—trumps the other two: "I will please those below longer than those here, for there I will lie forever" (7). While Antigone puts her love for her brother and the eternal power of the gods above the earthly power of the state, Ismene reaches for the hierarchy of gender to argue that the gods may forgive women who have been coerced into passivity by more powerful men. Antigone then rejects her sister, invoking a fourth hierarchy—that between friends and enemies—and casts her sister on the side of the enemies: "[Y]ou will earn my hatred" (9), she says, condemning Ismene for choosing the king over her own family.

This last hierarchy is in fact the one that launched the action of the play in the first place. Polyneices, fighting his brother for authority over Thebes, has married a foreign wife who has helped him to raise an army. Creon denies Polyneices a burial precisely on the grounds that he has been an enemy, not a friend, to Thebes.[11]

These forms may seem to organize the antagonisms in *Antigone*, but they also immediately disorganize them. Antigone is moved by loyalty to the private sphere of the family over the public domain of the state, and she insists that this loyalty is so good and so precious that there can be no shame in it, so she speaks out publicly against the king. In the process, she becomes a public spokesperson for the preeminence of the private sphere. And in speaking out publicly, she violates norms of femininity and becomes masculine in Creon's eyes, an act which in turn threatens to feminize him. "She boasts and laughs at what she has done," he complains. "Surely I am not the man now—she is!—if victory goes to her without punishment" (37). All along, Antigone's defiance rests partly on her sense that she is speaking publicly for the people of Thebes, acting in solidarity with the collective, and indeed she accuses Creon of putting his own private desires before those of the state—precisely what he has accused her of doing.

These kinds of ironic reversals recur throughout the play. Antigone, who has decided that Ismene is an enemy of the family, refuses to accept her sister's plea for solidarity, though it is precisely her insistence on the solidarity of the family that has led Antigone to reject Ismene in the first place. Antigone's supposed dedication to "the pure form of siblinghood," as Stefani Engelstein has argued, actually becomes "the elevation of one sibling above another, of Polyneices over Ismene."[12] Butler writes of her own surprise at finding how thoroughly the text's famous binaries falter and collapse: "how [Antigone's] actions compel others to regard her as 'manly' and thus cast doubt on the way kinship might underwrite gender, how her language most closely approximates Creon's, the language of sovereign authority and action, and how Creon himself assumes his sovereignty only by virtue of the kinship line that enables that succession, how he becomes, finally, unmanned by Antigone's defiance, and finally by his own actions, at once abrogating the norms that secure his place in kinship and in sovereignty" (6).

Butler and others have taken these ironies as inspiration to pursue a deconstructive style of argument, and to show how what are asserted as foundational rules and norms, such as stable kinship norms, turn out to depend on deviations and transgressions—their "constitutive outside." My own approach is complementary, in the sense that it too points us to a recognition that binaries necessarily waver and fail, and it too refuses to posit any single law or concept as foundational. But methodologically, the formalist approach I propose here is quite different.

I begin by understanding each form to have its own logic, its own principle of imposing order. Thus the opposition between friends and enemies offers a marked and distinct hierarchy, one that legitimizes war and violent punishments enacted by the state against criminals. Similar in form, gender operates as a binary division, the masculine predominating over the feminine. The opposition between the public realm of the collective and the private realm of the family and that between gods and humans also work by dividing the field of experience into two unequal parts. But these various binaries, though formally alike, do not map perfectly onto one another: an enemy may be feminine or masculine; a citizen who is loyal to the gods may be disloyal to the state; and a king who serves his own people may be dishonoring the gods.

The next step for the formalist reader, then, is to consider what happens to these hierarchies when they run into one another. The dramatic action of the play can be traced to a series of moments when characters choose one hierarchy over another: Antigone is obedient to the gods and disobedient to the state. She upholds one hierarchy (gods, humans) and so violates another (king, subjects). But in the process she happens to bring other hierarchies into play: she begins as feminine (lower) and an enemy of the state (lower) who favors the particular ties of kinship (lower), but by speaking out against the king becomes a public actor (higher), who is loyal to the gods (higher) who are on the side of the people (higher). Which means that her single choice of one hierarchy over another manages to transform a whole series of others, as low (woman, family, enemy of the state) becomes high (on the side of the Theban people and the gods), while high (man, state, public) is cast low (enemy of the gods and the people). The monarchy itself can grow tangled in its own binary forms: the state exerts laws that supersede any loyalty to kin, but it is the logic of kinship that controls the line of succession and assigns the head of state in the first place.

Antigone's choice of one hierarchy over another both inverts the usual order and blurs and disorders other hierarchies. For example, in choosing not to hide her choice of the gods over human laws, Antigone becomes public and so crosses the gender binary, suddenly appearing manly. She also undoes two other hierarchies, turning private loyalty into a public act, and in honoring the brother who was an enemy of the people, makes herself their friend. In the process, she manages to fracture even the organic form of the individual: she sets herself against herself (in the sense that she is willing to die to preserve her well-being) and sets Creon against Creon (in the sense that his commitment to the state undoes his commitment to the state). By choosing one hierarchy that happens to violate another hierarchy, then, Antigone becomes at once high and low, masculine and feminine, public and private, friend and enemy to the Theban people, self and not-self. Her end in this context is perfectly appropriate to her radically unsettled status: she is both killed and left to die, both entombed and alive.

Two minor characters in the play, less defiant than Antigone, try to work within the hierarchical structures that organize experience, but they find that it is impossible to harmonize them all. Haemon, Creon's son and Antigone's betrothed, struggles to be loyal to all of the contending parties: his father, his wife to be, the gods, the state, *and* the family. Pleading absolute friendship to his father and the state, he warns the king to honor the gods by forgiving his future wife. That is, he believes that he is being loyal to the king-state-father and tries to protect these higher terms in three hierarchies from the harm that will come from punishing an enemy of the state because she is also the friend of the gods and of Haemon himself. If it were true in this case, as it is often claimed, that hierarchies align in Western culture to produce powerful ideological and cultural formations, Haemon would not run into trouble. But he does. Creon, who had argued at first that the gods were on the side of the state, now, in his struggle against Antigone, assumes that Haemon's invocation of the gods must put his son on the side of the enemy. The friend-enemy hierarchy dominates Creon's logic so powerfully that he willingly sets himself against all allies of Antigone, including the gods and his own son, condemning him as the "slave of a woman!" (55)—lower than the low. Far from consolidating powerful hierarchies and showing how well they work in concert, Sophocles's representation of Haemon suggests that it is literally impossible to uphold the father, the gods, the king, masculinity, and the state all at once.

Meanwhile, Ismene too attempts simply to be loyal. Her fear for her sister's well-being marks her, from Antigone's perspective, as a cowardly friend to the state and traitor to the family, while from Creon's vantage point she appears loyal to her family and disloyal to the state. Ismene's single-minded attachment to the person of her sister, in other words, marks her confusingly as both public and private, both friend and enemy, because Antigone's actions have already blurred the division between the two spheres.

In a world in which binaries are so snarled together that they are constantly transforming one, it becomes impossible to choose a single hierarchy to organize the world. The hierarchies break down not because they are internally contradictory but because their encounters with other hierarchies unsettle them. Antigone's defiant speech and actions weaken Creon, raising her and lowering him. Since he insists that men are superior to women, the fact that she bests him, in his logic, makes her manly. In theory, the logic could just as easily go the other way: according to patriarchal reasoning, one could argue that her words are meaningless because they issue from the mouth of a woman, and women do not and cannot speak publicly. The space of formal collisions is in this sense an aleatory one—unpredictable even as each form tries to preserve its own logic—because it is not clear at any moment which form organizes all the others.

To be sure, one could argue that the whole Sophoclean system rests on an ultimate hierarchical binary: gods and humans. In the end, the drama punishes Creon for his hubris. But the gods' role in relation to the other hierarchies in the drama remains thoroughly indeterminate. The characters raise the question of whether the gods will side with ancient kinship customs or with the state—it could go either way. Creon insists that the gods will reward anyone who dedicates himself to the good of the *polis*: "Can you see the gods honouring evil men? Impossible!" (23). The friend of the state will be the friend of the gods. But Antigone is convinced that the gods will appreciate those who honor their laws over those of human beings: the friend of the gods can be an enemy of the state. Even the chorus changes its mind about the relation between humans and gods. Given the play's punishment of all concerned—Polyneices, Antigone, Creon, Haemon, Ismene, Eurydice, and all of Thebes, which is "sick" by the end of the drama—it is not clear that any position can lay claim to being on the side of the gods. Tragedy, famously, does not set wrong against right, but right against right. The gods are on all sides, and on none.

What Sophocles offers us, then, is a conflict among contending forms that disorders their logic without ever resettling them or simply inverting them. Nor does he imply that any single hierarchy grounds or organizes all of the others, offering a desirable or stable form for the future. The play's promiscuous punishing suggests, moreover, that the implications of the struggles between forms cannot be contained: the consequences of colliding hierarchies go everywhere. Ismene, trying simply to preserve her sister, and Haemon, trying to serve traditional hierarchies, are both victims of the unsettled order, caught up in the logic of contending forms. Antigone's initial choice throws persons, intentions, and all kinds of hierarchical ordering principles into disarray, as a woman becomes masculine, private turns public, a king becomes "less than nothing," and a single-minded devotion to the good of the *polis* ends up sickening the city.

The play is a valuable thought experiment for the formalist method I propose here, because it asks what consequences are likely to ensue when the binary forms that structure political experience come into conflict. My reading does not rely on traditional literary formalist methods, which would focus on the ways in which rhythm, metaphor, and dramatic structure come together in a taut unity. But it would also be a mistake to claim that literary form does not matter at all to this reading. I have privileged one form over others—dramatic narrative form, or the conflictual unfolding of events from an initial decision. In asking what might plausibly follow from a complex starting circumstance, Sophocles puts forward a set of ideas about how forms work. Thus a time-bound literary form allows us to think through the social work of nonliterary forms, as they carry their affordances with them into the tragedy.

Most philosophers and political theorists approach *Antigone* as a way to consider ethical or political choices and their consequences: should one choose kinship ties or state laws, the particularity of the brother or the generality of the *polis*? The form of tragedy would seem to be ideally suited to such philosophical questions: resting on a conflict between genuine alternatives, rather than vilifying or idealizing one position or another, tragedy asks how we might come to terms with opposing notions of the good.[13] Both a conventional philosophical reading and my own formalist one move easily between the forms of the drama and the forms of the world. And what is crucial to note here is that even highly political interpretations, ones that are more or less uninterested in the aesthetic, *use* the form of the drama to help to shape their own theories of the world. It is impossible to think ethics or politics outside of discursive forms such as argumentation, description, and presentation. Dramatic form affords some kinds of political and philosophical thinking that are foreclosed by other forms. *Antigone* is valuable, then, not only as an autotelic artwork, beautifully crafted as a totality—though it is certainly that—but also as a formal model for political relationships, one that restructures our attention and invites us to think anew about the power of hierarchies to organize our world.

Gender

Gender emerges as one of several powerful hierarchical binaries in *Antigone*, one that can be upended and reversed in relation to other hierarchies. Now I want to extend this claim, moving beyond a formal model in which multiple hierarchies collide, to consider a set of circumstances in which other kinds of forms, too, work with and against gender norms. In the last two chapters, we have seen wholes unsettling other wholes and rhythms colliding with rhythms, but in the world it is not only similar forms that meet. The rest of this book will consider how unlike forms encounter one another: what happens, for instance, when an event or experience is being organized simultaneously by rhythms, wholes, and hierarchies? As in Sophoclean trag-edy, these formal collisions can produce strange and aleatory possibilities. Gender is a good place to start, because, as we will see, it regularly forces hierarchies into relation with numerous other forms and shows how hierar-chical power can be destabilized in these encounters.

Although literary and cultural studies scholars do not typically refer to gender as a form, theorists such as Foucault and Butler have given us strong reason to do so. These thinkers have argued persuasively that gender does not emerge out of given or prior sex distinctions, but is repeatedly asserted and reasserted through attention to norms and deviations. Gender's "appa-ratus" entails the policing, the enforcement, of its binary structure. Thus any body, any practice, any genre or style could be gendered masculine or feminine, or some combination of the two, and penalized from moving out of its proper sphere.[14] To put this another way: the masculine-feminine binary is an organizing rule, an abstract, generalizable principle that can impose order here and there, on a multiplicity of social materials. Like enclosures and rhythms, it is capable of being repeated across time and space. This is by no means to claim that these forms are universal, or that they transcend particularity to give us access to some deep truth or value. But we have learned from decades of feminist scholarship that the gender binary does not belong to a single culture or context. And just about any-where it goes, gender is an organizing principle by which social groups come to be organized in a hierarchy, one high and one low, one wielding power and the other coerced into service. Thus it makes sense to think of gender as one of many iterable structures or patterns that are constantly shaping experience. It is more like a literary form than a fact of nature, a made or crafted shaping of materials.

This understanding of gender as a simple form might seem to go against scholarship in the past few decades, which has emphasized its complexity and multiplicity.[15] Intersectional analysis made the case that gender struc-tures social experience only in the context of other vectors of oppression and discrimination, such as race, class, sexuality, and disability.[16] Rejecting simplistic accounts of gender, scholars of the nineteenth-century United States have gone so far as to reject the category of "separate spheres" alto-gether. As Cathy Davidson explains, the gender binary "is simply too crude an instrument—too rigid and totalizing—for understanding the different, complicated ways that nineteenth-century American society or literary production functioned." She claims that it is a convenient "metaphor" that allows contemporary scholars to think simplistically about nineteenth-century culture. And so she calls for its dismissal.[17]

Davidson is right to be concerned that the gender binary is too simple, too orderly, too all-encompassing to describe the complexities of nineteenth-century social life. And yet I would argue that this is not in itself a reason to stop thinking about gender in binary terms. What if the binary is crude but also sometimes operative? What if gender functions *as* a binary, and sometimes powerfully? After all, it may be precisely because identity categories are characteristically simple that they can spread and be generalized. As Jane Gallop puts it, "with most of the workings of gender and/ or authority, the crude and schematic is usually all too apt."[18] The gender binary has force, in short, *because* it is reductive.

Simplicity is not itself a reason to cast gender off as an analytical category. But Davidson's worry that the gender binary leads to a reductive account of socio-political and cultural experience has force. It is my contention that the problem is not that gender itself is simplistic, but that it is too clear-cut if we consider it in isolation. If we look for the ways in which gender divides the social world in two, it will appear that it imposes its uncomplicated order on social materials. But part of what makes social experience complex is the fact that the gender binary is always working with and against other identity categories, such as race, class, and sexuality. And not only other identities: gender also encounters other forms—forms of knowledge, forms of narrative, forms of subjectivity, space, administration, education, repetition, circulation, collectivity, worship, and intimacy, among many others.

Let us continue our look at gender, then, by investigating in more detail the very form rejected by recent Americanist scholars like Davidson—the "separate spheres" associated most closely with the nineteenth century. The metaphor of "separate spheres" suggests that the gender hierarchy overlaps with another form, a bounded whole, or to be precise, two bounded wholes. One is the masculine, public realm of commerce and public life, the other the feminine, private sphere of home and family. "Separate spheres" evokes not only a clear binary, then, but also two spatially delineable forms. And although this is often only a figure, the idea of separate spheres for masculine and feminine activity has certainly imposed its order on literal spatial arrangements, containing women within domestic walls, for example, and preventing them from speaking in political forums.[19]

Since spaces are often gendered, and since gender is conceptualized as a space, it is tempting to understand gender simply through the form of the spatial container. And yet, the gender binary also regulates temporal experience. Contemporary societies urge girls not to begin sexual activity too soon and not to postpone marriage too long, while expecting boys to separate from their mothers and seek autonomy earlier than their female counterparts. Gender can also organize tempos of labor. Women around the world often undertake a "double workday," performing paid labor as well as unpaid domestic work.[20] On nineteenth-century slave plantations in the United States, gender often organized both the workday and the lifecycle, as older women looked after infants so that their mothers could labor through the daylight hours. And gender can also impose its order on definitions of maturity. For centuries in Europe, young boys grew out of dresses and gowns and into trousers, a custom known as "breeching." And after WWI, the British Parliament passed a law allowing women who were household-ers to vote, but they had to be over 30, while men could begin to vote at 21.

If the gender binary operates *across* both bounded spaces and temporal rhythms, we need to think the relations among three different forms: first, the hierarchical form of gender arranges social materials into two levels of power and authority, with the masculine occupying the higher rank and the feminine the lower. This hierarchy then also divides sociocultural spaces into separate containers coded masculine and feminine, and it imposes its order on time as well, generating rhythms marked as masculine and femi-nine. While containers organize space and rhythms regulate time, hierarchy is the form that creates domination and oppression, producing the most painful material effects. Politically, then, we might well assume that hierar-chy is the form of social organization that matters most.

But when forms overlap and collide, hierarchy does not always dom-inate the formal field. Let me offer an example from nineteenth-century Britain. I draw here from Teresa Mangum's intriguing work on aging. As Victorian men grew old, Mangum tells us, they outlived their active roles as agents in the public realm. The aging nineteenth-century British male faced "if not an outright loss of sexual identity then a lapse into a state akin to helpless femininity." Images of older men often figured them as feeble, useless, and pitiable, their alignment with femininity entailing a painful loss of personhood. But not always: "this feminization . . . sometimes signals moral, spiritual and domestic fulfillment. The tolerance for a gentler, more maternal masculinity in old age helps to explain the appeal of characters like Dickens's reformed Scrooge in *A Christmas Carol* (1843) [or] Job Legh (who is single-handedly raising his granddaughter) in Gaskell's *Mary Bar-ton* (1848)."[21]

In short, the temporal rhythm of the masculine lifespan, characterized by the familiar ages of man—infancy, childhood, youth, maturity, and old age—overlapped with the spatial containments organizing the masculine public and feminine private spheres and produced uncertain effects for gen-der identity and masculine privilege. Did the domestic sphere appreciate in value when the old man came to inhabit it, or did his relegation to the feminine sphere of the home render him comparatively worthless? Was he masculine or feminine, contemptible or admirable, emptied of authority or filled with care? Or to ask this another way: when hierarchy encounters rhythm and bounded whole, is it possible to predict which will organize experience? Will the higher term in the hierarchy retain its status despite the depredations of time and the containment of domestic space, even raising the domestic to a new height, or will the rhythm of aging and the confinement to the home succeed in bringing the man down in the social hierarchy to the feminine side of the gender binary?

The aleatory paths of colliding gendered forms are not limited to the Victorian context. Recent economists and sociologists note an ongoing transnational phenomenon they call the "family gap" in wages: men with children earn more than men without, and they are held to a substantially lower standard at work than non-fathers, while precisely the reverse is true for women.[22] Given traditions of discrimination against women in the workplace, it is not surprising to hear that mothers earn less than childless women, but why are men with children rewarded over those without? On the one hand, sociologists contend that the powerful stereotype of the male breadwinner continues to account for the pay differential, but they also note that fathers are allowed to take more time off work than their childless counterparts and are rewarded for doing so, suggesting some social returns for fathers who adopt a domestic role.[23] In this example, rather than lowering men in the social hierarchy, paternal care and responsibility for children literally raises the value of the domestic sphere.

In other cases, the opposite may result: when men become full-time home-makers, their association with conventionally feminine domesticity may diminish their status.[24] Together, what these examples suggest is that the relations among bounded wholes, rhythms, and hierarchy are unstable because their collisions genuinely afford multiple outcomes. And what this means is that hierarchy does not always organize political life: it can be disturbed and rerouted by forms as various as the arc of aging and domestic space.

Bureaucracy

Up to this point, I have been working with hierarchical forms that take the shape of simple binaries: higher and lower. *Antigone* suggests that even simple, traditional binaries, when thrown together, can have uncertain and deforming effects. But in the past two centuries, a much more complex hierarchical form has become a common organizing experience globally:

the bureaucratic ladder. Max Weber famously described its multiple "levels of graded authority," composing "a firmly ordered system of super- and subordination in which there is a supervision of the lower officers by the higher ones."[25] This formal chain of command leads from the production line worker to the CEO, and from the bottom rung of the military or civil service to the highest-ranking official. It is the kind of pecking order that organizes labor unions, colonial administration, church leadership, political parties, universities, government agencies, and corporations—public and private, official and unofficial, left and right, national and transnational. It is also one of the most widely reviled of social forms, though in contradictory ways, as it stands simultaneously for "bungling inefficiency and threatening power": "Incompetence, red tape and feather-bedding on the one side; manipulation, obstructionism and Byzantine intrigue on the other."[26]

With their endless rules and record-keeping, bureaucracies seem to drown us in mere formalities—procedures sustained for the sake of procedure itself. Yet, at the same time, these records do keep track of our bodies, our medical and psychological health, our education, our credit ratings, our citizenship, creating a storehouse of knowledge that can be used for or against us. These bureaucratic records, with their combined connotations of uselessness and power, have given us one of the most common contemporary meanings of the word *form*: the endless forms—tax forms, immigration forms, registration forms, evaluation forms—that monitor individuals whose lives come into contact with modern institutions. This meaning of *form* strangely haunts—and is haunted by—its aesthetic other. That is, bureaucracies come under attack for being self-perpetuating, for producing endless red tape, until it seems as if the business of bureaucracies is to create pure formalities, their forms meaningless—*pro forma*. But this, in turn, suggests an understanding of bureaucracies as autotelic bodies—self-contained and autonomous, referring only to themselves. We are not far, it seems, from the perfection of Immanuel Kant's aesthetics, which casts art as an end in itself, both useless and powerful.

This understanding of bureaucracy as dedicated entirely to serving its own ends is certainly what infuriates Dickens in his scathing portrait of government in *Little Dorrit*, where the Circumlocution Office sends Arthur Clennam back and forth between departments with the express purpose of frustrating business of any kind. One official obligingly tells him: "I can give you plenty of forms to fill up. Lots of 'em here. You can have a dozen if you like. But you'll never go on with it."[27] The law receives similar treatment in *Bleak House*. When the case of Jarndyce and Jarndyce finally comes to an end, the result is enormous waste in the form of "great bundles of paper":

"bundles in bags, bundles too large to be got into any bags, immense masses of papers of all shapes and no shapes, which the bearers staggered under, and threw down for the time being, anyhow, on the Hall pavement, while they went back to bring out more."[28] Dickens popularizes an understanding of bureaucracies as inward-looking and self-perpetuating.

The hierarchy of the bureaucratic world in Dickens is especially maddening. After one employee in the Circumlocution Office offers a particularly convoluted set of instructions to Arthur Clennam, we learn that this official "fully understood the Department to be a politico diplomatico hocus pocus piece of machinery, for the assistance of nobs in keeping off the snobs. This dashing young Barnacle, in a word, was likely to become a statesman, and to make a figure" (119–20). It is precisely his understanding of bureaucracy as purposeless that will help young Barnacle to climb its ladder and achieve his own purposes. According to Dickens, then, self-serving individuals devote themselves to advancing in the hierarchy, and as they do so the hierarchy itself dominates to the exclusion of other values, forms, and purposes. Thus bureaucracy becomes *pro forma* indeed—existing solely to perpetuate its own hierarchical structure.

Of course there is another and even grimmer side to bureaucracies. Dostoevsky, Kafka, Orwell, and such films as *Ikuru* and *Brazil* show them as nightmarish in their capacity to control our lives. Unappreciated workers perform meaningless work, governed by the inexplicable decisions of faceless managers in distant, high-level departments. *The Adjustment Bureau*, a 2011 film, imagines a secret bureaucracy, topped by a shadowy figure called the Chairman, that determines the life of every living person according to "the plan."

Both the self-perpetuating and the threatening power of bureaucratic organizations crop up often in the popular imagination: from police procedurals to newspaper accounts to fiction. These representations of criminal, welfare, immigration, psychiatric, and credit organizations, with their forms and records, workers and managers, repeatedly remind us that such organizations produce serious material effects, determining everything from health and unemployment benefits to prison terms and deportation.

I have listed here just a few examples among many, simply to suggest that bureaucracy plays an important role in modern understandings of power. What many thinkers from Dickens and Weber onward have shared is a sense that it is dominated by a single form—the hierarchy—that subordinates us all to its maddening ladder-like logic. Those at the top of a bureaucracy issue give unaccountable commands; those lower down take orders while seeking to rise; outsiders are mystified, frustrated, and disempowered. But it is the main argument of this book that to isolate a single form and to assume its dominance is almost always an act of oversimplification. Something much more complex, formally speaking, happens in the day-to-day operations of bureaucracies.

I want to suggest that a formalist approach invites a more productive understanding than Dickens or Orwell of the intricacies of bureaucratic power. To grasp the overlapping of multiple forms in the workings of bureaucratic organizations, I turn here to the work of Robert Jackall, a sociologist who studied a large US corporation in the early 1980s. One aspect of the organization he noticed was that it was structured by two different management hierarchies: line and staff. Those on the line were the workers and managers actively involved in production; staff were those who acted in an advisory capacity, offering technical or organizational expertise, environmental oversight, or legal guidance. The two sets of managers, Jackall found, were locked in a constant competition:

> The more freedom staff have to intervene in the line . . . the more they are feared and resented by line management. For line managers, independent staff represent either an unwelcome "rules and procedures mentality" into situations where line managers feel they have to be alert to the exigencies of the market, or, alternatively, as power threats to vested interests backed by some authority. In the "decentralized" organizations prevalent today in the corporate world, however, most staff are entirely dependent on the line and must market their technical, legal, or organizational skills to line managers exactly as an outside firm must do. The continual necessity for staff to sell their technical expertise helps keep them in check since line managers, pleading budgetary stringency or any number of other acceptable rationales, can thwart or ignore proffered assistance.[29]

At any given time, either of the management hierarchies could be "higher" than the other. As the hierarchies encountered one another, the managers regularly came into conflict over the rules and procedures that governed everyday operations. And this ongoing tension was not the only power struggle shaping the organization's day-to-day work. This corporation, like many others, was divided into specialized units including production, sales, marketing, and finance. Although ultimately they were all supposed to be contributing to a larger whole, in fact these units were constantly "at cross-purposes," vying with one another for authority (37). Meanwhile, some managers made alliances and built "fealty relationships" that cut across rival hierarchies and allowed them to negotiate backroom deals. Often these alliances were more important than profits and losses: "You can lose money and still be an insider; you can make money and still be an outsider," one manager explained (66). The hierarchies were also regularly turned upside down, as managers' success turned out to be dependent on the accomplishments of their underlings (46).

In short, far from being structured as the single ladder described by Weber's "firmly ordered system of super- and sub-ordination, in which there is a supervision of the lower officers by the higher ones," the bureaucracy as it appears in Jackall pits multiple hierarchies against one another, encourages alliances that traverse competing divisions and hierarchies, and holds managers accountable for the work done by their subordinates. All of this contributes to an environment of perpetual uncertainty: it is rarely clear who is rising and how, which unit commands the most respect and resources, and whether line or staff will at any moment get the upper hand. Not surprisingly, then, no single strategy will guarantee advancement: neither capitulation to norms, teamwork, deception, clandestine negotiation, displays of creativity, socializing with the right people, nor cutthroat competitiveness. Any one of these may work at one moment and fail at another.

The resulting anxiety fosters an intense focus on the workings of the hierarchy itself, as managers become consumed with ascending the corporation's ladder. In this sense, Jackall agrees with Dickens: bureaucratic hierarchies foster an obsession with advancement at the expense of other values and purposes. For Jackall, climbing high in the corporation requires a high tolerance for moral ambiguity, a willingness to take advantage of others' misfortunes, and "the brazen nerve that allows one to pretend that there is nothing wrong even when the world is crumbling" (219). But Jackall is more precise than Dickens in his analysis of the forms that produce this damaging ethos. For Dickens, bureaucracy's structures and rules are so maddeningly complex as to be altogether irrelevant—not worth representing—with the exception of the ladder to be climbed, which motivates ambitious bureaucrats. Jackall, by contrast, is meticulous in his attention to the pecking orders, units, and alliances that together, in complex and unpredictable collisions, produce opportunities for advancement and stagnation, integrity and corruption.

While Jackall's study only reinforces the familiar sense that reforms are likely to be frustrated and ethically minded workers likely to languish or fail altogether, his work does unsettle two conventional assumptions about the power of hierarchical forms. First, he exposes the multiple hierarchies that struggle against one another even within a single organization, while they also run up against alternative forms—alliances, networks, and coteries. To speak of "the career ladder" is therefore to simplify a formal landscape composed of multiple vertical and horizontal forms constantly intersecting, disrupting, and rerouting one another. If Weber's bureaucrat is a "discretionless single cog in an ever-moving mechanism which prescribes to him an essentially fixed route of march,"[30] Jackall's bureaucrat has more agency (in the sense that she can choose a coterie over a hierarchy if she likes), less control (in the sense that she cannot work with the grain of all of the many forms that crisscross the organization), and less direction (in the sense that she has to make a difficult choice between making a deal with a manager in a different department or focusing instead on pleasing her immediate superior).

The second contribution Jackall makes is to show that bureaucracies are not so self-enclosed—so autotelic—as we are in the habit of imagining. Multiple forms, sometimes even shaped by more than one hierarchy, will structure any given organization, and since organizations typically interact, each hierarchy will work in a context where many forms are operating. In *The External Control of Organizations*, Jeffrey Pfeffer and Gerald R. Salancik show how complex these interacting forms can be: "Organizations are linked to environments by federations, associations, customer-supplier relationships, competitive relationships and a socio-legal apparatus defining and controlling the limits of these relationships. . . . This is true whether we are talking about public organizations, private organizations, small or large organizations, or organizations which are bureaucratic or organic."[31] Ecological rather than autotelic, a bureaucracy cannot revolve solely around its own self-serving purposes, and all bureaucrats have to look not only up but also around, considering external pressures and forms beyond the ladder.

For example, one company Jackall studied experienced a large environmental disaster in the late 1970s. After substantial public outcry, the management instituted serious reforms to prevent a future incident. But just a few years later, during an economic downturn, "Brown," the company head, decided to lay off the environmental staff.

> Brown himself said at a managerial meeting that good staff simply create work to justify their own existence. Many line managers echoed this opinion. More to the point, the feeling was that work on environmental issues had lost any urgency in the Reagan era. The Environmental Protection Agency (EPA) was dead. Moreover, the only real threat to corporations on environmental issues was in the courts, which, however, judge

past actions, not present practices. By the time the courts get to cases generated by contemporary practices, typically in fifteen years, those executives presently in charge will have moved on, leaving any problems their policies might create to others. (33)

Brown makes his decision at the crossroads of three different bureaucracies—his own company, a regulatory agency, and the courts. In this example, he takes advantage of their conflicting forms to make a terrifying choice. Seeking to please the CEO, he sets about trimming the company budget. In the competition between the line managers and their staff counterparts, he chooses the more efficient line. To justify this choice he turns to another hierarchy—the relationship between the executive branch of government and a regulatory agency. The new president, he thinks, will bring down the agency, a move legitimated by a popular opinion that is swinging in an antiregulatory direction. The only other body that might shape the corporation is the judiciary, and here Brown cannily, if immorally, sets two temporal forms side by side, arguing that the courts, given the slow rhythm at which they operate, will not be able to act in time to disturb the quick tempo of corporate leadership. Given three different bureaucracies and three contending forms—at least two hierarchical structures and a pair of rhythms—he concludes that he can make the expedient decision to lay off his environmental staff.

Brown finds room for agency amid pressures from competing forms—his position in a management hierarchy, the constraints of environmental regulatory rules, a new presidency, the tide of public opinion, and the courts—deliberately setting their forms against one another in an effort to make the decision that will best serve his company's interests, and his own. Ironically, this decision gets Brown demoted, plunging him down the hierarchy of the very company he has so carefully sought to serve. Not unlike Creon's fate, Brown's freedom to act amid contending hierarchies brings about his own demise. A kind of hubris, in both cases, allows these leaders to imagine that competing forms can be fully understood and harnessed to their own ends. To be sure, the story does not always end tragically for corporate protagonists. Jackall, at the end of his book, notes that a few at the top are highly rewarded for "the ability to read the inner logic of events, to see and do what has to be done" (219). But along the way he also observes that some who do not understand the "inner logic" rise, while others who read it well fall. The contingency of colliding forms—in a world structured by numerous nonhomologous rhythms, shapes, and hierarchies—can derail even the most ruthlessly strategic striver after success.

So much, then, for understanding colliding forms. It does not guarantee a climb up the corporate ladder. But my goal here is different from Mr. Brown's. I want to understand the workings of forms in ways that do justice to their capacity for disorganization as well as for organization, and from that starting-point to consider what an effective politics might look like. If hierarchies do not always organize other forms—if they can be disrupted by containers, rhythms, and other hierarchies—then authority may well prove surprisingly fragile. And at the very least, exerting power is no simple matter of the position one holds in a hierarchy, and we cannot assume that certain actors will always organize the social world successfully to their own ends. Amid the complex and aleatory overlapping of social forms, there are always opportunities for unexpected and ideologically unsettling outcomes.

Gender, Bureaucracy

So: what happens when the two major hierarchical forms we have analyzed so far—gender and bureaucracy—encounter one another? We might assume that we know the story all too well: glass ceilings limit the capacity of women to ascend, and any job that becomes too closely associated with women loses status, causing wages to sink. But even here the collision of the two hierarchies can produce some deforming and unpredictable effects. In an influential feminist study, Rosabeth Moss Kanter did research on the first women sales-workers and managers in a US corporation in the 1970s. She was particularly interested in what happened in a "skewed" workforce, where there was a large majority of a single group, which she calls the "dominants," and a small minority of another, the "tokens."

The preponderance of male workers at the higher levels of Kanter's corporation had everything to do with the continuing power of separate spheres. Professional women who had risen in the corporation were rare, because bourgeois women were expected to stay at home, in the private sphere. But their rarity in the office had a paradoxical effect: the fact that there were so few women made each highly visible, constantly noticed, gossiped about, and evaluated. They became inescapably "public creatures," as Kanter puts it.[32] The very binary form that marked women as private thus *also* produced their fate as public characters. This reversal then forced the women "tokens" to exaggerate their public side:

> Many of the tokens seemed to have developed a capacity often observed among marginal or subordinate peoples: to project a public persona that hid inner feelings. Although some junior management men at Indisco,

including several fast trackers, were quite open about their lack of commitment to the company and dissatisfaction with aspects of its style, the women felt they could not afford to voice any negative sentiments. They played by a different set of rules, one that maintained the split between public persona and private self. (385)

Women—traditionally the bearers of the internal (emotion, the home, the private)—had to suppress inner feelings to become insiders in the public world outside of the home, while masculine insiders, traditionally bearers of the external (reason, the workplace, the public), could afford to express their inner feelings because they were so firmly on the inside of the outside.

If a token woman in the bureaucratic hierarchy could unsettle the logic of separate spheres, Kanter considered what happened when offices hired two women, rather than a single token. She tracked three different scenarios. In the first:

One woman was characteristically set up as superior, the other as inferior—exaggerating traits in both cases. One was identified as the success, the other as the failure. The one given the success label felt relieved to be included and praised, recognizing that alliance with the identified failure would jeopardize her acceptance. The consequence, in one office, was that the identified success stayed away from the other woman and did not give her any help with her performance, withholding criticism she had heard that might have been useful, and the second woman soon left. (394)

Here, the men in the office split the two women apart by forming a new hierarchy. One woman became doubly subordinate—lower than all the men and then cast further down below her sole female counterpart, who was complicit in the hierarchy between women because it seemed to draw attention away from her role in the hierarchy between men and women, despite the fact that it was the male-female hierarchy that had created her anxious and subordinate status in the first place.

In the second case, the male coworkers treated the women as "an automatic pair," dividing the workplace into masculine and feminine domains, and seeing themselves as "relieved of the responsibility for interacting with or supporting the women." Turning to the logic of the bounded whole, the men opted to separate the workplace into clearly delineated spheres, and in this case their formal choice reinforced the gender hierarchy. The women treated in this way were often alarmed by being forced into isolation together and so sometimes turned against one another, "trying to create difference and distance between them and becoming extremely competitive" (394).

The third situation Kanter describes emerged when the two women developed an alliance,

> and refused to be turned against each other. Strong identification with the feminist cause or with other women was behind such alliances. Allied, two tokens could reduce some of the pressures and avoid some of the traps in their position. They could share the burden of representing womankind, and they could each be active on some pieces of "the woman's slot" while leaving time free to demonstrate other abilities and interests. (394)

By understanding themselves structurally, as part of a subordinated group in a large-scale gender hierarchy, pairs of women could create and sustain their own antihierarchical form: an alliance of equals. This alliance then helped them to counter the typical problems of tokenism, reducing their sense of isolation and vulnerability to criticism. Peer partnership became literally an emancipatory form, freeing up time for women to do something other than play strictly gendered roles. Freedom thus meant not an escape from all constraints, but a strategic deployment of the form of the allied pair.

Based on this study, Kanter called for an increase in the proportion of minority workers to "dominants." Her research has since been contested, with other scholars arguing that numbers alone cannot counter discrimination, since a larger proportion of a minority group in the workplace can provoke backlash, actually increasing sexual harassment, wage disparities, and the insistence on glass ceilings.[33] But Kanter's work remains compelling as a formalist study of power. It shows that when hierarchies collide, they reroute and deform as much as they organize, unsettling divisions between public and private and masculine and feminine. Her study also makes clear that the structure of the pair, when it interacts with the other hierarchies in play—the career ladder, the gender binary—carries unpredictable effects with the potential to produce new hierarchies, competitions, *or* alliances.

Contending Hierarchies

In these corporate examples, as in my reading of Sophocles, I have asked what outcomes can plausibly or predictably ensue when hierarchies encounter other forms as well as each other. The results are more aleatory than conventional accounts of power usually suggest: the binary form of gender sorts masculine from feminine in ways that powerfully subordinate, yes, but that also strain and unsettle the logic of other binaries, creating openings for the inversion, breakdown, and transformation of public and private, feeling and reason, friend and enemy, power and powerlessness. But so far, the vast majority of our colliding hierarchies have ended tragically, and our only happy outcome has emerged from a rejection of hierarchy altogether in favor of egalitarian alliance. While I wholeheartedly embrace equality as a formal alternative to hierarchy, I want to conclude by suggesting that hierarchies themselves can overlap and clash to surprisingly productive and emancipatory effect, producing political opportunities as well as tragic endings.

In this conclusion, I am drawing on the work of Bruce Robbins, who makes a fascinating point about overlapping hierarchies in his 2007 book, *Upward Mobility and the Common Good*. Here he argues that upward mobility stories are not exactly, or only, narratives in which impoverished or marginalized characters betray their roots to climb a class ladder at the expense of those they leave behind. Rather, they are stories that "by focusing on the passage *between* identities and how one gets from here to there . . . reveal something important about power."[34] To be precise, these narratives reveal the processes of mediation by which particular characters rise in the social hierarchy. Whether depending on loving individual benefactors or social institutions, protagonists who climb the social ladder recognize not their own capacity for self-making but their interdependence, and this recognition, Robbins argues, fosters a desire for the kind of social mediation best enacted by the welfare state.

At the end of the book, Robbins disagrees with Gayatri Spivak's influential reading of *Jane Eyre*, departing from her especially strongly when it comes to how hierarchies work. Spivak makes the case that the dark-skinned, Caribbean-born Bertha must fall so that Jane may rise. It is Bertha's exclusion that allows Jane to take her place at the center of the social world, as a legitimate insider. The narrative thus sacrifices the Third World woman for the sake of the First World protagonist.[35] Since Spivak, many other critics have returned to *Jane Eyre* to consider the text's support for racist and imperialist ideologies.[36] But Robbins offers a different response. Rather than conceding that Jane's success depends on Bertha's rejection and expulsion, he suggests that we need to disaggregate two hierarchies: class on the one hand and the global center/periphery—or First World/Third world—divide on the other. Spivak, he writes, seems unwilling to admit . . . that if the international division of labor takes some political representativeness away from the working-class European, it also *bestows* some political representativeness upon the middle-class non-European. It is only the core/periphery disparity dictated by the international division of labor that gives the middle-class postcolonial any right at all to speak for fellow nationals, a right that a more orthodox Marxism, seeing in such a figure only another member of the bourgeoisie, would deny her. This is a large point. . . . It suggests the possibility that upward mobility stories may not after all be built on the absolute necessity of betraying and sacrificing some Bertha Mason or some representative of Third World indigeneity. (239)

To put this another way, both Spivak and traditional Marxism have fused together two hierarchical forms, bourgeoisie/proletariat and center/periphery, assuming that they work together in a coordinated way. Robbins urges us to separate them, and argues that something important happens at the point where they cross: the middle-class person from the global South can become a center-periphery mediator, a "First World/Third World go-between" (242). It is at the junction of two overlapping hierarchies that Spivak herself can become a mediating figure, taking advantage of her class status and professional success to act as a powerfully critical voice on behalf of the Third World. That is, Spivak's power is itself an effect of two forms, two hierarchies, as class meets the First World/Third World divide.

Robbins's broadest argument rests on the presumption that there is no need to assume that one person's rise necessarily comes at the expense of another. A missionary's efforts at conversion, a woman's chance at meaningful social action, a professor's opportunity to shape students and public debate, the work of the welfare state to provide an opportunity to leave poverty behind: all of these mediating acts seek to raise certain people in the social hierarchy, but they are not all dictated or dominated by a single master-hierarchy: European imperialism or bourgeois power. To the contrary, one hierarchy might unsettle another, as Spivak herself seeks to do when she takes advantage of her class status and professional success to speak as a critical voice on behalf of women in the Third World. And in the end, Robbins suggests that we teachers surely know this already. We try to help our students rise not, typically, in order to make them superior to others, but to teach them the critical skills and knowledge that make for responsible citizenship, which will, in turn, help to raise everyone else. That is, we struggle to be mediators of social mobility for the common good.

My own goal, here, is to contribute to Robbins's persuasive argument by articulating the formal logic that underlies his claims. To assume that a European woman's meaningful career necessarily comes at the expense of an indigenous other, or that a man's choice of the domestic sphere will always come at the expense of his power, is to assume a master-hierarchy of values that works like a zero-sum game: a gain in one place always entails losses elsewhere. And this is simply not how hierarchies—or indeed forms in general—work. They are just as likely to unsettle one another, their collisions as liable to produce gains in odd places as to reinforce given structures of power. Robbins is right to reject the zero-sum game, that is, because no single hierarchy governs all others, nor do they all work together, successfully reinforcing Western imperialism, or the ruling class, or patriarchy. In fact, where two powerful hierarchies cross—bourgeoisie/proletariat and center/periphery—we find one of academia's most influential voices speaking on behalf of the global South.

At one intriguing moment, Robbins considers the crossing of two other hierarchies that have concerned us in this chapter: gender and professional advancement. Reading *Jane Eyre*, he urges us to think about St John's invitation to bring Jane to India as opening up the imaginative possibility of an alternative ending: "He offers her . . . what she is ready to consider meaningful and desirable work—work whose desirability for Jane comes in part from the fact that it might not *require* marriage, the fact that it replaces marriage with otherwise unavailable possibilities for personal autonomy and socially significant action" (64). Robbins insists that the text "registers this disruptive energy" even while it does not fulfill this narrative possibility (65). Not dissimilarly, Deirdre David sees Jane as the prototype for a colonial administrator, recasting the ambition and dedication that St John admires in her as well suited to the bureaucratic ladder that will soon be in place. It is in fact only St John's insistence on the strict superiority and power of the husband within marriage that precludes this outcome for Jane. Thus St John's gender hierarchy is all that forecloses a totally different kind of future: an ending that promises not the hierarchical divisions of gender but the equally hierarchical pleasures of ambition, climbing the ladder in the service of a meaningful career.

Despite their shared interest in an implied alternative ending in which Jane Eyre rejects marriage for work, Robbins and David introduce different hierarchies as they spin out their implied narratives. For Robbins, St John's proposal allows Jane and the reader to imagine a life of relative autonomy, where work ranks above marriage; while for David, Jane's prospective career might grant her freedom and autonomy, but only at the expense of colonized peoples. What most differentiates the two readings is a decision about where the story of hierarchical forms stops: Robbins stops sooner than David, with one hierarchy, the choice of work and autonomy; David's narrative lasts longer, imagining that Jane's choice would support a new hierarchy.

Is this what critics do? Do we spin out implied stories in which new forms take shape beyond a narrative's end? This probably does not sound like our usual account of literary reading, but I want to suggest, in closing, that most politically minded critics do precisely this. They attend to the political forms within the text in order to generalize them beyond the text's own example, extending the political ordering principles that are at work in the text to understand its implied rules for ordering the extratextual world. It is the portability of political form that permits these readings to happen at all, and it is our own ideas about how these forms operate in the world that guide or govern our assessment of the politics of literary texts. This means that acts of political reading routinely rely on implicit models of the plausible unfolding of forms.

Let us stick with *Jane Eyre* for the moment. Critics have never come to a consensus about the narrative's conclusion. For some readers, Jane's willingness to rank erotic love above a life of painful service is liberatory, while for others her choice to sink into domestic oblivion, contrasted with St John's heroic ending, is a disappointment.[37] Some readers have embraced Jane's assertion of the "here and now" as part of the secularizing project of the realist novel, while others have celebrated her resistance to St John as an alternative spiritual mission that entails a new and radical Christian feminism.[38]

What is happening here, I want to suggest, is not so much divergent *interpretations* of the text as an array of competing hierarchies on the part of both the text and its readers. There are two major sources of dispute among critics. The first emerges from the fact that this is a novel that offers real irresolution around some of its own hierarchies of value: while the text is perfectly clear about some of its hierarchies—such as the superiority of Britishness and the usefulness of a colonizing mission—it is unwilling to rank, clearly and finally, the relative merits of individual autonomy, erotic passion, ambition, the pleasures of home, respectable marriage, meaningful work, and religious service. In fact it is by offering a number of unresolved hierarchies that the novel unleashes the "disruptive energy" that it does not ultimately settle into any fixed or conclusive relation. It is this irresolution that allows us readers to spin out multiple implied social worlds.

The second source of dispute stems from the critics' own differences over values: Does a woman's insistence on erotic pleasure in a patriarchal context have more or less significance than her embrace of a domestic sphere over ambition and broader social action? Does Jane's ranking of earthly pleasures over otherworldly rewards matter more or less than her language of spiritual mission and her willingness to give the last word to the text's missionary? It might well make sense for us to debate those questions apart from literary texts, since these are questions that are less about Charlotte Brontë than about our own hierarchies of value.

In the end, the methodological point is not to decide, once and for all, on a particular text's hierarchy of values, or on our own, but to become clear-eyed about the ways that the vertical form of the hierarchy structures acts of literary reading. As we struggle to reveal the text's distinctions of privilege and priority, we also grapple with ethical, political, and professional hierarchies that organize nontextual worlds. Do we rank the human costs of imperialism far higher than a middle-class female character's opportunity for career advancement? Can hierarchies of value coexist? What happens when they operate together? If a new formalism has one lesson to offer, it is this: a close analysis of contending and colliding hierarchies invites us to rethink effective political action.

V

NETWORK

Sprawling and spreading, networks might seem altogether formless, perhaps even the antithesis of form. For some influential theorists, in fact, it is their resistance to form that makes networks emancipatory—politically productive. Gilles Deleuze and Félix Guattari famously offer up the rhizome as a network that connects any point to any other, and argue for it as a disorganizing, destabilizing answer to the more conventional unifying form of the tree, with its binary branches that all reach back to a common root, fixing a single order. "Nothing is beautiful or loving or political aside from underground stems and aerial roots," they write.[1] Ella Shohat claims, too, that the ever-spreading reach of networks is politically valuable: only networked flows and circulations will allow us "to transcend some of the politically debilitating effects of disciplinary and community boundaries."[2] In this tradition, networks usefully confound containing forms.

Many literary and cultural critics have grown interested in networks in the past decade, using the concept to describe powerful social facts, such as transnational markets, transportation, and print culture. Most have defined networks loosely and generally as "connectivity."[3] Recently, however, as network theory has emerged across disciplines, humanists, including Patrick Jagoda, Patrick Joyce, and Franco Moretti, have begun to turn to studies of networks in mathematics, physics, and sociology to show how these connective configurations follow knowable rules and patterns. While it is certainly true that networks do not fit formal models of unified shape or wholeness,[4] even apparently chaotic networks depend on surprisingly systematic ordering principles, "the most famous one being the so-called 'small-world' property, or 'six degrees of separation': the uncanny rapidity with which one can reach any vertex in the network from any other vertex."[5] Critics have started to think through Mark Granovetter's influential thesis about the "strength of weak ties"—the notion that people one knows only slightly can bring one access to a wider range of information and resources than those in one's close-knit circle, who, precisely because of their intimacy, share overlapping knowledge and contacts.[6] Cultural studies has also started to import such terms as *path length*, which counts the number of links that separate nodes; *network centrality*, which analyzes the popularity and importance of a node to the whole network; *hubs*, objects or persons that play a role in more than one cluster of nodes; and *hinges*, nodes that connect otherwise separate groups.[7]

This new vocabulary suggests that we can understand networks as distinct forms—as defined patterns of interconnection and exchange that organize social and aesthetic experience. Though they are not self-enclosed totalities, networks have structural properties that can be analyzed in formal terms. And an attention to the patterns governing networks will allow us to think in newly rigorous ways about political power and social experience.

In previous chapters, I have considered what happens when just two or three forms meet: when national boundaries meet narrative closure, or when the gender hierarchy encounters the arc of aging and the enclosures of domestic space. As a form that first and foremost affords connectedness, the network provides a way to understand how many other formal elements—including wholes, rhythms, and hierarchies—link up in larger formations. Specifically, network organization allows us to consider how many formal elements connect to create nations or cultures. It is thus a form absolutely crucial to our grasp of significant assemblages—including society itself.

Networks are useful, Bruno Latour suggests, because they allow us to refuse metaphysical assumptions about causality in favor of observing linkages between objects, bodies, and discourses. Latour asks us simply to notice points of contact between actors as well as the routes actors take.[8] By tracing the actual and possible paths that forms follow, we can practice a large-scale cultural studies method that starts not by presuming causality, but rather by attending to specific patterns of contact between forms. What connects different forms? What routes do they take once they have encountered one another?

The term *network* derives from the language of metallurgy and textiles used in the sixteenth century to describe objects made out of fabric or metal fibers interlaced as in a net or web. Something like *text*, the roots of the term imply interwoven strands moving in multiple directions rather than directed toward a single end.[9] The concept of the network has since expanded to include animal and plant tissues, natural crystalline structures, and, since the nineteenth century, social relationships—including any string or structure of interconnections, from transportation and communication systems to property, business, professional associations, and even literature itself.[10] Defined in the most straightforward way, a network is "a set of connections that link [discrete] elements."[11] The identity of those elements and the particular ways in which they connect can vary vastly, from computers to organic tissue to city planning to friendships.

Literary and cultural studies scholars who have been interested in networks have typically focused on one at a time: the slave trade, the print marketplace, the telegraph, global capital. Jonathan Grossman's fascinating new *Charles Dickens's Networks* singles out transportation networks from others—including communications, politics, religion, and economics—in order to "sharpen" our understanding of the specificity of passenger transport.[12] Even Manuel Castells, one of the most influential theorists of the complexity of our globally networked society, imagines a remarkably streamlined and coherent single kind of network at the heart of it all: "Technology *is* society."[13]

To be sure, it is clarifying and practical to isolate a single network and pursue its impact, since when networks are thrown together they can seem messy or incoherent. But it is also misleading to treat them as separate. I draw here on the work of sociologist Michael Mann, who has argued, unlike Castells, that "[o]verlapping interaction networks are the historical norm." Mann makes the case that networks are not the effects of modernity, technological innovation, or globalization. In ancient empires, for example, "the mass of the people participated overwhelmingly in small-scale local interaction networks yet were also involved in two other networks, provided by the erratic powers of a distant state, and the rather more consistent, but still shallow, power of semiautonomous local notables." It is the rule, not the exception, to be enmeshed at one and the same time in economic exchanges, legal systems, military alliances, churches, communications, transportation, and linguistic meanings, all "powerful, sociospatially different networks."[14]

A formalist approach advocates paying careful attention to the multiplicity of networks and especially to their differences. Some networks are densely local, such as social relationships in a village; others, like shipping routes, put vast spaces between nodes. Some are centralized, like the Catholic Church; others have multiple hubs, like air transportation. Some are utopian, transnational, and discursive, such as Leela Gandhi's "affective communities";[15] others, like the federal prison system, are material and coercive. Some, such as global finance, are complex, linking numerous institutions, people, and places; others are simple—two children communicating across a wire tied between tin cans. Some cross boundaries more readily than others: religious communities can cross oceans; railroads cannot. All networks afford connectivity; all create links between disconnected nodes.

Politically, they are neither consistently emancipatory—freeing us from a fixed or dominant order—nor always threatening—trouncing sovereignty or dissolving protective boundaries. Their power to organize depends on the particular patterns of each network and the ways that its arrangements collide with other networks and other forms.

I will begin this chapter with an investigation of encounters between unified wholes and networked connections, a set of relations that, I will argue, has been absolutely fundamental to cultural studies, from early twentieth-century anthropology to recent scholarship on global flows. Our understanding of cultures has itself depended on a shifting and largely un-articulated set of assumptions about what happens when these two forms are overlaid. Some theorists, like Shohat, have assumed that circulatory flows, transnational migration, and economic exchanges are always and nec-essarily opposed to wholes and enclosures, including cultural and national boundaries, while others have imagined that they work together, reinforc-ing one another's power. Turning to a formalist analysis, I will ask how specifically these forms clash and collide, and if and when they are capable of working in concert.

I will then turn to the overlapping of multiple networks, which is a far more ordinary fact of social life—and a more unsettled and unsettling one—than literary and cultural studies has recognized. Here I develop my own understanding of networked form through two readings, one nonfic-tion and the other fiction. The former is Trish Loughran's study of print cul-ture in early America, *The Republic in Print*, which makes the case that mul-tiple, overlapping networks—mail, print, money, and roads—interrupted each other and frustrated the work of consolidating a new nation. The sec-ond is Charles Dickens's *Bleak House*, a novel that casts social relations as a complex heaping of networks that not only stretch across space but also un-fold over time. Attentive to multiple principles of interconnection as they spread and overlap, Dickens uses narrative form to convey society itself as a network of dynamically unfolding networks.

Network, Whole

Implicitly as well as explicitly, cultural studies has been fascinated by net-works for a long time. Early twentieth-century anthropologists understood cultures in terms of harmonious relations between the whole and the net-work. That is, they saw any given culture as a coherent network of meanings, practices, and values that allowed one to grasp the wholeness of a particular way of life. For Franz Boas, Bronislaw Malinowski, and others, cultures were not just an accumulation of details that happen to be observable in a particular place but rather "the wholes in which everything is somehow related to everything else," the "network underlying or permeating or hovering above surface phenomena."[16] Cultural studies continues to invoke this notion of culture, according to James Buzard, even as it has come under strong critique by anthropologists.[17]

We can see one clear example in the work of Catherine Gallagher and Stephen Greenblatt, who claim in *Practicing New Historicism* that they are fascinated "with the possibility of treating all of the written and visual traces of a particular culture as a mutually intelligible network of signs."[18] Referring to "the invisible cohesion" of "the cultural matrix," they imagine cultures as composed of networks that flow within the boundaries of a knowable whole:

> We are intensely interested in tracking the social energies that circulate very broadly through a culture, flowing back and forth between margins and center, passing from zones designated as art to zones apparently indifferent or hostile to art, pressing up from below to transform exalted spheres and down from on high to colonize the low. . . . [This approach grows out of] a fascination with the entire range of diverse expressions by which a culture makes itself manifest. (13)

That "a culture" should have a "center" and an "entire range of diverse expressions" implies a wholeness, a unity; that it is crisscrossed by "social energies" that "circulate" and "flow" suggests that there can be no apprehension of culture without networked movement. The "culture" that is the focus of historicist cultural studies emerges here as precisely a harmonious cooperation of network and whole.

Recent critical work suggests that this New Historicist model of culture is now obsolete. First of all, anthropologists have come to agree that there is no such thing as a self-enclosed culture—certainly never one that can appear as such. In James Clifford's classic argument, we rely on observers and informants, mobile points of contact between cultures, to gain access to the most isolated of villages. Traditional anthropology typically effaced the means by which the ethnographer came and went from the site, "the boat, the land rover, the mission airplane," any of which were evidence of "systematic prior and ongoing contacts and commerce with exterior places and forces which are not part of the field." Clifford notes, too, that many kinds of things pass through remote sites: armies, tourists, television, objects for sale.[19] People and goods leave and return.

Attention to economic, transportation, and communication networks has therefore been crucial to undermining the ideal of authentic, isolated, self-contained cultures. Recent studies of migration and diaspora, transnational trade routes, contact zones, and traveling cultures have focused on the network's capacity to trouble or crack open bounded totalities.[20] And as scholars have paid an increasing attention to networks, they have tended to refuse the harmonious overlaying of wholes and networks in favor of a conflictual relation. Some critics consider wholeness to be a myth that networks helpfully shatter. Others adopt wholeness as a troubling reality that can and should be violated by networked extension. And still others want to hold onto the older form of the rooted community as a safeguard against global capital and the homogenization of linguistic and cultural experience worldwide.[21] In all of these cases, critics insist that networks breach the form of the bounded whole.

And yet, what both earlier and later conceptualizations of culture share is an implicit reliance on these two major forms to grasp cultural experience: it is the relation of networks and wholes that allows us to grasp culture as an object of study. For Boas, Gallagher, and Greenblatt, it is the wholeness of a culture that allows its network of crisscrossing connections to become perceptible in the first place, and they see boundaries as capable of containing networks. For most theorists of globalization and cultural encounter, on the other hand, including Shohat and Clifford, networks are the forms that rupture or defy enclosed totalities and allow us to understand border-crossing circulations and transmissions.

So: which is it? Are networks containable or uncontainable by bounded shapes? I want to suggest that a formalist approach is exactly what we need to answer this question—an attention to specific encounters between bounded wholes and network sprawl. Theoretically, networks are capable of unending expansion: once there is a link between two nodes, there is a network, and it can grow simply by linking to new nodes. Thus the network form affords a certain infinite extensiveness. But in practice, many networks are limited. Some operate as deliberately closed systems, such as Local Area Networks (LANs), which link a finite number of computers. And even networks that do expand can be governed by strict rules: a kinship network makes potentially endless new links by marriage, reproduction, and adoption, but all of these are controlled by the state, religious institutions, and custom, which routinely set powerful constraints on which particular nodes may link to each network. It is true that some networks can cross and even undermine the boundaries of containing shapes. Indeed, it is networks of this kind that most often make their way into popular culture: multinational capital, disease, terrorist networks, and the world wide web, which violate national boundaries in frightening ways. But these do not represent all networks. Consider, for example, transportation systems—roads, railroads, canals. These are expandable in theory, but each addition requires infrastructural investment, and sometimes complex international treaties. Roads and railroads cannot cross large bodies of water, and some objects and bodies are not permitted to cross national borders, even when the means of access exist. Expansions are often abandoned or delayed. In short, some networks cannot cross boundaries at all, and many do not cross easily.

And so, when it comes to the relationship between wholes and networks, it is not always clear which form will dominate. Some networks can be contained; others thwart containment. Global capital itself actually requires both networked sprawl and containing boundaries. Multinational corporations, always on the lookout for favorable economic conditions around the world, have the power to move from place to place, frequently displacing local economies and shaping the political agendas of individual nation-states as they demand land, access, and special tax provisions. In this respect the global flow of capital challenges the sovereignty of the nation-state. But states, for their part, continue to keep strict control on the mobility of workers across national borders, and enforce laws that protect corporate property—both boundaries that are crucial to the success of multinational enterprises.[22] When we consider terrorist networks, the picture becomes more complex still. Often operating outside of the logic of the nation-state, terrorists have inspired nations to build ever-higher walls and other barriers to try to exclude or contain them. Thus national boundaries continue to operate powerfully—and sometimes more powerfully than ever—in the face of transnational networks.[23]

In recent years we have been inclined to assume that networks always violate the bounded enclosures that either imprison or protect us. But let me offer a last example—a much more conventionally literary one—of a mutually sustaining encounter between a bounded shape and a sprawling network. This is the case of Emily Dickinson, who famously secluded herself in a bedroom in her father's house in Amherst, Massachusetts, and spent most of her adult life there, leaving the house only once, it was rumored, "to see a new church, when she crept out by night, & viewed it by moonlight."[24] Most critics, understanding the poet either as anxious and agoraphobic or as socially rebellious and independent, have emphasized the link between her physical enclosure and her intense interiority. But as Diana Fuss argues, this containing space also enabled a wide-ranging network:

The domain of privacy in which Dickinson is said to have been imprisoned or entombed actually offered the poet ample opportunity for intellectual growth; neither a space of confinement nor of death, Dickinson's bedroom proffered ready entry into the public world of letters. It is one of the great paradoxes of this poet's interior life that the more she withdrew, the wider her circle of acquaintances became. The Homestead bedroom was the place where Dickinson composed the vast majority of her seventeen hundred and seventy-five poems and an estimated ten thousand letters, of which more than a thousand survive. Here Dickinson communicated with her "private public," developing a public persona *as* a private poet.[25]

Like the Wienhausen nuns we met in the first chapter, Dickinson was not controlled by a single form—feminine containment in one enclosed, private space—but by multiple forms, which overlapped to provide surprising opportunities. It is true that she retreated to the privacy of her bedroom, confined and immobile. But a network of letters and books passed through this room, as the networks of print circulation and the postal system enabled Dickinson to link herself to nodes near and far.

The poet's confinement actually freed her in crucial ways from social responsibilities and domestic duties. Her father's public stature as treasurer of Amherst College, a one-term congressman, and prominent local citizen meant that the house was "crowded daily with the members of this world, the high and the low," who exhausted the daughters of the house with their perpetual visits and requests.[26] When the family hired a servant and installed Franklin stoves, Fuss argues, Dickinson could retreat with relief from the demands of both household and visitors. Thus Dickinson's strategic embrace of a bounded enclosure allowed her to resist the draining networks of kinship and local society while permitting her to take part in a larger, more sprawling and energizing network: a transnational literary community.

Together, what these examples make clear is that networks and enclosures are constantly meeting, sometimes sustaining and reinforcing one another, at other times creating threats and obstacles. It shows that neither form has the final organizing word—neither always regulates the other. But that is not to say that we must throw up our hands in ignorance or apathy. What a formalist analysis affords is an interest in the specificity of each form—what kind of network is it? what rules govern it?—and a grasp of what the affordances of each network can entail for other forms. Which networks can jeopardize, stabilize, or reroute bounded unities, and how exactly do they do so? Which enclosures successfully contain networks, and why? Rather than assuming that "culture" entails a neat containment of networks by shapes, or conversely, that networks always destroy or disregard boundaries, a formalist method offers the tools to track the particular range of ways in which these forms run up against each other and the consequences their encounters bring into the world.

Network, Network, Whole

Although literary critics have returned again and again to the relations between networks and bounded wholes, they have paid scant attention to the overlapping of multiple networks. In one notable exception, Trish Loughran offers a beautiful example of a society both organized and disorganized by a collision of different kinds of networks.[27] In fact, she invites us to think both about the relationships between overlapping networks and also about their impact on the wholeness of the nation, offering a critique of scholars such as Benedict Anderson and Michael Warner, who have assumed a causal link between the emergence of a communications network on the one hand and the formation of a shared national consciousness on the other. Instead of arguing that networks of print production give rise to a common and homogenizing attachment to the nation-state, Loughran shows how, in the United States, networks frustrated and obstructed the wholeness of the nation between the 1770s and the 1870s. Here, I will build on her work to underscore the formal terms of her argument and to suggest that her study offers a powerful example of the collision of networked and bounded forms.

Loughran begins by exploring the prerevolutionary postal system, which was supposed to unite the colonies. The British imposed a tax on all colonial mail, and in 1773, eager to collect on each item posted, they sent out an inspector named Hugh Finlay to figure out how to improve the efficiency of the system. What Finlay discovered, in terms I will borrow here from network theory, was neither a *centralized network*, where all paths successfully pointed back from the colonies to the Crown, nor a smoothly running *distributed network*, where all points could connect with one another, but rather a series of local *network clusters*, where the *hinges* between small groups of nodes were often missing or broken. Separated by bad weather, purposeful delays, and impassable roads, sometimes kept in a ruined state to frustrate rival colonies' trade (as happened between New Hampshire and Massachusetts), network clusters often failed to connect. Add to this that colonial mail deliverers typically resented the British tax and frequently carried letters to friends and neighbors privately, and we can see that a tax-free, local network was superimposed on the centralized imperial network, whose hub was thousands of miles distant. As multiple networks operated in detached and overlapping forms, they thwarted both British rule and a coherently unified alternative.

A similar set of difficulties beset national print culture in the early Republic. Though the states were now better connected than they had been a decade earlier, in 1787, Loughran writes, "a functional market zone, or unified field of exchange, had still not materialized across the landmass of eastern North America. Indeed ... there were few roads, no rails, and, in fact, very little money in the United States" (17). Without good hinges to connect scattered local networks both before and after the Revolution, there could be no centralized or powerfully influential national print culture—and consequently, Loughran concludes, no real sense of a shared national consciousness either:

> [T]exts of this period leave a compelling record of the ways in which the potential unity of a still emerging American book market was routinely disrupted by material circumstances that were local in origin and localizing in effect—including, among others, geographic isolation, competing political affiliations, regional identification and diversity, and temporal lags in the production and dissemination of texts themselves. (22)

The problem was not that it was too hard to organize a network: it was that there were *too many* networks, each with its own logic, overlapping and running into one another—town, regional, print, and political networks, all working at once. Add to this a social rhythm that got in the way of national coherence—temporal lags in the circulation of print—and one begins to see why the nation could not cohere into a bounded whole. It failed to take a clear shape because there were simply too many organizing patterns at work, no one of them dominating or controlling the others.

Thus Benedict Anderson's famous presumption that print culture can erase local difference in favor of "formal homogeneity," Loughran argues, emerges in the early United States as nothing more than a fantasy.[28] One could certainly *imagine* the nation as a unity—understanding it in formal terms as a unified whole—but its multiple print, postal, economic, and regional networks, with their different organizing principles, broken links, and temporal delays, did more to hinder the nation from assuming a whole, unifying shape than to foster that reality.

Network, Whole, Narrative

I want to turn now to Charles Dickens's *Bleak House* (1854), another text that takes up the daunting challenge of understanding life in a world organized by mulitple networks, and pushes this to a dramatic new level of complexity and nuance. As with *Antigone*, I am deliberately taking a fictional text as a model for understanding the social, an experiment in apprehending society through—and as—multiple contending forms. The point here is less to use formalist methods to read Dickens than to use Dickens to throw light on the operations of social form. If this seems like literary criticism turned upside-down, that is certainly part of my purpose. I have not understood literary texts in this book as reflections or expressions of prior social forms, but rather as sites, like social situations, where multiple forms cross and collide, inviting us to think in new ways about power. Some forms move surprisingly easily across social and literary contexts, and narratives are among the very best forms for identifying and tracking the unfolding of relations among different forms.

Bleak House is a highly unusual narrative in that it organizes experience around a heaping of separate but overlapping networks. Dickens, like Loughran, is interested in thinking through the relationship of sprawling networks to the bounded shape of a nation. But like Sophocles, he uses a specific literary form to make sense of these worrying social arrangements—in this case, the long narrative arc of the multiplot novel. *Bleak House* invites a careful analysis of the ways that the time-bound form of narrative collides with the overlaying of multiple networks. Network theorists in literary and cultural studies have rarely launched this kind of analysis. On the face of it, the networked crisscrossing among nodes in a system would seem to be best represented by synchronic forms, such as charts and maps. And although scientists and social scientists have recently begun to experiment with time-slicing to visualize networks unfolding, humanists interested in networks have almost always privileged space over time.[29] I argue here that Dickens makes brilliant use of the affordances of narrative form to conceptualize the ways that networks unfold temporally. This is a case where network theory and narrative theory can transform one another: networks expand and alter the usual conventions of narrative form, while narrative develops and challenges existing theories of networks and social power. By incorporating networks into the novel, *Bleak House* might seem to pave the way for recent "network narrative" films, as David Bordwell calls them, which are organized around political, technological, economic, and social networks, such as *Traffic*, *Syriana*, and *Babel*.[30] But I will argue, here, that the nineteenth-century novel is more successful than these feature films at analyzing the complexity and power of networked social experience.

"Why, Esther," says John Jarndyce, after Sir Leicester Dedlock has left the house, "our visitor and you are the last persons on earth I should have thought of connecting together!"[31] *Bleak House*, deeply interested in the possibilities of interconnections between far-flung lives, joins haughty aristocrats to crossing sweepers and bricklayers, by way of philanthropists, soldiers, dancing masters, doctors, suitors, and lawyers.

But what exactly are the principles of interconnection in the novel? Rather than limiting what counts as a network interaction to actual words passed between characters, as Franco Moretti does, or restricting it to appearances in the same scene, as Jean-Baptiste Michel and others do, I want to follow Dickens's lead in imagining the enormous variety of connectors that link people.[32] The most obvious principle of interconnection in *Bleak House* is the lawsuit of Jarndyce and Jarndyce, which successfully keeps characters in the dark about their relations to each other, and certainly does not demand any face-to-face contact between them or their simultaneous presence on the scene. But the novel also imagines numerous other ways that characters are connected, some of which, like disease, depend on physical contact. As Jo passes smallpox to Esther, the contagion itself becomes a point of contact that links social actors across groups. The network of philanthropies is a third organizing principle, bringing Esther into contact with Caddy Jellyby and Mrs. Chadband into relation to Mr. Guppy. There is also the aristocratic social-political network, which links Lady Dedlock to the world of fashion and Sir Leicester Dedlock to parliamentary debates about social reform. And there is "rumor," which "persists in flitting and chattering about town" (690). Crucially, the novel is interested in connecting patterns of kinship, the most important being the secret tie that links Sir Leicester Dedlock to Esther via Nemo and Lady Dedlock. The absence of face-to-face contact for many pages does not make this connection any less significant. Other organizing kinship networks are at work in the novel too, such as the one linking Trooper George to the Ironmaster and another that connects Mrs. Jellyby to Mr. Turveydrop. There is also the space of the city itself, which links characters like Charley and Gridley by mere proximity. "London." is the famous first sentence of the novel, and the city can itself be understood as a network, a set of interconnected streets and buildings, linked largely by sheer contiguity. And because of the larger networks of transportation and communication that crisscross it, London is always linked to adjacent sites: its streets prove contiguous with rural roads, as Jenny and Liz show us when they leave Tom-All-Alone's for Hertfordshire, where they will play a role in Lady's Dedlock's flight back into the city, the site of her death.

Importantly, too, the city does not work *only* as a principle of adjacency: it also fosters connections between characters and institutions. In one maddeningly complex example, Mr Bucket happens upon Jenny and Liz at Tom-All-Alone's while looking for Jo to identify the veiled lady at Tulkinghorn's chambers. Here the urban space of the city collects the rural bricklayers, who know Esther through Mrs Pardiggle of Jarndyce's philanthropic network; Jo, who holds the key to a set of mysteries about Nemo and Lady Dedlock, and whose poverty brings him to Tom-All-Alone's, which turns out to be part of the Jarndyce and Jarndyce suit; and Snagsby, Tulkinghorn, and Bucket, who are working to piece together the link between Lady Dedlock and Nemo. The city emerges in this example as a kind of meta-network, linking and assembling other principles of interconnection.

Now, one might argue that for Dickens all of these networks stop at the borders of the nation: *Bleak House* can absorb the landed aristocracy, the rural poor, and even the industrial north, but it explicitly and pointedly refuses to take in the Empire. And yet, the network's formal capacity for extension and contiguity pushes against even Dickens's deliberate nationalism. Despite Mrs. Jellyby's clear moral failure to concentrate her attention on national needs, Dickens finds himself strangely following her lead when, in one passage, he links Jo to networks that spread to distant places on the globe:

> Jo comes out of Tom-all-Alone's, meeting the tardy morning which is always late in getting down there, and munches his dirty bit of bread as he comes along. His way lying through many streets, and the houses not yet being open, he sits down to breakfast on the door-step of the Society for the Propagation of the Gospel in Foreign Parts, and gives it a brush when he has finished, as an acknowledgment of the accommodation. He admires the size of the edifice, and wonders what it's all about. He has no idea, poor wretch, of the spiritual destitution of a coral reef in the Pacific, or what it costs to look up the precious souls among the coco-nuts and bread-fruit. (198–99)

Jo sits on a doorstep—an accident of the city as a network, since this specific doorstep just happens to be in close proximity to Jo when it is time for breakfast. But then the doorstep turns out to be itself a node linked to another set of nodes, since it adjoins a building that houses an institution that itself reaches out as far as a "coral reef in the Pacific," sending books and bodies around the world. The Gospel in Foreign Parts is uncannily like Dickens's own fiction, which would almost instantly reach India, Canada, Australia, and the United States thanks to networks of shipping, roads, railroads, print circulation, and colonial administration. Thus the nationalistic *Bleak House* reaches beyond national borders through networks both inside and outside of the text. Jo does not know anything about the connection between himself and "Foreign Parts," but this is no hindrance to the operation of a network; indeed, most of the characters in *Bleak House* are entirely unaware of their function as nodes in a dense overlapping of networks, but they are linked nonetheless to far-flung strangers in remote places through multiple webs of interconnection.

How could they be aware of them all? At one and the same time, characters in the novel are linked through the law, disease, economics, class, gossip, the family tree, city streets, rural roads, and even global print and philanthropic networks. Let me pause for a moment to note the strangeness of this list, its puzzling incoherence: some of these links are voluntary, others coercive; some follow the procedures of state institutions, others thrive on sheer proximity. Some—like the law and class relations—are hierarchical, while others—like rumor and urban space—can be fluid and egalitarian.

Each character acts as a node in at least one distributed network, in which any point can connect to any other without needing to go through any central site or in any fixed order, but what makes this novel so interesting and so complex is that almost all of the characters act as nodes in *more than one* different distributed network at a time. These networks are both separate and overlapping: each has its own logic, its own way of organizing and linking the social world, but each is also capable of connecting the same groups of characters as the others. Crucially, too, these principles of interconnection are not homologous, and in fact actually have the potential to derail and subvert one another. When Esther catches Jo's smallpox, she worries that she has become unmarriageable—unable to take her place as a new node in a kinship network. Mrs. Rouncewell commits herself willingly to serving an aristocratic hierarchy; and yet her position in a kinship system links her to the bourgeois Ironmaster, who is bent on replacing aristocratic power with capitalism, and to Trooper George, her favorite son, for whom she is ultimately willing to sacrifice the Dedlock family name.

In order to capture these many contending networks, Dickens expands the usual affordances of the novel. Depending on how you count them, between fifty and seventy characters populate *Bleak House*. To investigate far-reaching and overlapping networks—disease, urban streets, global philanthropy, the lawsuit, and so on—the novel needs to present lots and lots of nodes, and to link them along multiple pathways. Such layered interconnection would simply not be possible with the ordinary number of novelistic characters: Jane Austen's three or four families, for example, or the marriageable woman caught between two suitors in the marriage plot. And so Dickens dramatically expands the conventional affordances of the novel by multiplying the usual number of characters.

Bleak House then uses networks to reconceptualize character. Most conventional novels that seek to capture a whole society use characters to stand for entire social groups—the dissipated aristocrat, the honest laborer—but this one goes to some trouble to stress that characters are less important because they are exemplary or synecdochical than because they play crucial roles in social, economic, and institutional networks. For example, Jo first appears in *Bleak House* not because he is a typical abandoned child forced to work on the streets, but because he is a point of contact between a dead man and the law. That is, the novel introduces us to Jo for the first time at the inquest into Nemo's death, and he is called to testify because a witness claims he is the only person Nemo has been seen talking to. Jo then reappears in the text, over and over, not because he represents poverty or childhood or social marginality, but because his literal location in the city at specific times and places makes him relevant to a murder investigation, efforts at urban reform, and even the institution of marriage. Jo's appearance in the novel is an effect of his role as a node in multiple networks.

By organizing the narrative around networks rather than persons, *Bleak House* does for character something like what Marx did for commodities: casting narrative persons less as powerful or symbolic agents in their own right than as moments in which complex and invisible social forces cross. Network form therefore prompts a rethinking of novelistic character. For example, caught up in the passage of contagion, legal inquiry, and urban space, Jo is shocked by his own apparent importance on the one hand and his total insignificance on the other. How can he be both entirely neglected by the social world and yet also unable to escape the webs of interconnection that necessarily link him to that world?

Network theorists argue that in most networks there are some nodes—hubs—that are more highly linked than others; while most nodes cluster together around shared functions and purposes, a few important nodes are simultaneously part of many large clusters. It is not hard to identify the hubs in *Bleak House*: Jo, Esther, Woodcourt, Tulkinghorn, Bucket, and Miss Flite all appear in multiple clusters and provide links between clusters. But again, this is a surprising and strangely incoherent list. It names not only central and powerful figures, for those who are the sites of the most substantial traffic are not necessarily sources of either agency or authority. Some are simply proximate—in the right place at the right time—while others become unconscious bearers of connectability—disease or a secret love affair. Thus it is no accident that hubs are not necessarily centers of power: as the example of Jo makes clear, it is perfectly possible to function as a highly trafficked point of social intersection without having any control over the social oneself.

While the network invites Dickens to expand the usual affordances of narrative, narrative allows him to offer a shrewd understanding of networks. In this chapter, I have already touched on a few examples of the ways in which temporal rhythms collide with and reshape network arrangements—temporal delays in print and post, the addition of new nodes to the family, and the constant threat that multinational corporations will shift to newly favorable sites. By making use of a formal feature of the Victorian novel that has not often been theorized—sheer length[33]—Dickens puts an especially loose and baggy narrative form to use to theorize networks in canny and persuasive ways.

The length of *Bleak House* affords some insight into networks that is precluded by shorter narrative forms, including the spate of recent "network narrative" films that struggle to represent globalized networks of politics, economics, and technology. These films, such as *Traffic* (2000), *Syriana* (2005), and *Babel* (2006), all rely on what network theorists call *chain networks*, where one event prompts another in a sequence of effects—more like dominoes than like the Internet. *Babel* might look like an exception at first, but it pretends to be more complex than it is by telling three of its four main stories as if they were simultaneous, when they are in fact sequential: reordering the plot gives you quite a straightforward cause-and-effect narrative. *Bleak House*, by contrast, relies on the more complex model of distributed networks, where the links between nodes arise in any order—anyone can run into almost anyone else on the streets of London—and this complicates and multiplies not only possibilities for causal relationships but for social relationships altogether, including unlikely ties between members of apparently far-flung social groups. After all, any number of distributed networks, from gossip to disease to urban space, can end up linking someone like Jo the lowly crossing sweeper to someone as remote as the haughty Sir Leicester Dedlock. The films, much simpler in plot because of their restricted length, all rely on a single principle of interconnection, like the drug trade or the oil industry, to undergird their plots, whereas Dickens layers on multiple principles of interconnection, linking the same individuals over and over again through different channels.

In the process, *Bleak House* offers a better formal understanding of one particular network—the family—than do Hollywood's network narratives. *Traffic, Syriana,* and *Babel* all imagine the breakup of the family as the worst kind of violence wrought by networks. The restoration of the safety and integrity of the family becomes both the primary catalyst for plotted action and the primary source of thematic meaning. Formally speaking, the family emerges in these films as a singular unit, a whole, which can be threatened by networks. By contrast, consider the biggest secret in *Bleak House*—the link between Esther and her mother: this is the secret of an intimate, family relationship. But it does not begin as such in the novel's telling: Esther and Lady Dedlock first appear as two distant points, only gradually brought together as linked nodes in the consciousness of both readers and characters. By beginning with a social and geographical gap between two people who are ignorant of one another's existence, Dickens exposes not so much the splitting apart of families *by* networks but families *as networks,* in which the nodes are not always already fused together, but rather connected by paths that can be interrupted and stretched by other forms. *Bleak House* refuses to unify the family, then, and instead conceives of it as one of many networks, taking its place alongside the law, philanthropy, class hierarchy, and disease. In the process, the novel asks us not only to rethink character, but also relation, breaking apart even intimate ties to reveal them as networked forms.

Dickens then skillfully takes this analysis of the family a step farther, using narrative form to work through the dynamic unfolding of kinship networks over time. Consider one of the novel's minor characters, Mrs. Badger, who is absurdly proud of having had three distinguished husbands: the first a naval captain, the second a professor "of European reputation," and the third a surgeon. What Mrs. Badger makes clear is that a husband is not first and foremost a particular person but a position in a kinship network, and specifically a *replaceable* node. "Replaceable" also describes Esther's two husbands, one of whom replaces himself and his house with another husband and another house in one of the most unsettling moments in the text.

Dickens's interest in replaceability allows us to understand exactly how he brings narrative and network together. As anyone who has ever tried to make a genealogical chart will know, the family is never graspable as a whole. It stretches indefinitely across time and space. Distant branches connect ever outward, as marriage creates links to other families, old generations stretch back into the past indefinitely, and generations yet to come will continue to add nodes. And as Mrs. Badger suggests, the nodes of the family network are best figured as positions that can be endlessly emptied and refilled: new people supplant previous husbands and wives, sons and daughters, sisters, cousins, grandparents. In short, the nodes repeatedly replace themselves, and in so doing replicate the network in ways that stretch the institution of the family itself across time. Or to put this another way: the temporal unfurling of networks cannot be "turned into space" without distorting our understanding of the form in some crucial ways. Engaged in a constant process of self-renewal, the networked form of kinship is never whole, but always emerging, perpetually in process.

The narrative form best suited to conveying this resistance to totality, I want to suggest, is plotted suspense. At first glance, these two impulses—the sprawling, ever-emerging and overlapping network, and the teleological drive of suspenseful narrative—might seem starkly opposed. Most classic readings of detective fiction suggest that endings are deferred in order to provide the eventual satisfactions of understanding and order. This is quite the reverse of the network, which is happy to lose us in its constantly crisscrossing maze. But conventional readings of detective fiction have missed the importance of the narrative middle by too strongly favoring the analysis of closure.[34] The suspense of the middle occurs when a narrative clearly signals that it is holding something back. Such moments might indicate that we are missing a crucial piece of information—like a secret—or they might deliberately prolong an uncertain process, holding off the outcome—a chase, a threat, a flirtation.

Bleak House offers multiple sources of suspense—family secrets, a mysterious murder, a baffling lawsuit, and a frantic midnight pursuit—and so insists that we spend hours and hours in the experience of uncertainty, the experience specifically of *withheld* knowledge. At any given moment, we know that we cannot grasp crucial pathways between nodes, and this points us to our more generalized ignorance of networks. We cannot ever apprehend the totality of the networks that organize us.

This is a formal fact of networks. Because these sprawling, overlapping, and indefinitely expanding processes of interconnectedness, from law to disease to kinship, can never be fully grasped all at once, the emphasis on withholding knowledge may actually be essential to the task of representing multiple distributed networks. Or to put this another way: in order to represent a world of networks, the text must refuse totality. *Bleak House* uses the suspense of its long middle to demonstrate that at any moment our knowledge of social interconnections can only be partial: we may intuit the overwhelmingly complex webs of social interconnections in glimpses and hints, but the networks that connect rich and poor, city and world, the dead and the living, are never fully present to consciousness. Since the overlapping of social networks approaches a magnitude and a complexity so great that their wholeness defies full knowledge, Dickens opts for a narrative form that suggests and withholds—that is, the narrative of suspense.

By repeatedly offering and also suspending a knowledge of the networked social world, he hints that his novel is not—and indeed could never be—complete or encompassing. In any network, nodes can be replaced, and they can gather links to new nodes. To capture a moment, one must struggle to grasp the multiple systems of interconnection—constantly unfolding and expanding and overlapping—that constitute local instantiations of the social. Since these different systems emerge, expand, and develop in different times and places and at different rates, any apprehension of a cultural network must be responsive not only to multiple networks but also to their multiple temporalities. Thus *Bleak House* suggests that any historically particular event or institution or person is to be found at the crossing of numerous networks. The novel's massive scale might be necessary to the evocation of multiple distributed networks, but it still cannot really capture the social as a single, overarching meta-network, since so many of the networks Dickens describes extend beyond any temporal or spatial boundaries that one might try to set for them.

Bleak House, by organizing itself around such uncontainable networks, constantly runs up against the limits of its own capacity for representation. As Henry James put it so famously in the preface to *Roderick Hudson*, "Really, universally, relations stop nowhere."[35] Yet Dickens refuses to be a Jamesian artist, choosing "eternally but to draw, by a geometry of his own, the circle within which [relations] shall happily *appear* to [stop]" (vii). Instead, *Bleak House* gestures to the very fact that relations constantly break the boundaries of representation. Far from claiming to capture the family, the city, or the nation, Dickens points us instead to a model of social interconnection that is larger and longer than even this dauntingly expansive novel itself could manage. Again and again, the networked plot hints at immeasurable durations and extensions that lie beyond its own considerable reach. The vastness of *Bleak House* affords not individual agency, not the primacy of families, and not the wholeness of the nation, but a kind of narratively networked sublime.

And what is perhaps most strange and compelling, in the end, is that this sublime complexity captures something all too ordinary at work. All of us, along with other species and objects, are located at the crossings of multiple unfolding networks that are perpetually linking bodies, ideas, and things through numerous channels at different rates and across different kinds of spaces. As they pattern relationships, networks—social, economic, electronic, ecological, viral, bacterial, legal, familial, national, and transnational—also run up against other forms, including territorial boundaries, which they sometimes cross and which at other times bring them to a halt. We may have become accustomed to thinking about communications, transportation, and economic networks as powerful connectors that consolidate nations or enable globalization, but a formalist approach reveals many opportunities, large and small, to hamper networks and their coordinating power. The bounded shape of the nation-state can work both with and against capital flow. Multiple communications networks can disrupt as well as unite a nation. And minor forms can sometimes work against major ones—a local mail carrier can weaken a centralized network of imperial power by superimposing another, more local network, and a woman poet can retreat to the boundaries of her bedroom to block the encroachment of some very tiresome social networks in favor of a richer, more expansive world.

VI

THE WIRE

Most accounts of social relationships in literary and cultural studies encourage us to focus our attention on the ways that a couple of formations intersect at any given moment: imperialism and the novel, for example, or the law and print culture. But what happens if we change the scale of our formal perspective and begin with many forms? Paying attention to numerous overlapping social forms may seem daunting, if not impossible, but if it is in fact true that forms very often find their organizing power compromised, rerouted, or deflected by their encounters with other forms, then a formalist cultural studies interested in how power works will need to take account of what happens when a great many social, political, natural, and aesthetic forms encounter one another. What would such a formalist cultural studies look like?

I am going to make the eccentric claim here that it could look something like David Simon's superb television series, *The Wire* (2002–2008). The method I have favored in this book entails not only analysis but also detailed description—a willingness to observe and follow the impact of different kinds of forms on one another—and *The Wire* is a rare exploration of the ways that social experience can be structured and also rendered radically unpredictable by the dense overlapping of large numbers of social forms. When the series began, it looked something like a conventional television cop drama, with a police force pitted against drug dealers, but it widened its emphasis with each season to take in new institutions: first unions, then city politics, then education, and finally the press. Though the focus shifted with the seasons, the series built intersections with earlier institutions rather than replacing them, probing the sites and moments where they overlap, influence one another, and collide.

There are numerous bounded wholes and enclosures in *The Wire*, including prison cells, foster homes, administrative offices, and "Hamsterdam," a designated zone for legalized drugs. These take shape amid many conflicting and colliding social rhythms, from the testing of schoolchildren to the fast tempo of news stories and the slower movement of election cycles. Hierarchies matter here, too, of course. The series explores not only points of contact between the uncannily parallel, highly bureaucratic organizations of police force and drug dealers, but also other bureaucracies, including the law, education, and politics. These major institutions are ordered and disordered by different structuring hierarchies—racial, administrative, and generational. Finally, networks are perhaps the most noteworthy of all of *The Wire's* forms, as the name of the whole series suggests. There is the web of economic transactions, which links Barksdale drug money to downtown real estate and international terrorism. There are social networks organized by class, from the boys in the pit to political fundraisers. There is the space of the city, which brings characters like Jimmy McNulty and Stringer Bell into contact through the accident of sheer proximity. There is gossip, which cascades up and down the social ladder. There are small-scale social groups, including the boxing ring and the Narcotics Anonymous group, which often cross paths with the organized network of Baltimore churches. And there is kinship, from the Barksdale code of family loyalty to Wallace's grandmother down at the shore.

All of these are structured according to different organizing principles, which run up against one another in unexpected and often frustrating ways. But together they produce experience, and do so from childhood onward. *The Wire* makes clear that children at Tilghman Middle School do not begin outside of political forms and institutions and move into them as they mature; rather, we see how even before birth the patterns of family and school are already meeting and informing one another, and how both are rerouted and reshaped in encounters with electoral politics, drug trafficking, police administration, social services, and the law. Each child's story emerges out of a complex collision of social forms that can never be limited to one or two dominant social principles—race, economics, the city, the family, politics, the law, or education—but takes shape amid the pressures of all of these and their constantly colliding patterns. Thus *The Wire* allows us to ask what happens if we change the scale of our formal perspective to begin with an account not of two or three forms only—marriage and career, or meter and the state—but of vast numbers of social forms meeting one another.

There is something perverse, to be sure, in finding a theory of the social world not in science, not in philosophy, not in experience, but in fiction. *The Wire* may be realist in some ways, but it is obviously not the real: it is constructed and stylized, and it is hardly free of ideology or narrative artifice. And yet, to turn to *The Wire* as a theorization of the social is to be faithful to the roots of the word *theory*, which comes from the Greek word for "a looking at," "spectacle," or "contemplation." *Theoria* entails the possibility that one might be able to extrapolate generalizable rules about the world from the experience of a spectacle, and here I am suggesting that there is in *The Wire* precisely this potential for theorizing the social.

Sociologists Anmol Chaddha and William Julius Wilson agree, pointing to the particular affordances of fiction that can elude conventional sociological scholarship, a field that acknowledges the power of multiple social forms but nonetheless tends to isolate one pattern at a time for analysis:

> As a work of fiction, *The Wire* does not replace rigorous academic scholarship on the problems of urban inequality and poverty. But ... the show demonstrates the interconnectedness of systemic urban inequality in a way that can be very difficult to illustrate in academic works. Due to the structure of academic research, scholarly works tend to focus on many of these issues in relative isolation. A number of excellent studies analyze the impacts of deindustrialization, crime and incarceration, and the education system on urban inequality. It is often implicitly understood among scholars that these are deeply intertwined, but an in-depth analysis of any one of these topics requires such focused attention that other important factors necessarily receive less discussion.[1]

The Wire emerges as valuable here for its capacity to represent multiple forms operating at once, providing a serious analytical alternative to the usual scholarly attention to one or two forms at a time.

I will pay my closest attention in this chapter to a formal element of *The Wire* not always understood to lend itself to theory: its plot. Here I am following the lead of Fredric Jameson, who argues that in this series "plot construction ... has a theoretical or philosophical dimension."[2] And it is no accident that the particular plotting of this television drama should prompt a new respect for the powers of plot generally. Not unlike *Bleak House*, *The Wire* expands the usual affordances of its medium by intertwining over one hundred characters in multiple intricate sequences that overlap and reshape one another. It links apparently distant or disconnected characters, showing how a homeless heroin addict in Baltimore can have an impact on Russian drug smugglers and the governor of Maryland. And like *Bleak House*, but unlike almost any other fictional text, it dramatically expands the usual number of characters while also connecting them to each other through *multiple* channels. There is no single principle of interconnection that links each to every other. The sheer complexity and intricacy of *The Wire*'s plot are therefore truly striking—and indeed different from almost all conventional storylines.

Despite Jameson's recognition of the importance of plotted form here, his analysis of the series remains formally unconvincing. He argues that small moments in *The Wire*'s plot introduce "a slight rift or crack" into its "realism," which, according to Jameson, is all about "necessity": "why it had to happen like that and why reality is both the irresistible force and the unmovable obstacle." He contends that realist plots have certain, inexorable outcomes, while the plots of utopias open out unusual or unexpected possibilities. *The Wire* converts one into the other, Jameson argues, as "the Utopian future here and there breaks through, before reality and the present again close it down" (371–72). But he gives us no way to distinguish between these two kinds of plot: that is, what is it that makes one sequence of events necessary and another implausible and fantastic if both structure experience in the same text? How could one plot "break through" the other, if both are organizing elements of the same overarching narrative? Jameson himself distinguishes between them based on convention: some plotted arcs are familiar and recognizable and therefore realist; others, more unusual and surprising, are for him utopian.

But it is the genius of *The Wire* to show that *both* kinds of plot are plausible. The series presents all manner of outcomes looming at all times, imagining multiple possible paths immanent in every formal encounter, some conventional, others more surprising. I propose, then, to flip Jameson's argument upside down. Rather than seeing realism as closing down strange and unfamiliar plots, we can understand *The Wire* as making strange, unconventional plots plausible—realist. My own reading departs from Jameson's interest in genre to come much closer to that of sociologists like Wilson, who explains that *The Wire* "shows incredible imagination and understanding about the way the world works."[3] Fiction it is, certainly—artful and stylized, without question. But in and through its plot it seeks to track the plausible unfolding of events as forms collide.

Plotting matters in particular to our capacity to think about causality. As I have said before, narrative is an ideal form for avoiding metaphysical truth-claims about causes: it presents causality in something of the same way that it actually appears to us in the world, through an experience of unfolding. And serialized television seems especially well suited for this, since, unlike many novels, no obtrusive omniscient narrator intervenes to tell us why something has happened, and since, like the novel but unlike conventional film, it has hours and hours and hours to unfold relationships. The narrative affords hundreds of social forms, tracking them as they cooperate, come into conflict, and overlap, without positing a single deep structure or original cause. And since forms can move across contexts, taking their own range of affordances with them, the plot gives us a way to theorize the relations among forms that appear both inside and outside of fiction.

The Wire is famously bleak, and its critics—perhaps most notably Slavoj Žižek—have condemned it for its "fatalistic world view."[4] It might therefore seem politically ineffective, even counterproductive, to turn to David Simon's series for a theory of social forms. Most outcomes for the characters are tragic or ironic, and no entirely restructured alternatives take shape. Sometimes characters mourn for the old days, suggesting a break between past and present. Both the unions and the newspapers have seen better times. But the series also ironizes such nostalgic sentiments. In one case, Bodie, a drug dealer who is no older than sixteen or seventeen, looks with regret at his eighth-grade lookouts who are off to play with pigeons: "Young 'uns don't got a scrap of work ethic nowadays. If it wasn't for us pops I wouldn't even bother."[5] Similarly, Wee-Bay, who has killed many times, longs for the good old days under Avon Barksdale, before Marlo's rise to power: "[W]e did that shit right; word was your bond; man looked out for his own, knowing he in a family. . . . But today, it's all fucked up."[6] In a series that ends by suggesting that its young characters are about to replicate the lives of their predecessors—with Michael as the new Omar, and Duquon as the new Bubbles—the repetitiveness of patterns seems to triumph over attempts to generate genuine difference. Or to put this another way: although the world of Baltimore may have changed over time, *The Wire* focuses our attention on institutional rhythms of replication and substitution that stretch forward and backward in time rather than on moments of dramatic change or rupture.

But it would also be a mistake to claim that *The Wire* gives us no way to think social relations outside of a too-abstract capitalism or tragic fate, which decrees that all is predetermined. To the contrary, we are repeatedly, even insistently, shown how things work, with openings to multiple alternatives at every turn. And how things work is relentlessly a matter of form. Patterns and arrangements structure experience in such complicated ways that they often derail happy endings, but at the same time they do not altogether foreclose the possibility of events turning out otherwise. Indeed, *The Wire* repeatedly imagines the ways that forms might work together for genuine social change. If those get disrupted, the source cannot always be traced back to a single structure of power—economics, politics, or race— but rather to the overlapping of multiple forms.

I will consider forms in *The Wire* in the same order that I have used to structure this book as a whole: bounded wholes, rhythms, hierarchies, and networks. This order is arbitrary in the sense that none of these is primary or basic: each can be nested inside the other—wholes can contain rhythms and hierarchies networks. In fact, *The Wire* helps us to see how interdependent these forms must always be. But for the sake of intelligibility, I want to build my case by focusing on one at a time, and only then exploring their interdependence. My reading will focus almost exclusively on the arc of the series' interconnected plots, since it is my contention that *The Wire*—though notable for its rich characterization, its excellent acting, its refusal of simple stereotypes, and even its soundtrack—is truly exceptional in its attention to the ways that multiple social forms unfold in relation to one another, their encounters producing serious, painful, and occasionally promising effects.

Whole

Many bounded wholes organize experience in *The Wire*. Most of these are literal spatial enclosures, from homes, offices, and city limits to shipping containers, public meeting spaces, bars, stash houses, and prison cells. Like the unified wholes we encountered earlier, all of these have boundaries that distinguish inside from outside; all afford protection or imprisonment, inclusion and exclusion. Drug dealers fight over the limits of their turf, and police identify strongly with either Eastern or Western districts. I will begin here by focusing briefly on three different examples of encounters between spatial containers, as illustrative—rather than exhaustive—of *The Wire*'s interest in the power of various contending and colliding enclosures to organize and disorganize experience.

Perhaps the most notable example of the power of bounded enclosures appears as an experiment in season 3, when Bunny Colvin creates Hamsterdam, a strictly bounded trio of urban zones where drug dealers and users can behave as they wish, safe from police interference. These enclosed spaces take the drug trade off the usual street corners, distributed throughout poor neighborhoods in the city, and allow public health groups, who now have easy, centralized access to addicts, to begin to distribute condoms and offer needle exchanges and rehabilitation programs. Hamsterdam then has consequences for other enclosures, both small and large. First of all, neighborhood boys, once hired by drug dealers to stand on the corners and act as lookouts, now have nothing to do and so drift into a different kind of contained space, Dennis "Cutty" Wise's community-run boxing ring. Second, Mayor Clarence Royce is momentarily impressed by the success of the zones, and his delay in shutting them down helps to bring about his defeat in the next election, catapulting Tommy Carcetti into leadership of the city and eventually the state. Where one might expect the leader of the larger, official political space—the city—to define the smaller, experimental one—Hamsterdam—in fact the mere existence of the free zones shifts power relations in Baltimore and eventually Maryland as a whole, suggesting that minor forms have consequences for major ones. These three defined spaces, each a container with clear boundaries, one nested within the next—Hamsterdam, Baltimore, and Maryland—are formally similar, but that does not mean that they are coordinated to the same political or organizational ends.

In season 2, the relation of enclosures again suggests that the smallest containers can affect the largest scales of political power. At the start, police commander Stan Valchek is furious that Frank Sobotka of the dockworker's union has bested him in a small-time quarrel over who gets to install a new stained-glass window in a local church. Seeking to win a power struggle over a single parish church, Valchek calls in favors at the Baltimore police department to launch an investigation into Sobotka's finances. Sobotka turns out to be taking money from an international smuggling ring, and the police department and soon the FBI turn their attention to larger targets than the Baltimore-based union boss. Valchek has called in both Baltimore and federal law enforcement to prevail in a neighborhood fight, only to find that the city, national law enforcement, and transnational networks have their own logics, which unfold well beyond his control. The politics of a single church triggers the sequence that ensues, but as the parish overlaps with other jurisdictions—the city police, the national FBI, and global trade and terror agents—major forms end up engulfing minor ones.

In my third example, we see how bounded shapes can collide to trigger a far-reaching sequence of events. When the Barksdale solider, Wee-Bay Brice, willingly accepts a life sentence for the sake of the organization, he is enclosed for life in a prison. In exchange, the Barksdales support and protect Wee-Bay's girlfriend De'Londa and their son Namond in an expensively furnished home. But the Barksdale drug crew is soon driven off their territory by Marlo's ruthless new team of dealers. Having lost their turf, the Barksdales say that they can no longer pay for Wee-Bay's home. De'Londa responds by sending Namond into the streets to sell drugs, where he is driven off his own corner territory by rivals, fails in the business, and as punishment is thrown out of his mother's home. Thanks to an academic experiment happening in Namond's school, where children who are especially troublesome are enclosed in a separate classroom, the boy comes to the attention of former police officer Bunny Colvin, forced into retirement because of his own experiments with bounded wholes. Bunny offers Namond temporary sanctuary and eventually a new home. Here, then, each bounded space has an impact on the next. An enclosed prison cell is exchanged for a protected home, which is endangered when drug-turf boundaries are breached, which causes Namond to be ejected from his home. But Namond is also one of the few characters who has a happy ending in the series, and he succeeds because the school's reorganization of space happens to propel him into two new protected enclosures, Bunny's classroom and his adoptive home: without those, his fate would be like that of his homeless peers, Randy and Duquon. No single form dominates or causes this sequence of events: not the home, not the school, not the drug territory, not the prison cell. But all of these enclosures play a part in the organization of Namond's story, which is literally unthinkable without them.

Rhythm

The Wire is as interested in the collision of social rhythms and tempos as it is in the overlap of bounded spaces, offering up an impossibly complex assemblage of temporalities. The plot layers routine police assessments of crime statistics on top of biennial political campaigns on top of annual school testing on top of the daily deadlines of newspapers. Narratively speaking, it is often impossible to determine whether the events represented are sequential or simultaneous: *fabula* can be hard to deduce from *sjuzhet*. To be sure, as it constantly cuts back and forth between plots and between institutions—moving rapidly from the newsroom to the classroom to the mayor's office to the home to the street-corner—each particular episode does imply a temporal unfolding. We tend to see shots that take place in the morning, followed by those during the day, evening, and then night. But are the morning scenes taking place at the same time, or consecutively? Similarly, seasons change, but we rarely have a sense of precise dates, or of the spans of time that pass between episodes. The series seems to resist temporal exactness, preferring to capture a feeling of simultaneous recurrence, patterns of repetition all going on at once, rather than events following each other in any precise order.

As the plot unfolds, we see how each institution has its own temporal rhythms, and often multiple rhythms, overlaid one on the other. Mrs. Sampson, a teacher at Tilghman Middle School, describes one school tempo: "You can tell the days by [the kids'] faces. The best day is Wednesday. That's the farthest they get from home, from whatever's going on in the streets. You see smiles, then. Monday is angry. Tuesdays they're caught between Monday and Wednesday, so it could go either way. Thursdays, they're feeling that weekend coming. Friday is bad again."[7] The school is also organized temporally by grade level. One of the most painful moments in *The Wire* is Duquon's graduation from middle school. Part of a beleaguered school system's attempt to show that its students are advancing academically, Duquon is suddenly expected to move forward to the ninth grade at mid-year. This interrupts the widespread practice of routine social promotion—which moves children forward with their peers by age, rather than academic level—and it will prove catastrophic for Duquon. He is not ready for the socially mature world of high school and so drops out altogether, only to learn that there are no good alternatives. He is not yet old enough to find paid work in a legitimate business, and so, cast out of the bounds of home, his middle-school cohort, and the workplace, both too old and too young, he faces a bleak future of drug addiction and homelessness. This is the formal power of temporal organization both at its most mundane—Duquon's promotion is, after all, just a routine bureaucratic action—and at its most tragic.

The Wire often represents characters caught between social tempos, surprised by the effects of multiple rhythms colliding. In one example, Lester Freamon and Kima Greggs, having tracked drug dealers' donations to high-ranking political officials, decide to take advantage of the primary election to hand out subpoenas, reasoning that the election cycle will make people pay attention to them. And pay attention they do. Kima is kicked out of Major Crimes, and finds herself on the bottom rung of the ladder, a novice, in Homicide. When the mayor fears that a scandal will erupt around the murder of a state's witness, he puts pressure on Police Commissioner Burrell to slow down the investigation, so Burrell puts Kima—the inexperienced rookie—on the case. The press gets hold of the story, interviewing candidate Tony Gray who takes advantage of the situation to humiliate Kima, showing her up as a naive know-nothing. "What the fuck I ever do to him?" she asks.[8] But to see this as an interpersonal drama is a mistake; it is actually a case of colliding temporal forms. Kima has been caught at the junction of contending tempos that include the pace of two different police investigations, the timing of a mayoral primary, her own newness at the job, and the daily news cycle.

Kima is not the only worker on *The Wire* to turn over—to be replaced and to replace others. Some of the most powerful temporal forms in the series are patterns of surrogation. As soon as characters die, get fired, or go to jail, others replace them—in the police bureaucracy, the drug trade, and even the family. The police in *The Wire* complain that death and jail can never put an end to the drug trade, because the dealers are endlessly replaced; this means that their own jobs will never be done; so they too are

endlessly replaceable. *The Wire* also makes it clear that these surrogations are not limited to official organizations. In season 3, we see McNulty at a baseball game: his ex-wife Elana has taken up with a new man, a wealthy downtown lawyer, whose seats are far better than his own, much to his sons' disappointment when they switch from maternal to paternal custody. This scene suggests that the realm of private, intimate relationships is hardly safe from institutionalized patterns of turnover. Indeed, we might think of the many foster and adoptive parents in the series, including the four substitute fathers in season 4—Colvin, Carver, Prez, and Bubbles—each of whom considers taking on a kind of parental role in relation to one of the boys—Namond, Randy, Duquon, and Sherrod. The family clearly involves its own processes of surrogation.

The series thus shows how all of the major institutions it represents endure across time. There are no dramatic historical breaks on *The Wire* precisely because the many institutions that impose order on experience—family, school, government, business—operate by way of iterable patterns of surrogation and replacement. This is not the same as fatalism or stasis: institutions can introduce a new pattern of student promotion, decline over time through lost business, or shift workers to new positions. We can see the repercussions of these changes as new forms encounter other forms both inside and outside of a particular institution, but it is a crucial aspect of social rhythm that institutions replicate themselves across time through repetition and substitution.

Hierarchy

One of the most powerful institutional forms that endure through patterns of replaceability in *The Wire* is the vertical form of the hierarchy, which crops up everywhere, from racism to the bureaucratic hierarchies of the police force, political campaign, and, most startlingly, drug organizations. Part of what makes *The Wire* so brilliant is its revelation that the bureaucratic forms of modern institutions are so pervasive that they have come to organize not only official institutions but underworld activity as well.[9] The business of drugs turns out to produce the same kinds of pecking orders, promotions and demotions, incentives for good work, quality assessments, and business mergers as the routines of official institutions. Stringer Bell's borrowing of *Robert's Rules of Order* for his cross-Baltimore drug consortium is perhaps the most elegant instance of the pervasive spread of bureaucratic forms. And what this means is that the most powerful institutions portrayed on *The Wire*—not only the police force and the drug trade, but city politics, the school system, and the newspaper—are, without exception, structured according to remarkably similar hierarchical forms. The choices made by *The Wire*'s characters—from police lieutenants to mid-level drug dealers, from city council members to kids in the boxing ring—are, in most cases, strategic attempts to retain their positions or to reach up the ladder to occupy a higher rank. Just about everyone can report to a superior, snitch on a peer, or be demoted. *The Wire* draws our attention, over and over, to the hierarchical structuring of experience.

Season 3, for example, opens with police detectives planning to arrest a mid-level dealer. They expect him to be replaced with a garrulous underling whose chatter, they hope, will give the whole game away. "What makes you think they'll promote the wrong man?" asks the police commissioner. "*We* do it all the time," Daniels responds. Burrell laughs, but it is worth noting that he also uses this point to turn the conversation to the question of Daniels's own promotion, telling him that his wife's run for office—to replace the mayor's ally—is prompting the mayor to hold up Daniels's career move.[10] Each of the persons in question—Drac, Marla Daniels, Cedric Daniels—has the potential to take the position of another in a hierarchy, just as Burrell and the mayor are trying to hold on to their own high-ranking spots. All are vulnerable, and no place in any of these pecking orders will remain empty for long.

Importantly, however, even the bureaucratic hierarchy does not emerge in *The Wire* as a single source of clear power. Bureaucratic institutions turn out to be neither monolithic panoptic nor simply hierarchical structures—as we might expect—but rather complex and uneven overlappings of norms and practices that work against each other as often as they work together. A crucial part of the plotted tension of season 1, for instance, revolves around the question of whether Lieutenant Daniels will seek his own promotion, pleasing his bosses at the expense of the drug case, or whether he will choose to value his detectives' work, pursuing the investigation and risking his career. The outcome feels genuinely uncertain. And crucially, we come to learn that it is not just Daniels's choice that is involved here: Carver, his underling, is secretly reporting all of his lieutenant's choices to the Deputy of Operations, thereby securing his own promotion while undermining both the success of the case and the choices of his own immediate superior. Meanwhile, McNulty is constantly challenging Daniels's authority by investigating the case in his own way, typically dragging his partner Bunk Moreland into the process by invoking the value of the peer partnership over the chain of command. None of these characters chooses to work outside of the bureaucracy altogether: rather, each favors one aspect of bureaucratic organization over others. In the process, they come into conflict in ways that are enabled by precisely the bureaucratic forms that also frustrate them. Thus the text refuses the narrative logic of personal intentions as well as the logic of monolithic institutional power, opting instead for the intricate interweaving of competing bureaucratic forms—multiple hierarchies and alliances—as they organize, constrain, and overwhelm individual ends.

Unpredictable consequences ensue when multiple vertical forms meet in *The Wire*. Marla and Cedric Daniels separate when he refuses to pursue an ambitious rise up the career ladder, and she pursues her own political ambitions instead, running for city council. Daniels agrees to support her, only to find his own career further damaged by his wife's decision to run against one of the mayor's close political allies. But when the mayor, under pressure from the Hamsterdam debacle, is forced to switch allegiances, he lends his support to Marla Daniels and gives Cedric a career boost. This eventually changes the career trajectory of Bill Rawls, whose sole and ruthless aim is to rise in the bureaucracy of the police department. Rawls is horrified to discover that Cedric Daniels may be promoted over his head because the white mayor, Tommy Carcetti, needs an African-American police commissioner to solidify support for his administration. The majority black Baltimore population, he is told, will not stand for a white commissioner working for a white mayor. "It's funny how it works out," Daniels says. "All those years I'm trying to climb the ladder, kissing ass, covering ass, doing what I'm told. I finally let some of it out, say what I really think, and I'm going from lieutenant to colonel in little more than a year."[11] This unpredictability has been the effect of a formal collision: the hierarchies of gender, race, and bureaucracy. The gendered hierarchy of the Daniels marriage—where the wife serves the husband's career—runs into trouble when the husband's place in the police bureaucracy stagnates. The wife takes her husband's failure as a reason to pursue her own rise, only to find herself, thanks to political matters beyond her knowledge and control, propelling her former husband far beyond anything either of them had ever expected. Meanwhile, Rawls, who has been single-mindedly dedicated to climbing the career ladder, finds that the hierarchy of race—here inverted from the norm in majority black Baltimore—allows him to be outstripped by the much less ambitious Daniels. In the final montage, we see the conventional hierarchies of race and career ambition restored, as Daniels's refusal to manipulate crime statistics thrusts him out of the police force altogether, and Rawls is rewarded for loyalty to Carcetti by being named state commissioner. But we do not see the links in the chain that produce this conventional ending. Instead, *The Wire* has shown, closely and carefully, how effectively hierarchies can throw one another into disarray.[12]

Network

We have seen how bounded wholes, rhythms, and hierarchies produce tangled and unexpected effects in *The Wire*'s Baltimore. But what is it that connects all the pieces, joins all the participants, creates the larger plot structure? This brings us to our last form: the network. Several critics have argued that the real protagonist of the show is the city of Baltimore, which is portrayed as an overlapping set of networks, each operating according to its own principles of interconnection. Others have said that the real agent is capitalism. "Follow the money," says Lester Freamon, tracking economic links from nodes in the Barksdale drug business to downtown real estate and electoral politics. Information, too, has power, and it too moves along network paths: phone calls among drug dealers prompt the detectives' desire for wiretapping technology to reveal the structure of the drug business, and gossip and informants provide crucial hinges between police and drug dealers when the wiretap fails. There are other networks that exert power here: official, institutional networks, such as the legal system, which brings together police officers, judges, lawyers, prison guards, witnesses, convicts, and informants; and illegal networks, including the consortium of drug dealers organized by Stringer Bell, which links up East and West Baltimore, and has connections to unions, politicians, corner kids, Russian prostitutes, and global smugglers. This final example points to the impossibility of thoroughly disconnecting different networks: the drug trade must overlap with other economic transactions and run up against the legal system, while taking place on city streets and drawing on ties of kinship. And yet, while there is no question that these networks overlap and link together, they also follow discrete principles of interconnection: kinship is not the same as the city streets and will never be, but both provide crucial connections. The multiple networks that tie the city together—trade, the legal system, and the circulation of information, among others—often reach beyond its boundaries, so that the shape of the city fails to contain its many networks.

Networks on *The Wire* link other social forms, including enclosures (connecting the school to the prison cell, for instance) and hierarchies (as when drug dealing kingpins contribute to the campaign war chests of ambitious politicians). They also link temporal patterns: as the detectives investigate links between drugs and politics during the election season, both police officers and politicians know that they can leak stories to a press always hungry for something juicy for the evening news cycle. Networks can have rhythms of their own (gossip can move fast; court cases can be slowed down by missing witnesses); and they can be organized hierarchically (as in the legal system or the drug trade). Networks thus not only connect but overlap with other forms.

Like bounded shapes, rhythms, and hierarchies, networks also collide with one another on *The Wire*. In one example, Bubbles, a former police informant, runs into Prez, a former police officer, at Tilghman Middle School. Crossing paths in the same enclosed space, Bubbles assumes that Prez is working as an undercover cop, but in fact the paths that link them this time are less obvious. Bubbles is there to try to educate his young business associate, Sherrod, who refuses to be contained by the school walls, while Prez has left the police force to teach eighth grade after mistakenly shooting a black cop and being publicly accused of racism. Cutty, too, crosses their paths at the school, having been hired as a seasonal truant enforcer through the recommendation of the Deacon, whose exceptionally expansive network reaches across politicians, school administrators, police officers, and the poor people of the west side. ("A good church man is always up in everybody's shit," as the Deacon himself puts it.[13]) The space of the school is thus crisscrossed by networks that gather together people who have been joined before by the network of law enforcement.

Consider, for another example, the fate of D'Angelo Barksdale, who is caught, at the end of season 1, between his position in the family and his potential to act as a hinge between the network of drug dealers and the courts. The family is a powerful structuring principle for Dee: the fact that he is Avon Barksdale's nephew means that he has often bypassed the usual business hierarchies and reaped special privileges. But Avon also requires that D'Angelo accept a twenty-year jail term for the sake of the family. After Dee has made up his mind to refuse the family, informing on the Barksdale crew to the police, and promising a huge career-clinching victory for those trying to prosecute Avon, his mother visits him in jail: "How the fuck you gonna start over without your peoples?" she asks.[14] The outcome, at this moment, is very much in question. D'Angelo could plausibly go either way. Following a pause of powerful suspense, Dee yields to his mother, choosing the power of kinship networks over the safeguards of police protection.

The Wire favors those characters who understand the power of network forms. The police who do street rips, gathering up small-time dealers, never get anywhere: it is only a knowledge of drug dealing hubs that will allow police work to progress. The most successful and sympathetic detectives, like Freamon, use the networking technology of the wiretap to uncover knowledge of the drug dealers' networks, as the drug kingpins themselves try to conceal the nodes that claim the most network centrality, and to expose only the least networked nodes. Stringer Bell grasps the value and power of linking East and West Baltimore drug rings, while Avon remains tied to habits of family and neighborhood loyalty. Omar's remarkable freedom and power comes not least from his knowledge of the major drug dealers' networks, which he gains by constant observation. Good journalists, we learn in season 5, always have robust networks that cross institutions, including the mayor's office and the police force. Even Bubbles, poor and marginal, is one of *The Wire*'s most beloved characters, one whose importance to the plot rests on his willingness to act as a hinge between networks of law enforcement and drug dealers.

Why is a knowledge of networks so crucial in *The Wire*? Since networks can always make one vulnerable—a schoolboy witness, willing to make the link between streets and police force, could take down a whole criminal operation—a knowledge of network links is absolutely crucial to maintaining or unsettling a fragile hold on power. But *The Wire* also suggests that knowledge of network links is essential to understanding the ways that the social world works. What makes things happen in Baltimore, *The Wire* suggests, is no single social group or form—not money or politics or race or the family or the social elite—but the many webs of small and subtle interconnections that can link a low-level cop to the mayor, via police bureaucracy, daily news cycles, and the classroom. To understand how Avon Barksdale is brought down or Carcetti propelled to power requires a careful tracing of the connecting links between forms both major and minor.

Every plot sequence in *The Wire* follows a networked logic, inviting us to track the surprisingly byzantine paths between social forms as they coordinate, transform, or block one another. Or to put this another way: one cannot understand "the social" outside of the many intricate and open-ended plots depicted by *The Wire*. Any attempt to isolate the power of education or poverty or drugs will be doomed to failure, since the crucial fact is that none of these work in isolation. *The Wire* imagines that the process of capturing social experience will not lie in stories that follow a sequence of separate institutional forms—one narrative about a hospital, another about lawyers, a third about a school—but through attention to the many points where forms collide.

Knowing Forms

The Wire's plot appears so complex that it often seems to thwart both knowledge and action. The characters themselves, though often highly mindful of hierarchies, are largely unaware of other formal overlaps and collisions. This ignorance can lead to tragedy, as for example when Assistant Principal Marcia Donnelley tries to separate the bounded spaces of home and school definitively, warning Prez away from seeing Duquon as his own child:

> You and your wife, you don't have children, do you? . . . Well, have some. For better or for worse, they're yours for life. The kids in this school aren't yours. You do your piece with them, and you let them go. Because there'll be plenty more coming up behind Duquon, and they're gonna need your help too.[15]

For Donnelly, the teacher's children belong in the middle-class home, whereas the children in the school are endlessly replaceable, interchangeable units in a perpetual process of institutional turnover. But Donnelly turns out to be wrong: it is soon after this scene that Bunny Colvin will successfully cross the divide between home and school, working out a deal with Wee-Bay to take Namond into his own family. He substitutes himself as father in the kinship network, while he moves Namond between the enclosures of school and home. It is intriguing, too, that he manages to convince Wee-Bay to be replaced by pointing to him out that Namond will now be able to slot himself into a place in the social hierarchy that would never have been open to him if Wee-Bay had remained his father. Namond now can climb the social ladder thanks to his new home, while Duquon, thanks to Mrs. Donnelly's logic of strict separation of shapes, remains one of many interchangeable units of black poverty and neglect.

Another tragic example of what can happen when no one is conscious of the collision of forms, is the story of Randy Wagstaff, who has been acting as a lookout for a sexual encounter in the middle school. Caught, he is terrified that his foster mother will throw him out of her house and he will end up in a group home, so he confesses to the assistant principal that he knows about a murder. Three forms help to govern Randy's fate—the boys' bathroom, his foster home, and the group home—all of which are bounded spaces that have the capacity to exclude as well as include, to imprison as well as protect. His fear of being shifted from one enclosure to another to another prompts him to divulge crucial knowledge of a crime, and so involves the police department. There, Ellis Carver, who has offered to act as the boy's foster father but is stymied by social services, passes Randy on to Herc, who is eager to get himself out of trouble with his superiors, hoping that information from Randy will allow him to climb the career ladder by delivering up drug kingpin Marlo Stanfield. Herc decides that Randy cannot help him rise, and casually leaks the information that Randy is a snitch to one of Marlo's people, who immediately reports this fact to his superiors. Randy emerges as a threatening hinge with the potential to link the police to the drug dealer's network. Marlo destroys the boy's home and foster mother, and Randy finds himself in precisely the group home he has most desperately wanted to avoid. Caught among at least three bounded wholes and three hierarchies—the school administration, the police bureaucracy, and the drug trade—Randy ends up trapped and brutalized in a home that is all too much like a prison.

Both characters and critics bewail the power of what they call "the system" portrayed on *The Wire*, but it is crucial to note that "the system" is less an organized or integrated single structure than it is precisely this heaped assortment of wholes, rhythms, hierarchies, and networks.[16] The police administration fails because it depends on a simple model of individual responsibility—guilt and innocence that can be known through the arrest and prosecution of small-time drug deals on street corners but does not begin to grasp the crisscrossing forms that produce social experience. On the other hand, large-scale, abstract theories of capitalism fail too. Patrick Jagoda argues that *The Wire* insists on a particular kind of "distributed thought" suitable to networks rather than "a grand theory of capitalism":

> Theories of a seamless social totality too easily produce stability out of dynamic processes. *The Wire*, however, teems with contradictions and instabilities. The series carefully attends to the controversies, contradictions, and messy complexities of American social life. The connections that make up social networks, after all, are rarely smooth and continuous. Every political ecology—every socially embedded system of accumulation—is a precarious, tottering structure.[17]

Jagoda's invocation of a complex "political ecology" here is powerful, and I think he is right to see *The Wire* as demanding a specific kind of "distributed thought." But it is important to recall, too, that the series also reaches well beyond the network form alone as a way of understanding the social.

By shifting its focus from the power of individuals or elite groups to the intricate "political ecology" of a whole world of contending forms, *The Wire* allows us to see networks as linking other forms, but also derailing them and being derailed by them.

Along the way, the series, like *Bleak House*, offers an unconventional account of agency. Individual characters do have some power to make choices—D'Angelo can choose to snitch on the Barksdales, Stringer Bell can opt for the warrior ethic or the business model he has adopted from corporate practice, and Tommy Carcetti can choose between the schools' budget shortfall and the collapse of police morale—but these examples all suggest that individual decisions matter only within environments of colliding forms where no individual or elite group controls either procedures or outcomes. It is not just that small players like Dee cannot dictate their own fates: no one—including the mayor and the police commissioner—can predict what will happen or exert a clear control over outcomes. Indeed, as new characters replace old ones in positions of power and authority, they typically find themselves becoming like their predecessors, against their best intentions. This is true of Carcetti when he replaces Royce, but it is also true of McNulty in season 5, when he has a brief stint as a supervisor and finds himself acting strangely like the supervisors he has so loved to resist in the past. While it is certainly the case that some characters have positions of high status or belong to powerful elites, then, it does not follow that their intentions wholly determine events. And if characters have limited agency, what limits them are precisely preexisting social forms: bureaucratic hierarchies that are themselves shaped by electorates organized by race; bounded spaces that include drug territories, prison cells, city limits, and group homes; and social tempos that constantly overlap, from budget cycles and school calendars to election campaigns and court cases. Far from an ideologically coherent society with power lodged in the hands of a few, *The Wire* gives us a social world constantly unsettled by the bewildering and unexpected effects of clashes among wholes, rhythms, hierarchies, and networks.

The few characters who recognize the power and significance of multiple forms—Lester Freamon, Bunny Colvin, and Omar Little—all make strategic decisions which, temporarily at least, permit outcomes that frustrate or elude the conventional distribution of power. Freamon manages to link politicians to drug smugglers by following the tracks of economic and information networks, briefly exposing a corrupt elite. Colvin reshapes the city and the world of the corner boys into new bounded wholes until he is brought down by the mayor, and he succeeds in offering one of those boys a safe home and promising future. Omar remains comparatively free, the consummate outsider, refusing to join hierarchies and always escaping from enclosing shapes. But he works the network all the same, showing us that he understands well how both hierarchies and networks operate. All of these are sympathetic, even heroic. They are the show's epistemological and ethical exemplars, and they perform a reading of the social that is nothing other than a canny formalism.

NOTES

Preface

1 Michel Foucault, "The Politics of Contemporary Life," in *Politics, Philosophy, Culture: Interviews and Other Writings, 1977–1984*, ed. Lawrence D. Kritzman (London and New York: Routledge, 1988), 168.

I Introduction: The Affordances of Form

1 Charlotte Brontë, *Jane Eyre* (1847) (Harmondsworth: Penguin, 1996), 54–55, 98.
2 Janis McLarren Caldwell, for example, argues that Cowan Bridge School, "the institution that inspired Lowood," shaped Charlotte Brontë's repeated novelistic focus on maturation. *Literature and Medicine in Nineteenth-Century Britain* (Cambridge: Cambridge University Press, 2004), 97. David Amigoni claims that Lowood is "emblematic of Foucault's case for the disciplinary turn which characterized nineteenth-century institutions." *The English Novel and Prose Narrative* (Edinburgh: Edinburgh University Press, 2000), 64.
3 Angela Leighton's *On Form* tracks many of these contradictory meanings (Oxford University Press, 2007), 1–29.
4 Here I am both building on Rancière, who helpfully turns our attention to distribution as the enforcement of categories and inequalities, and also departing from his terms. He does not use the term *form*, and he distinguishes the work of distribution, which he calls *police*, from *politics*, which only erupts in moments of unsettling redistribution. I choose to call both of these *politics*, following convention in literary and cultural studies, where politics encompasses both enforcement and resistance.
5 John Milton, "The Verse," preface to *Paradise Lost* (1674), in *The Major Works* (Oxford: Oxford University Press, 2003), 355.
6 Richard Aldington, *Some Imagist Poets: An Anthology* (Boston and New York: Houghton Mifflin, 1915), vi–vii.
7 Terry Eagleton argues that the Brontës created mythical resolutions to real social conflicts through narrative closure in *Myths of Power* (1975) (Houndmills: Palgrave Macmillan, 2005). Stephen Greenblatt's famous New Historicist essay, "Invisible Bullets," ends with the claim that "the form itself" of Shakespeare's drama "contains the radical doubts it continually provokes," in *Political Shakespeare*, eds. Jonathan Dollimore and Alan Sinfield (Manchester and New York: Manchester University Press, 1994), 45. Most recently, Marxist-formalist Alex Woloch brilliantly rethinks the problem of character in the novel by arguing that nineteenth-century novels are organized around enclosed character-systems. *The One v. the Many* (Princeton: Princeton University Press, 2003). An attention to forms as constraints emerges in other schools of thought as well. Feminist poststructuralist Luce Irigaray decries Western thought for its long history of insisting on the constraints of form. *This Sex Which Is Not One*, trans. Catherine Porter (Ithaca, NY and London: Cornell University Press, 1985), 26.

8   Aristotle (*Poetics*) launches this tradition of thought in the West, with his attention to the structuring of tragedy and epic poetry. Al-Farahidi (786–718 BCE) is said to be the first writer to describe the patterns of syllables in Arabic verse. Sanskrit prosody begins with Pingala's *Chandaḥśāstra*, dating to around the first century BCE or CE, a time when poets were shifting from Vedic to classical Sanskrit meter. A century of interesting work in theories of narrative form begins with Vladimir Propp's *Morphology of the Folktale* (1928) and moves up through Gerard Genette's *Figures* (1967–70), Roland Barthes's *S/Z* (1970), and Peter Brooks's *Reading for the Plot* (1984), and reaches our own time in the works of Marie-Laure Ryan, Robyn Warhol, and David Herman, among many others.

9   Kimberlé Williams Crenshaw was the first to theorize intersectionality in "Mapping the Margins: Intersectionality, Identity Politics, and Violence against Women of Color," *Stanford Law Review* 43, no. 6 (July 1991): 1241–99.

10   Wai-Chee Dimock traces an "epic spiral" that moves from Virgil and Dante to Henry James in *Through Other Continents: American Literature across Deep Time* (Princeton: Princeton University Press, 2006). Frances Ferguson argues that forms are surprisingly stable across audiences. "*Emma* and the Impact of Form," *Modern Language Quarterly* 61 (March 2000): 160. And Franco Moretti has been asking which forms travel successfully across space, and which do not, in *Distant Reading* (London and New York: Verso, 2013).

11   See Michel Foucault, *Discipline and Punish: The Birth of the Prison*, trans. Alan Sheridan (London: Penguin, 1977), 137, 141, 156–57.

12   For Walter Benjamin, the idea of totality in art was "false" and seductive, and particularly dangerous when the fascists used it to create a totality out of the masses of people themselves. See "The Work of Art in the Age of Mechanical Reproduction," in *Film Theory and Criticism*, eds. Gerald Mast and Marshall Cohen (New York: Oxford University Press, 1974), 869–70.

13   In one recent example among many, Matt Cohen writes that "a virulent racism structures many of [Edwin Rice] Burrough's Tarzan novels," in *Brother Men* (Durham, NC and London: Duke University Press, 2005), 31.

14   Susan Wolfson, *Formal Charges: The Shaping of Poetry in British Romanticism* (Stanford: Stanford University Press, 1997); Heather Dubrow, "The Politics of Aesthetics: Recuperating Formalism and the Country House Poem," in *Renaissance Literature and Its Formal Engagements*, ed. Mark David Rasmussen (Houndmills: Palgrave, 2002): 67–88.

15   Most design theorists emphasize the relations between an object and its users; I am more interested in the ways that affordance allows us to think about both constraint and capability—that is, what actions or thoughts are made possible or impossible by the fact of a form. First used by perceptual psychologist J. J. Gibson ("The Theory of Affordances," in R. E. Shaw and J. Bransford, eds., *Perceiving, Acting, and Knowing* [Hillsdale, NJ: Lawrence Erlbaum Associates, 1977]: 67–82), the term *affordance* became widely used thanks to Donald Norman's *Design of Everyday Things* (New York: Doubleday, 1990).

16   Dante Gabriel Rossetti, *The House of Life* (1881) (Portland, ME: Thomas B. Mosher, 1908), xiii.

17   Catherine D. Clark and Janeen M. Hill, "Reconciling the Tension between the Tenure and Biological Clocks to Increase the Recruitment and Retention of Women in Academia," *Forum on Public Policy* (spring 2010): online at http://www.forumonpublicpolicy.com/spring2010.vol2010/spring2010archive/clark.pdf.

18   Caitlin Rosenthal, "Fundamental Freedom or Fringe Benefit? Rice University and the Administrative History of Tenure, 1935–1963." *Journal of Academic Freedom* 2 (2011): 1–24.

19   As Attorney General, Robert F. Kennedy reduced the sentence of a man who had been sentenced to forty years for robbing a bank. He was moved by the story of the man's poverty and the fact that he had turned himself into the authorities out of remorse. Arthur Schlesinger, Jr., *Robert Kennedy and His Times* (New York: Mariner Books, 2002), 394.

20 Gilles Deleuze and Félix Guattari influentially celebrated constant processes of change over any graspable structured order—shifting "aggregates of intensities," in *A Thousand Plateaux: Capitalism and Schizophrenia*, trans. Brian Massumi (Minneapolis: University of Minnesota Press, 1987), 15. Literary and cultural studies scholars have continued to stress plasticity, multiplicity, heterogeneity, instability, elusiveness, slippages, and contradictions—all ways of refusing and unsettling the binary forms of an essentialized contemporary heteronormativity. See, for example, Carolyn Dinshaw, *Getting Medieval: Sexualities and Communities, Pre- and Post-Modern* (Durham, NC and London: Duke University Press, 1999), and Carla Freccero, *Queer/Early/Modern* (Durham, NC and London: Duke University Press, 2006).

21 Henry S. Turner, "Lessons from Literature for the Historian of Science (and Vice Versa): Reflections on 'Form,'" *Isis* 101 (2010): 582. Turner argues that form "is an attribute of being, of ontology."

22 Bruno Latour too argues that form is best defined as the material medium that connects things, people, and ideas to each other. One example he offers is voting. Nothing if not material, the pieces of paper, reports, check marks, accounts, and maps that connect things, people, and ideas at work in an election are what Latour calls "forms." Latour, *Reassembling the Social* (Oxford: Oxford University Press, 2005), 223.

23 Stefanie Markovits, "Form Things: Looking at Genre through Victorian Diamonds," *Victorian Studies* 52, no. 4 (summer 2010): 598.

24 Herbert F. Tucker, "Of Moments and Monuments: Spacetime in Nineteenth-Century Poetry," *Modern Language Quarterly* 58 (1997): 289.

25 Wolfson is responding to Jerome McGann's now-classic reading of Romantic writers in *The Romantic Ideology* (Chicago: University of Chicago Press, 1985). Susan Wolfson, *Formal Charges*, 19, 14, 231.

26 These alternative economic forms did not survive without a struggle: private utilities did everything they could, including launching advertising campaigns filled with outright lies, to drive the cooperative and state-owned enterprises from the market. Marc Schneiberg looks at the sites where they endured nonetheless and notes that they flourished most often in places where there were "legacy effects"—holdovers from previous times that managed to last effectively into the present. "What's on the Path? Path Dependence, Organizational Diversity and the Problem of Institutional Change in the US Economy, 1900–1950," *Socio-Economic Review* (2007): 66, 72.

27 For an example of the fusing of genre and form, see Jason Mittell, "All in the Game: The Wire, Serial Storytelling, and Procedural Logic": electronic book review (March 18, 2011): http://www.electronicbookreview.com/thread/firstperson/serial. See also my response to Mittell: "From Genre to Form" (electronic book review, May 1, 2011): http://www.electronicbookreview.com/thread/firstperson/serialrip.

28 For a brilliant account of the plasticity and historical situatedness of a genre and its effects, see Carolyn Williams, *Gilbert and Sullivan: Gender, Genre, Parody* (New York: Columbia University Press, 2011). Dimock also argues against the stability and simple endurance of genre: "bending and pulling and stretching are unavoidable, for what genre is dealing with is a volatile body of material, still developing, and still in transit, in some unknown and unpredictable direction." *Through Other Continents*, 73–74.

29 Ferguson, "*Emma* and the Impact of Form," 160.

30 Hayden V. White, *The Content of the Form* (Baltimore and London: Johns Hopkins University Press, 1990), x.

31 By 1896, fifty editions of the novel had been published in England alone. Beverly Lyon Clark, *Regendering the School Story: Sassy Sissies and Tattling Tomboys* (New York and London: Garland, 1996), 11.

32 Thomas Hughes, *Tom Brown's Schooldays* (1857) (Oxford: World's Classics, 1989), 57.

33 Moretti, *Distant Reading*, 59.
34 "The collection of such past and future orders is not a closed list or a predetermined sequence, governed by law-like constraints or tendencies. To understand the internal constitution and the occasional remaking of these orders requires a style of social analysis that breaks with the assumptions of deep-structure social theory and positivist social science." Roberto Mangabeira Unger, *False Necessity* (1987) (London and New York: Verso, 2001), 54. See also *Democracy Realized* (London and New York: Verso, 1998), 20.
35 See Rancière's account of Rosa Parks in *Hatred of Democracy*, trans. Steve Corcoran (London and New York: Verso, 2006), 61.
36 Carolyn Lesjak, "Reading Dialectically," *Criticism* 55 (spring 2013): 233–77.
37 Fredric Jameson, *Valences of the Dialectic* (London: Verso, 2009), 18.
38 David Hume, *An Enquiry Concerning Human Understanding* (1748) (Chicago: Open Court, 1907), 198, 210. It is possible to capture cause-and-effect relations in statistical charts and mathematical equations, but typically these modes of representation are accompanied by narratives. See, for example, Oxfam's 2009 report on the impact of the economic crisis on global poverty rates: http://www.oxfamblogs.org/fp2p/?p=282.
39 "Because they deal with fiction, literary theorists have been much freer in their enquiries about figuration than any social scientist." Latour, *Reassembling the Social*, 54–55.
40 Cleanth Brooks, "The Heresy of Paraphrase," in *The Well Wrought Urn* (New York: Reynal and Hitchcock, 1947), 176–96.
41 Gayatri Chakravorty Spivak, "Three Women's Texts and a Critique of Imperialism," *Critical Inquiry* 12, no. 1 (autumn 1985): 243–61.
42 Heather Love, "Close but Not Deep: Literary Ethics and the Descriptive Turn," *New Literary History* 41 (2010): 375, 378; see also Sharon Marcus and Stephen Best, "Surface Reading: An Introduction," *Representations* 108 (fall 2009): 11–12. I build here on the work of Marcus and Best, who confess to a "skepticism about the very project of freedom" and suggest that we focus our attention instead on "the ways that constraints structure existence" (18).

II Whole

1 Aristotle, *Poetics*, trans. S. H. Butcher and ed. Francis Fergusson (New York: Hill and Wang, 1961), 105. Samuel Taylor Coleridge, "On Poesy or Art," in J. Shawcross, *Biographia Literaria* 2 (Oxford: Clarendon Press, 1907), 255. Georg Lukács, "Form in a work is that which organizes into a closed whole the life given to it as subject matter." "Observations on the Theory of Literary History," quoted in Franco Moretti, *Signs Taken for Wonders: On the Sociology of Literary Forms* (London and New York: Verso, 1983), 10. William Wimsatt embraces "the priority of the whole to the parts, the congruence and interdependence of parts with parts and of parts with the whole, the uniqueness and irreplaceability of parts and their nonexistence prior to the aesthetic whole or outside of it": "Organic Form: Some Questions about a Metaphor," in *Romanticism: Vistas, Instances, Continuities*, eds. David Thorburn and Geoffrey Hartman (Ithaca, NY: Cornell University Press, 1973), 26. Peter Brooks writes that in narrative "the ultimate determinants of meaning lie *at the end*," in *Reading for the Plot: Design and Intention in Narrative* (Cambridge: Harvard University Press, 1984), 52; Fredric Jameson, *The Political Unconscious* (Ithaca, NY: Cornell University Press, 1981), 141; Alex Woloch, *The One v. the Many* (Princeton: Princeton University Press, 2003), 14; Eric Hayot, *On Literary Worlds* (Oxford: Oxford University Press, 2012), 45.
2 Kate Millett's famous feminist work, *Sexual Politics*, was one of the first really influential scholarly arguments to insist on political contexts over self-contained aesthetics (New York: Doubleday, 1969). A Marxist critique of formal unity that became a popular textbook was Terry Eagleton's *Literary Theory* (Oxford: Blackwell, 1983). Jacques Derrida

called into radical question the relationship between the inside of the work and the outside in *Dissemination*, trans. Barbara Johnson (Chicago: University of Chicago Press, 1981) and *The Truth in Painting*, trans. Geoff Bennington and Ian McLeod (Chicago: University of Chicago Press, 1987). For an elegant close reading that deliberately reveals the limits of self-enclosed formal unity, see Frank Lentricchia, "How to Do Things with Wallace Stevens," in *Close Reading: The Reader*, eds. Andrew DuBois and Frank Lentricchia (Durham, NC: Duke University Press, 2003): 136–55.

3   Luce Irigaray, *This Sex Which Is Not One*, trans. Catherine Porter (Ithaca, NY and London: Cornell University Press, 1985), 26.

4   Judith Butler, similarly, argues against the resurgence of what she calls a "Lacanian formalism," which posits the law of the Father and of heterosexual kinship relations as necessary to psychic survival. So fixed and powerfully constraining is this regulation of kinship that Butler casts formalism itself as the problem, capable of foreclosing "a highly constructivist and malleable account of social law": *Antigone's Claim* (New York: Columbia University Press, 2002), 75. Gilles Deleuze also makes a powerful case for the importance of difference over form in *Repetition and Difference*, trans. Paul Patton (London: The Athlone Press, 1994).

5   Marc Redfield, *Phantom Formations* (Ithaca, NY: Cornell University Press, 1996), 10.

6   Derrida, *Dissemination*, 133.

7   This is a recurring term in Butler's work. For one example, see *Bodies That Matter: On the Discursive Limits of "Sex"* (New York: Routledge, 1993), 194.

8   Paula P. Chu, to give just one example among many, argues that Asian American texts are valuable for "contesting, subverting, and complicating the predominant models for assimilation." *Assimilating Asians* (Durham, NC and London: Duke University Press, 2000), 4.

9   Arjun Appadurai points to media and migration as two contemporary social facts that rupture nation-states in *Modernity at Large* (Minneapolis: University of Minnesota Press, 1996), 2–3, and Dominic Richard David Thomas writes: "In the case of the Congo, the nation has been engineered top-down by ideologues and state-sponsored official literature, which has in turn been challenged by orality and non-official and diasporic literature," in *Nation-building, Propaganda, and Literature in Francophone Africa* (Bloomington: University of Indiana Press, 2002), 2.

10 Joanna Brooks, for example, argues for the value of "a narrative formula that summons meaning from randomness and disaster and uses this meaning as the basis for new, if temporary, forms of intimacy and relationship." "From Edwards to Baldwin: Heterodoxy, Discontinuity, and New Narratives of American Religious-Literary History," *American Literary History* 22 (summer 2010): 443.

11 Susan Wolfson, *Formal Charges* (Stanford: Stanford University Press, 1997), 10.

12 See Cary Wolfe's response to Judith Butler in *Before the Law: Humans and Other Animals in a Biopolitical Frame* (Chicago and London: University of Chicago Press, 2013), 16–21.

13 William Kurtz Wimsatt, *The Verbal Icon: Studies in the Meaning of Poetry* (Lexington: University of Kentucky Press, 1954), 202; William Empson, *Seven Types of Ambiguity* (New York: New Directions, 1947), xi; Ronald S. Crane, *The Languages of Criticism and Structure of Poetry* (Toronto: University of Toronto Press, 1957).

14 René Wellek and Austin Warren, *A Theory of Literature*, 3rd edition (New York: Harcourt Brace, 1970), 24.

15 Stephen Greenblatt, *Renaissance Self-Fashioning: From More to Shakespeare* (Chicago and London: University of Chicago Press, 1981).

16 Cleanth Brooks, *The Well Wrought Urn* (New York: Reynal and Hitchcock, 1947), 9, 10.

17 There are four urns in *The Well Wrought Urn*: the urn that contains the ashes of the phoenix in Shakespeare's poem, "The Phoenix and the Turtle"; Donne's "well-wrought urn" from

"The Canonization"; the "storied urn" from Gray's "Elegy Written in a Country Church-yard"; and Keats's Grecian Urn.

18 He says of Donne's "Canonization," "The poet has actually before our eyes built within the song the 'prettie room' with which he says the lovers can be content. *The poem itself is the well-wrought urn* which can hold the lovers' ashes" (16, my emphasis). Then, in the Gray chapter, "it is the whole Elegy that *is* his storied urn—it is the poem itself . . . all the lines of the poem, the whole poem, taken as a poetic structure" (112). As for Keats, "the urn itself as a formed thing, as an autonomous world" provides the model for reading the poem "*as a whole*" (149, 152).

19 See, for example, Eagleton, *Literary Theory*, 50; Thomas H. Schaub, *American Fiction in the Cold War* (Madison: University of Wisconsin Press, 1991), 36; and Tobin Siebers, *Cold War Criticism and the Politics of Skepticism* (Oxford: Oxford University Press, 1993), 30.

20 On Yeats, see Michael North, *The Political Aesthetic of Yeats, Eliot, and Pound* (Cambridge: Cambridge University Press, 1991), 21–72; on Daudet, see David Carroll, *French Literary Fascism* (Princeton: Princeton University Press, 1995), 103–104; on Lukács, see Timothy Bewes and Timothy Hall, *Georg Lukács: The Fundamental Dissonance of Existence* (London and New York: Continuum), 2011.

21 Mary Poovey, *Uneven Developments* (Chicago and London: University of Chicago Press, 1988), 15, 17.

22 "[A]lmost all of the literary criticism published in the U.S. since the 1940s is organized, either explicitly or implicitly, by the trope of the organic whole," including "poststructur-alism, whose practitioners have explicitly repudiated the totalization that the metaphor of the organic whole implies." Mary Poovey, "The Model System of Contemporary Literary Criticism," *Critical Inquiry* 27 (spring 2001): 435.

23 Mary Poovey, *Genres of the Credit Economy* (Chicago and London: University of Chicago Press, 2008), 340–43.

24 Mary Poovey, *Making a Social Body: British Cultural Formation, 1830–64* (Chicago and London: University of Chicago Press, 1995), 7–8.

25 Sven-Erik Liedman, "Is Content Embodied Form?" in *Embodiment in Cognition and Culture*, ed. John Michael Krois (Amsterdam and Philadelphia: John Benjamins, 2007), 128.

26 Meredith L. McGill, *American Literature and the Culture of Reprinting, 1834–1853* (Philadelphia: University of Pennsylvania Press, 2003).

27 Donald E. Pease, *The New American Exceptionalism* (Minneapolis: University of Minnesota Press, 2009).

28 Jorge Luis Borges, "Funes the Memorious," in *Labyrinths*, eds. Donald A. Yates and James E. Irby (New York: Modern Library, 1983), 63, 66, 65.

29 Elizabeth Makowski, *Canon Law and Cloistered Women: Periculoso and Its Commentators, 1298–1545* (Washington: Catholic University Press, 1997).

30 June L. Mecham, "A Northern Jerusalem," in *Defining the Holy: Sacred Space in Medieval and Early Modern Europe*, eds. Andrew Spicer and Sarah Hamilton (Aldershot: Ashgate, 2005), 141.

31 A hymn by John Oxenham, quoted in Peter C. Murray, *Methodists and the Crucible of Race, 1930–1975* (Columbia: University of Missouri Press, 2004), 8.

32 Terry Eagleton, *Myths of Power* (London: Macmillan, 1975), 32.

33 My thanks to Virginia Piper, who has been working this question out in her own inventive ways, for helping me to think through this question.

34 W. A. Craik, *Elizabeth Gaskell and the English Provincial Novel* (London: Methuen, 1975), 112. Susan Johnston, *Women and Domestic Experience in Victorian Political Fiction* (Westport, CT and London: Greenwood Press, 2001), 129. Catherine Gallagher, *The Industrial Reformation of English Fiction: Social Discourse and Narrative Form, 1832–1867* (Chicago and London: University of Chicago Press, 1985), 168. Barbara Leah Harman, *The Feminine*

Political Novel in Victorian England (Charlottesville and London: University of Virginia Press, 1998), 53.

35 Julia Sun-Joo Lee, *The American Slave Narrative and the Victorian Novel* (Oxford: Oxford University Press, 2010), 111.

36 Many writers in the eighteenth and nineteenth centuries brought the nation together with the idea of the family. To give just two examples: Edmund Burke (*Reflections on the Revolution in France* [London: J. Dodsley, 1790], 49) writes that the English, unlike the French, have wisely understood their nation as a family: "We have given to our frame of polity the image of a relation in blood, binding up the constitution of our country with our dearest domestic ties, adopting our fundamental laws into the bosom of our family affections, keeping inseparable and cherishing with the warmth of all their combined and mutually reflected charities our state, our hearths, our sepulchres, and our altars." Charles Dickens's *Bleak House* (1854) figures all of England as a series of interconnected familial links.

37 Anne McClintock, *Imperial Leather: Race, Gender, and Sexuality in the Colonial Context* (New York: Routledge, 1995), 45.

38 John Ruskin, *Sesame and Lilies: Two Lectures Delivered at Manchester in 1864* (New York: John Wiley, 1865), 90–91.

39 Amy Kaplan, "Manifest Domesticity," in *No More Separate Spheres!* Special issue of *American Literature* 70, no. 3 (1998): 582.

40 See "Bibliographical Note" to *The Complete Works of John Ruskin*, 39 vols., eds. E. T. Cook and Alexander Wedderburn (London: George Allen, 1905), vol. 18, 193–96.

41 George Gissing, *The Odd Women*, 3 vols. (London: Lawrence and Bullen, 1893), vo1. 2, 134.

42 Seth Koven, "How the Victorians Read *Sesame and Lilies*," in John Ruskin, *Sesame and Lilies*, ed., Deborah Nord (New Haven, CT and London: Yale University Press, 2002), 184–84.

43 Fred M. Fling described his first experience of a seminar in Leipzig, mentioning the members' need for a key to enter the rooms. "The German Historical Seminar," *The Academy: A Journal of Secondary Education* 4 (1889–1890): 132.

44 William Clark, *Academic Charisma and the Origins of the Research University* (Chicago and London: University of Chicago Press, 2006), 175–76.

45 Eckhardt Fuchs and Benedikt Stuchtey, *Across Cultural Borders: Historiography in Global Perspective* (Boston: Rowman and Littlefield, 2002), 190, 196.

46 The professor "puts himself down to the plane of his students. He criticises them, but must in turn be expected to be criticised by them; and the more open and fearless the criticism the better for both. The professor is here the friend, the equal. He leads the discussion, to be sure; but if there are keen, able, bright students present, he may often learn instead of teach." E.R.A. Seligman, "The Seminarium: Its Advantages and Limitations," *Annual Report of the Regents, University of the State of New York*, vol. 106 (Albany: James B. Lyon, 1893), 67.

47 James H. Canfield, "Seminar Method in Undergraduate Work," *Annual Report of the Regents, University of the State of New York*, vol. 106 (Albany: James B. Lyon, 1893), 78.

48 See, for example, Derek Bok, *Our Underachieving Colleges* (Princeton: Princeton University Press, 2006), 118.

49 Seligman, "The Seminarium," 63.

50 Ian Forman, "Lowly Freshmen Achieve Scholarly Recognition," *Boston Daily Globe* (November 18, 1959): 14–15.

51 http://www.stjohnscollege.edu/academic/seminar.shtml; http://college.georgetown.edu /persona/prospective/44356.html; http://wheatoncollege.edu/first-year-seminar/

52 http://www.bsos.umd.edu/socy/syllabi/socy729C_pcollins.pdf.

53 To give just a handful of examples, I. C. Fletcher's "The Social in the Long Nineteenth Century," History 8230, Georgia State University (autumn 2006); Edward Beasley's

"Seminar in Historical Methodology," History 601, San Diego State University (autumn 2008); and Claudia Klaver, "Nineteenth-Century Capitalism and the Victorian Novel," English 747, Syracuse University (http://english.syr.edu/faculty/syllabi/klaversyllabi/ENG747 .htm; no semester date given).

III Rhythm

1   Quoted in Michael Golston, *Rhythm and Race in Modernist Poetry and Science* (New York: Columbia University Press, 2008), 48.

2   Clarence Major, "Rhythm: A Hundred Years of African American Poetry," in *Necessary Distance: Essays and Criticism* (Minneapolis: Coffee House Press, 2001), 71.

3   Robert Fink, criticizing this tradition, in "Goal Directed Soul? Analyzing Rhythmic Teleology in African American Popular Music," *Journal of the American Musicological Society* 64 (spring 2011): 185. Anne Danielson, *Presence and Pleasure: The Funk Grooves of James Brown and Parliament* (Middletown, CT: Wesleyan University Press, 2006).

4   Martin Munro, *Different Drummers: Race and Rhythm in the Americas* (Berkeley and Los Angeles: University of California Press, 2010), 8–10.

5   Pierre Bourdieu, *The Logic of Practice*, trans. Richard Nice (Stanford: Stanford University Press, 1990), 75.

6   Karlheinz A. Geissler, "A Culture of Temporal Diversity," *Time and Society* 11, no. 1 (2002): 4, 3.

7   Evitar Zerubavel, *Hidden Rhythms: Schedules and Calendars in Social Life* (Berkeley and Los Angeles: University of California Press, 1985), 20.

8   Eviatar Zerubavel, "Easter and Passover: On Calendars and Group Identity," *American Sociological Review* 47 (April 1982): 288.

9   Johannes Fabian, *Time and the Other* (New York: Columbia University Press, 1983), 2.

10 I draw a great deal here from social scientists, who argue that "All rhythms are *multiple*, showing up in messy and heterogeneous form and rarely if ever alone. Any given site or activity, or any isolated moment in time, may be best thought of as a gateway or constriction through which multiple rhythms are flowing at once, some of which will be contradictory or dissonant in nature." Steven J. Jackson, David Ribes, and Ayse Bukyutur, "Exploring Collaborative Rhythm: Temporal Flow and Alignment in Collaborative Scientific Work" *Ideals@Illinois* (2010): https://www.ideals.illinois.edu/bitstream /handle/2142/14955/JacksonRibesBuyuktur_ExploringCollaborativeRhythm.pdf? sequence=2. Wanda J. Orlikowski and JoAnne Yates call this experience *pluritemporal.* "People enact a multiplicity and plurality of temporal structures, not all of which can be characterized in terms of the clock or deadlines." "It's about Time: Temporal Structuring in Organizations," *Organization Science* 13 (November–December 2002): 698.

11 Jackson, Ribes, and Bukyutur, "Exploring Collaborative Rhythm."

12 "The job of the critic," Dames explains, became "to avoid everywhere the temporal flow and affective identifications that make up novel reading." Nicholas Dames, *The Physiology of the Novel: Reading, Neural Science, and the Form of Victorian Fiction* (Oxford: Oxford University Press, 2007), 34, 48.

13 Influential works on the unfolding of narrative include Gotthold Ephraim Lessing, *Laocoön* (1766), trans. Edward Allen McCormick (Baltimore and London: Johns Hopkins University Press, 1984); Roland Barthes's *S/Z*, trans. Richard Miller (New York: Hill and Wang, 1974); D. A. Miller, *Narrative and Its Discontents* (Princeton: Princeton University Press, 1981); Peter Brooks, *Reading for the Plot* (New York: Knopf, 1984); Wendy Steiner, *Pictures of Romance* (Chicago and London: University of Chicago Press, 1988); and Brian Richardson's *Narrative Dynamics* (Columbus: Ohio State University Press, 2002). I will return to

poetic meter at the end of the chapter, but for a clear account of the temporal patterns of metrical form in general, see Derek Attridge, *Poetic Rhythm: An Introduction* (Cambridge: Cambridge University Press, 1995).

14 Like Dames, Catherine Gallagher ("Formalism and Time," *Modern Language Quarterly* 61 [March 2000]: 230–31) laments the fact that even narratologists and Russian formalists have favored stillness by drawing up graphs or charts that display the morphology or "overall shape" of a text, or by focusing on specific stylistic features, such as syntax or verb tenses. "They both give the impression of overcoming time, rising above or congealing it, and hence, whatever their virtues, they appear strangely at odds with the temporal nature of the analyzed work." Hilary Schor argues that even Peter Brooks, who attends to the dynamics of the middle, implicitly privileges the position of distanced retrospect: "The middle is something we find at the end, when we have rearranged the plot into story, when we know what the characters desired and how they achieved, or did not, fulfill-ment." "The Make-Believe of a Beginning," in *Narrative Middles*, eds. Caroline Levine and Mario Ortiz-Robles (Columbus: Ohio State University Press, 2011), 48.

15 As Munro writes, "If rhythm is considered to be primarily an element of sound—in speech, music, and poetry—it is a malleable concept that may be applied to other patterns of repetition and regularity, be they natural (the rhythms of the body, time, and the seasons) or manufactured (rhythms of work, machinery, industrial time, everyday life)." *Different Drummers*, 5–6.

16 It is urgent to think not only about increasingly significant global flows of capital, popula-tions, and power, but about the formal conflicts between tempos that these flows produce as the temporalities of supranational enterprises encounter and redirect the national and local rhythms of labor and leisure, electoral cycles, and democratic deliberation. Political economist Bob Jessop argues that "the fast, technocratic decision making of supranational institutions and nation state elites [has the] capacity to impose laws and regulations upon national communities [that] undermines the temporal rhythms of democratic delibera-tion whereby citizens decide for themselves the content of laws that regulate their polit-ical association." "Time and Space in the Globalization of Capital and their Implications for State Power," *Rethinking Marxism* (December 2010), 82. Communications scholar Wayne Hope also argues that the rhythms of social life across scales are colliding now to produce an extremely complex and unpredictable set of power formations. Global flows of information, which stress "acceleration, instantaneity, short-termism and transience" as well as "night time economies, flexible work practices and the diversification of work and leisure schedules," are coming into conflict with more familiar national tempos, at the same time that "state formations themselves may be riven by temporal conflict as fast, executive decisions overrule electoral cycles, legislative deliberation and judicial process." "Conflicting Temporalities: State, Nation, Economy and Democracy under Global Capi-talism," *Time and Society* 18 (2009): 78, 64.

17 This phrase comes from Eric Hayot, who launches a strong critique of periodization in *On Literary Worlds* (Oxford: Oxford University Press, 2012), 151.

18 Catherine Gallagher and Stephen Greenblatt, *Practicing New Historicism* (Chicago and London: University of Chicago Press, 2000), 13.

19 "One year, five years, ten years: these are the standard durations we use to 'contextualize' a text, on the assumption that these slices of time are integral, unified." Wai-Chee Dimock, "Nonbiological Clock: Literary History against Newtonian Mechanics," *South Atlantic Quarterly* 102 (winter 2003): 154–55.

20 Sharon Marcus, *Between Women; Friendship, Desire, and Marriage in Victorian England* (Princeton and Oxford: Princeton University Press, 2007).

21 Denise Gigante, *Life: Organic Form and Romanticism* (New Haven, CT and London: Yale University Press, 2009).

22 As Marcus puts it, "I have chosen 1830 and 1880 as my temporal borders because they constitute a distinct period in the history of marriage and sexuality" (6). And Gigante affirms: "Despite decades of historical challenge to the rubric of Romanticism as a shared intellectual project, the writers discussed here were all committed to defining and representing the incalculable, uncontrollable—often capricious, always ebullient—power of vitality" (3).

23 David Perkins, *Is Literary History Possible?* (Baltimore: The Johns Hopkins University Press, 1992), 64.

24 Decades ago, Alan Liu was already exposing the work of New Historicism as a continuation of New Critical formalism; despite their claims to historical specificity, the New Historicists kept returning to the same formal tension between unity and plurality across contexts. "The Power of Formalism: The New Historicism," *ELH* 56 (winter 1989): 721–71.

25 In telling his fascinating story about the institution of literary studies, Gerald Graff does not define or expand on the term, using it as if its meaning were self-evident. *Professing Literature: An Institutional History* (Chicago and London: University of Chicago Press, 1987).

26 Homer Brown, "Prologue," in *Cultural Institutions of the Novel*, eds. Deidre Shauna Lynch and William B. Warner (Durham, NC: Duke University Press, 1996): 19.

27 Allen Grossman makes a similar point in "Wordsworth's 'The Solitary Reaper': Notes on Poiesis, Pastoral, and Institution," *TriQuarterly* 116 (summer 2003): 277–99.

28 The classic text of the new institutionalism is Paul J. DiMaggio and Walter W. Powell, eds., *The New Institutionalism in Organizational Analysis* (Chicago and London: University of Chicago Press, 1991). For a sense of the heterogeneity of this scholarship, see Vivien Lowndes, "Varieties of New Institutionalism: A Critical Appraisal," *Public Administration* 74 (summer 1996): 181–97.

29 "When we think of institutions, we almost always think of buildings—church, school, bank are all names of common institutions but also of the material buildings in which they are housed and with which they are often confused.... An 'edifice' gives it not only an imposing presence but also a past and future, an appearance of duration and continuity." (Brown, "Prologue," 19–20.)

30 As Lowndes puts it, "All 'new institutionalist' perspectives highlight that institutions are not *things* but *processes*. Institutional rules have to be sustained over time. An ongoing process of institutionalization creates stability" ("Varieties of New Institutionalism," 193).

31 James G. March and Johan P. Olsen, "Elaborating the 'New Institutionalism,'" in *The Oxford Handbook of Political Institutions* (Oxford: Oxford University Press, 2006): 3.

32 Many new institutionalist scholars have argued that human agents play a crucial part in the making and maintenance of institutions, but in many cases we are so profoundly shaped by the institutions themselves that we cannot conceive of alternatives, and we continually reconstitute the institution according to familiar and increasingly entrenched patterns. "Institutions are resistant to redesign ultimately because they structure the very choices about reform that the individual is likely to make." Peter A. Hall and Rosemary C. R. Taylor, "Political Science and the Three New Institutionalisms," paper presented at the Max Planck Institut für Gesellschaftsforschung (May 9, 1996); online at http://www.mpifg.de/pu/mpifg_dp/dp96-6.pdf (8).

33 Political scientist Robert Grafstein argues that institutions thus lead a "double-life" as "both human products and social forces in their own right." "The Problem of Institutional Constraints," *Journal of Politics* 50 (1988): 577–78.

34 Joseph Roach, *Cities of the Dead* (New York: Columbia University Press, 1996), 2.

35 Gauri Viswanathan, *Masks of Conquest: Literary Study and British Rule in India* (New York: Columbia University Press, 1989).

36 Frances Stonor Saunders, *The Cultural Cold War* (New Press, 2001); Joel Whitney, "The *Paris Review*, the Cold War and the CIA," *Salon*, May 27, 2012; Michael Bérubé, *Rhetorical Occasions* (Chapel Hill: University of North Carolina Press, 2006), 130.

37 André Lecours, "New Institutionalism: Issues and Questions," in *New Institutionalism: Theory and Analysis*, ed. André Lecours (Toronto:University of Toronto Press, 2005), 9.

38 Graff, *Professing Literature*, 6–8.

39 Raymond Williams, *Marxism and Literature* (Oxford: Oxford University Press, 1977), 122–23.

40 "Every sign, linguistic or nonlinguistic, spoken or written (in the usual sense of this opposition), as a small or large unity, can be *cited*, put between quotation marks; thereby it can break with every given context, and engender infinitely new contexts in an absolutely nonsaturable fashion. This does not suppose that the mark is valid outside its context, but on the contrary that there are only contexts without any center of absolute anchoring. This citationality, duplication, or duplicity, this iterability of the mark is not an accident or an anomaly, but is that (normal/abnormal) without which a mark could no longer even have a so-called 'normal' functioning. What would a mark be that one could not cite? And whose origin could not be lost on the way?" Jacques Derrida, "Signature, Event, Context," from *Margins of Philosophy*, trans. Alan Bass (Chicago and London: University of Chicago Press, 1982), 320.

41 Marshall Brown, "Periods and Resistances," *Modern Language Quarterly* 62 (2001): 315.

42 Michel Foucault, *Discipline and Punish: The Birth of the Prison*, trans. Alan Sheridan (New York: Vintage, 1979), 183.

43 Joel Weiss and Robert S. Brown, "Telling Tales over Time: Constructing and Deconstructing the School Calendar," *Teachers College Record* 105 (December 2003): 1733.

44 Elena Silva, *On the Clock: Rethinking the Way Schools Use Time* (Washington, DC: Education Sector, 2007), 8.

45 "Editorial: Back to School Rules Don't Serve Students," *Roanoke Times* (August 19, 2008); online at http://ww2.roanoke.com/editorials/wb/173633/.

46 The trial proceedings have been published in Margit Rowell, ed., *Brancusi v. United States: The Historic Trial, 1928* (Paris: Adam Biro, 1999). All subsequent citations from the trial will refer to this edition. I tell a longer version of this story in *Provoking Democracy: Why We Need the Arts* (Oxford: Wiley-Blackwell, 2007), 150–65.

47 Anna Chave, *Constantin Brancusi: Shifting the Bases of Art* (New Haven, CT and London: Yale University Press, 1993), 201.

48 *New York City Sun* (February 24, 1927), quoted in Rowell, *Brancusi v. United States*, 133.

49 *New York American* (October 22, 1927), quoted in Rowell, 136.

50 *Providence Journal* (February 27, 1927), quoted in Rowell, 134.

51 *United States v. Olivotti*, 7 Ct. Cust. Appeals, 46 (1916).

52 H. R. Doc. No. 1505, 60th Cong., 2nd Sess. 7209 (1908).

53 Ronald Dworkin, *Law's Empire* (Cambridge: Harvard University Press, 1986), 225.

54 Roger Traynor writes: "Even if [a judge] confronts a truly unprecedented case, he still arrives at a decision in the context of judicial reasoning with recognizable ties to the past; by its kinship thereto it not only establishes the unprecedented case as a precedent for the future, but integrates it in the often rewoven but always unbroken line with the past." "Reasoning in a Circle of Law," in *Precedents, Statutes and Analysis of Legal Concepts*, ed. Scott Brewer (New York and London: Garland Press, 1998), 344.

55 See Howard Becker's classic argument in *Art Worlds* (Berkeley and Los Angeles: University of California Press, 1984).

56 Ivan Kreilkamp, "Victorian Poetry's Modernity," *Victorian Poetry* 14 (winter 2003): 609.

57 Coventry Patmore, *Essay on English Metrical Law* (1857), ed. Sister Mary Augustine Roth (Washington, DC: Catholic University Press of America, 1961), 8.

58 Alethea Hayter, *Mrs Browning: A Poet's Work and Its Setting* (London: Faber and Faber, 1962), 125. For other brief critical treatments, see Adrienne Munich, *Queen Victoria's Secrets* (New York: Columbia University Press, 1996), 15–22; and Margaret Homans, *Royal Representations: Queen Victoria and British Culture, 1837–1876* (Chicago and

London: University of Chicago Press, 1998), 33–34. Among the only scholars to have taken the poems seriously is Antony Harrison, who urges us to notice the surprisingly radical "irruptions" of dominant ideology that have hitherto gone unnoticed in Barrett Browning's poetry of the late 1830s, in *Victorian Poets and the Politics of Culture* (Charlottesville and London: University of Virginia Press, 1998), 83–85.

59 *The Complete Poetical Works of Elizabeth Barrett Browning* (Boston and New York: Houghton Mifflin, 1900), 54–55.

60 Barrett Browning is in fact casting the event in more idealized terms than the historical record would suggest. Her uncle William IV had been both ill and unpopular, and the young Victoria had been preparing carefully for her reign. Immediately after the news of her uncle's death, Victoria began to rebuff her mother and apparently greatly enjoyed her new position. See Helen Rappaport, *Queen Victoria: A Biographical Companion* (Santa Barbara: ABC-CLIO, 2003), 183, 360.

IV Hierarchy

1 Nicolas Verdier, "Hierarchy: A Short History of a Word in Western Thought," in Denise Pumain, *Hierarchy in Natural and Social Sciences* (Dordrecht: Spring, 2006), 13.

2 See, for example, Claude Lévi-Strauss, *The Raw and the Cooked* (1964), reprinted as *Mythologiques*, vol. 1, trans. John and Doreen Weightman (Chicago and London: University of Chicago Press, 1983).

3 Elizabeth Grosz, *Volatile Bodies* (Bloomington: Indiana University Press, 1994), 3.

4 Grosz writes: "The mind/body opposition has always been correlated with a number of other oppositional pairs" (*Volatile Bodies*, 3). Miguel López-Lozano explores the alignment of European/native with masculine/feminine and culture/nature in *Utopian Dreams, Apocalyptic Nightmares: Globalization in Recent Mexican and Chicano Narrative* (West Lafayette, IN: Purdue University Press, 2008), 12.

5 Judith Butler, *Undoing Gender* (New York and Abington: Routledge, 2004), 42–43.

6 International Astronomical Union, *Binary Stars as Critical Tools and Tests in Contemporary Astrophysics* (Cambridge: Cambridge University Press, 2007), 347.

7 Karl Marx, *Later Political Writings*, Terrell Carver, ed. (Cambridge: Cambridge University Press, 1996), 78.

8 Alexander Cooley, *Logics of Hierarchy: The Organization of Empire, States, and Military Occupations* (Ithaca, NY and London: Cornell University Press, 2005), x–xi, 2, 12.

9 G.W.F. Hegel, *The Phenomenology of Spirit*, trans. A. V. Miller (Oxford: Oxford University Press, 1977), 274–75.

10 Sophocles, *Antigone*, trans. David Franklin and John Harrison (Cambridge: Cambridge University Press, 2003), 7.

11 *Antigone* does not only set vertical hierarchies against one another; it also revolves around containers, such as the boundaries around a people. These shapes are quite literal spatial forms: after all, those who are buried in proper tombs are those marked as belonging within the boundaries of the *polis*. I will take up the relation between wholes and hierarchies again later in this chapter.

12 This recent reading puts its emphasis on relations among siblings as opposed to parents and children. Stefani Engelstein, "Sibling Logic; or, Antigone Again," *PMLA* 126, no. 1 (January 2011): 38–54.

13 Tragedy also, as Bonnie Honig argues, risks allowing "mortality and suffering" to seem like the shared ground of human experience—universal, perhaps even uniform across time and space. "Antigone's Two Laws: Greek Tragedy and the Politics of Humanism," *New Literary History* 41 (winter 2010): 3–4.

14 "To assume that gender always and exclusively means the matrix of 'masculine' and 'feminine' is precisely to miss the critical point that the production of that coherent binary is contingent, that it comes at a cost, and that those permutations of gender which do not fit the binary are as much as part of gender as its most normative instance.... Gender is the apparatus by which the production and normalization of masculine and feminine take place along the interstitial forms of hormonal, chromosomal, psychic, and performative that gender assumes." Butler, *Undoing Gender*, 42.

15 In 1988, Mary Poovey argued influentially that British femininity in the nineteenth century "was both internally contradictory and unevenly deployed [and so] open to a variety of readings that could be mobilized in contradictory practices." *Uneven Developments: The Ideological Work of Gender in Mid-Victorian England* (Chicago and London: University of Chicago Press, 1988), 15.

16 Kimberlé Crenshaw, "Mapping the Margins: Intersectionality, Identity Politics, and Violence against Women of Color," *Stanford Law Review* 43 (July 1991): 1241–99.

17 Cathy N. Davidson, "Preface: No More Separate Spheres!" *American Literature* 70 (1998): 445–46. See also Monika Maria Elbert, *Separate Spheres No More* (Tuscaloosa: University of Alabama Press, 2001).

18 Jane Gallop, *Anecdotal Theory* (Durham, NC: Duke University Press, 2002), 25.

19 Such gendered divisions of space also characterize many non-Western societies, as we can see in Pierre Bourdieu's early, still structuralist ethnographic work on domestic space in Kabylia, Algeria. Bourdieu observes that the house itself is coded as dark and gendered feminine, and women are expected to spend most of their time there, cooking and weaving. It is opposed to the light, masculine outside, where men search for food. But then, inside the house there are masculine, light areas, assigned to human-centered activities such as cooking and weaving, and feminine, dark ones where animals sleep and eat. And famously, Bourdieu argues that the interior reverses the codes of the exterior: the west, for example, coded light on the outside, is coded dark within. *The Logic of Practice*, trans. Richard Nice (Stanford: Stanford University Press, 1990), 271–83.

20 See, for example, Diane Elson, "Labor Markets as Gendered Institutions," *World Development* 27, no. 3 (1999): 611–27.

21 Teresa Mangum, "Growing Old: Age," in *A Companion to Victorian Literature and Culture*, ed. Herbert F. Tucker (Oxford: Blackwell, 1999), 99.

22 See, for example, Jane Waldfogel, "Understanding the 'Family Gap' in Pay for Women with Children," *Journal of Economic Perspectives* 12 (winter 1998): 137–56; and Shelley J. Correll, Stephen Benard, and In Paik, "Getting a Job: Is There a Motherhood Penalty?" *American Journal of Sociology* 112 (March 2007): 1297–1338.

23 Correll, Benard, and Paik, "Getting a Job," 1317.

24 Psychologists have shown that subjects largely prefer working fathers over full-time "house husbands." See Victoria L. Brescoll and Eric Luis Uhlmann, "Attitudes Toward Traditional and Nontraditional Parents," *Psychology of Women Quarterly* 29 (December 2005): 436–45.

25 Max Weber, "Bureaucracy," in *Essays in Sociology*, eds. H. H. Gerth and C. Wright Mills (Abingdon: Routledge, 1991), 197.

26 David Beetham, *Bureaucracy* (Minneapolis: University of Minnesota Press, 1996), 1.

27 Charles Dickens, *Little Dorrit* (1855–57), (New York: Modern Library, 2002), 119.

28 Charles Dickens, *Bleak House* (1854), ed. Sylvère Monod (New York: W. W. Norton, 1977), 759.

29 Robert Jackall, *Moral Mazes: The World of Corporate Managers*, 2nd ed. (Oxford: Oxford University Press, 2010), 37.

30 Weber, "Bureaucracy," 228.

31 Jeffrey Pfeffer and Gerald R. Salancik, *The External Control of Organizations: A Resource Dependence Perspective* (1978) (Stanford: Stanford University Press, 2003), 2.

32 Rosabeth Moss Kanter, "Men and Women of the Corporation," in Michael J. Handel, ed. *The Sociology of Organizations* (Thousand Oaks, CA and London: Sage, 2003), 384.

33 Janice D. Yoder, "Rethinking Tokenism: Looking beyond Numbers," in *Gender and Society* 5 (June 1991): 178–92.

34 Bruce Robbins, *Upward Mobility and the Common Good: Toward a Literary History of the Welfare State* (Princeton: Princeton University Press, 2007), xii.

35 Gayatri Chakravorty Spivak, "Three Women's Texts and a Critique of Imperialism," *Critical Inquiry* 12 (1985): 243–61.

36 See, for example, Deirdre David, *Rule Britannia* (Ithaca, NY and London: Cornell University Press, 1995); and Patricia McKee, "Racial Strategies in *Jane Eyre*," *Victorian Literature and Culture* 37 (2009): 67–83.

37 See, for example, Joyce Carol Oates, "Romance and Anti-Romance," in *Charlotte Brontë's Jane Eyre: A Casebook*, ed. Elsie B. Michie (Oxford: Oxford University Press, 2006), 202–3; and Rachel Blau DuPlessis, *Writing beyond the Ending* (Indianapolis: University of Indiana Press, 1985), 10.

38 Barry Qualls, *The Secular Pilgrims of Victorian Fiction* (Cambridge: Cambridge University Press, 1982); and Susan VanZanten Gallagher, "Jane Eyre and Christianity," in *Approaches to Teaching "Jane Eyre,"* eds. Diane Hoeveler and Beth Lau (New York: MLA Press, 1993), 62–68.

V Network

1 Gilles Deleuze and Félix Guattari, *A Thousand Plateaus: Capitalism and Schizophrenia*, trans. Brian Massumi (Minneapolis: University of Minnesota Press, 1987), 15.

2 Ella Shohat, "Columbus, Palestine and Arab-Jews: Toward a Relational Approach to Community Identity," in *Cultural Readings of Imperialism: Edward Said and the Gravity of History*, eds. Keith Ansell-Pearson, Benita Parry and Judith Squires (New York: St. Martin's, 1997), 88.

3 Jonathan H. Grossman, *Charles Dickens's Networks* (Oxford: Oxford University Press, 2012), 7. For other examples of literary scholarship on networks, see Cathy Davidson, *Revolution and the Word: The Rise of the Novel in America* (Oxford: Oxford University Press, 1986), 11, 39; Joseph R. Roach, *Cities of the Dead: Circum-Atlantic Performance* (New York and London: Columbia University Press, 1996), 9, 24, 39; and Jules David Law, *The Social Life of Fluids: Blood, Milk, and Water in the Victorian Novel* (Ithaca, NY and London: Cornell University Press, 2010), 28, 31, 152.

4 Patrick Jagoda notes that "networks, which are inherently transformable and extensible cannot be reproduced in their totalities." "Terror Networks and the Aesthetics of Interconnection," *Social Text* 105 (winter 2010): 66.

5 Franco Moretti, "Network Theory, Plot Analysis," *New Left Review* 68 (March–April 2011): 80; Jagoda, "Terror Networks," 65–89; and Patrick Joyce, *The State of Freedom: A Social History of the British State since 1800* (Cambridge: Cambridge University Press, 2013).

6 Mark S. Granovetter, "The Strength of Weak Ties," *Sociological Theory* 1 (1983): 201–33.

7 For example, see Graham Alexander Sack, "*Bleak House* and Weak Social Networks," online at http://www.columbia.edu/~gas2117/Bleak_House_Networks.pdf.

8 I borrow the term *assemblage* from Bruno Latour. *Reassembling the Social: An Introduction to Actor-Network Theory* (Oxford: Oxford University Press, 2005), 8.

9 Jacques Derrida in fact uses the image of the network to describe the act of reading. "The First Session," in *Acts of Literature*, trans. Derek Attridge (Routledge, 1992), 144.

10 See, for example, Hermione Lee, "Network of Allusion," *Essays in Criticism* 26 (October 1976): 355–63.

11 Mark Newman, Albert Lazlo Barabasi, and Duncan J. Watts, *The Structure and Dynamics of Networks* (Princeton: Princeton University Press, 2006), 2.

12 Jonathan Grossman, *Charles Dickens' Networks*, 8.

13 Manuel Castells, *The Rise of the Network Society*, 2 vols. (Oxford: Blackwell, 1996), vol. 1, 6.

14 Michael Mann, *The Sources of Social Power*, 2 vols. (Cambridge: Cambridge University Press, 1986), vol. 1, 16–17, 4.

15 Leela Gandhi, *Affective Communities: Anticolonial Thought, Fin-de-Siècle Radicalism, and the Politics of Friendship* (Durham, NC: Duke University Press, 2006).

16 James Buzard, *Disorienting Fiction: The Autoethnographic Work of Nineteenth-Century British Novels* (Princeton: Princeton University Press, 2005), 31, 30.

17 Buzard, *Disorienting Fiction*, 5, 31.

18 Catherine Gallagher and Stephen Greenblatt, *Practicing New Historicism* (Chicago and London: University of Chicago Press, 2001), 7.

19 James Clifford, "Traveling Cultures," in *Cultural Studies*, eds. Lawrence Grossberg, Cary Nelson, and Paula Treichler (New York and London: Routledge, 1992), 99–100.

20 Kamari Maxine Clarke's subtle study of transnational Yoruba networks, for example, points to conflicting and layered models of belonging, some having to do with place and others with displacement, unsettling any single ideal of an original West African "homeland" as a site of authenticity and rootedness. *Mapping Yoruba Networks: Power and Agency in the Making of Transnational Communities* (Durham, NC: Duke University Press, 2004).

21 For examples of these positions, see Roland Greene, "Not Works but Networks: Colonial Worlds in Comparative Literature," in *Comparative Literature in an Age of Globalization*, ed. Haun Saussy (Baltimore and London: Johns Hopkins University Press, 2006), 212–23; Jahan Ramazani, *A Transnational Poetics* (Chicago and London: University of Chicago Press, 2009); and Stephen Owen, "Stepping Forward and Back: Issues and Possibilities for 'World' Poetry," *Modern Philology* 100 (2003): 532–48.

22 See Ellen Meiksins Wood, *Empire of Capital* (London and New York: Verso, 2003).

23 Wendy Brown, *Walled States, Waning Sovereignty* (New York: Zone, 2010). Historian Rhys Jones suggests that the containment of networks in medieval Europe might actually have been a necessary precondition for stable state power to take hold: "we can use the boundedness of networks . . . as a measure of the maturity of state institutions within medieval societies." "Mann and Men in a Medieval State: The Geographies of Power in the Middle Ages," *Transactions of the Institute of British Geographers* 24, no. 1 (1999): 75.

24 Mabel Loomis Todd, quoted in Jay Leda, *The Years and Hours of Emily Dickinson*, 2 vols. (New Haven, CT and London: Yale University Press, 1960), 2: 357.

25 Diana Fuss, *The Sense of an Interior: Four Writers and the Rooms that Shaped Them* (New York and London: Routledge, 2004), 58–59.

26 Quoted in Fuss, *The Sense of an Interior*, 53.

27 Trish Loughran, *The Republic in Print: Print Culture in the Age of Nation-Building* (New York: Columbia University Press, 2007).

28 Loughran, *The Republic in Print*, 14. We might add to Loughran's account those networks, shapes, and tempos that did not even figure in the official world of the republic of Anglo-American print: the network of Iroquois nations, for example, or slave communities that continued to circulate African words, oral narratives, and songs among themselves.

29 Moretti, in his network analysis of the plot of *Hamlet*, describes the graphs of his results as "time turned into space" ("Network Theory," 82). Jagoda writes: "a great deal of post-structuralist theory that grapples with the network form operates in primarily spatial terms." "Terror Networks," 87n34. Even scientists have come to the problem of time in networks relatively recently. Newman, Barabasi, and Watts see the emphasis on temporal unfolding as the newest work in network theory, differing from conventional accounts in

that it "takes the view that networks are not static, but evolve in time according to various dynamical rules" (*The Structure and Dynamics of Networks*, 4).

30 David Bordwell, *The Way Hollywood Tells It: Story and Style in Modern Movies* (Berkeley and Los Angeles: University of California Press, 2006), 72–114.

31 Charles Dickens, *Bleak House* (1854), George Ford and Sylvère Monod, eds. (New York: W. W. Norton, 1977), 532.

32 Moretti, "Network Theory," 81–82; Jean-Baptiste Michel et al., "Quantitative Analysis of Culture Using Millions of Digitized Books," *Science* 331 (December 2010), 176–82.

33 Catherine Gallagher is a notable exception. See her "Formalism and Time," *Modern Language Quarterly* 61 (2000) 229–51.

34 Mario Ortiz-Robles and I have brought together a number of articles to make the argument for more attention to the middle of fictions in *Narrative Middles: Navigating the Nineteenth-Century Novel* (Columbus: Ohio State University Press, 2011).

35 Henry James, *Roderick Hudson* (1875), (Boston and New York: Houghton Mifflin, 1917, vii.

VI *The Wire*

1 Anmol Chaddha and and William Julius Wilson, "Way Down in the Hole": Systemic Urban Inequality and *The Wire*," *Critical Inquiry* 38 (fall 2011): 166.

2 Fredric Jameson, "Realism and Utopia in *The Wire*," *Criticism* 52 (fall 2010): 365.

3 Drake Bennett, "This Will Be on the Midterm. You Feel Me? Why So Many Colleges are Teaching *The Wire*," *Slate Magazine* (March 24, 2010); online at: http://www.slate.com/id/2245788s.

4 Slavoj Žižek, "*The Wire*, or the Clash of Civilisations in One Country," lecture at the Birkbeck Institute for the Humanities (February 24, 2012), online at: http://backdoorbroadcasting.net/2012/02/slavoj-zizek-the-wire-or-the-clash-of-civilisations-in-one-country/

5 Season 4, episode 1, "Boys of Summer," directed by Joe Chappell, written by David Simon and Ed Burns.

6 Season 4, episode 5, "Alliances," directed by David Platt, written by Ed Burns.

7 Season 5, episode 4, "React Quotes," directed by Agnieszka Holland, written by David Simon and David Mills.

8 Season 4, episode 5, "Alliances," directed by David Platt, written by Ed Burns.

9 As Mark Bowden puts it, "The heads of both organizations, official and criminal, wrestle with similar management and personnel issues, and resolve them with similarly cold self-interest. "The Angriest Man on Television," *Atlantic Monthly* 301 (January/February 2008), online at: http://www.theatlantic.com/magazine/archive/2008/01/the-angriest-man-in-television/306581/.

10 Season 3, episode 1, "Time after Time," directed by Ed Bianchi, written by David Simon.

11 Season 4, episode 8, "Corner Boys," directed by Agnieszka Holland, written by Ed Burns and Richard Price.

12 In another example, Norman Wilson, Carcetti's campaign manager, who stands to gain a significant career boost from a Carcetti victory—a top position in the new mayor's cabinet—confesses happily that he is going to vote for one of the two African-American candidates rather than for his own white boss, while acknowledging that many black Baltimoreans will be willing to cast a vote for a white candidate. Clearly, neither race nor the career ladder is absolutely predictive: when hierarchies meet, the results could go either way.

13 Season 4, episode 4, "Refugees," directed by Jim McKay, written by Ed Burns and Dennis Lehane.

14 Season 1, episode 13, "Sentencing," directed by Tim Van Patten, written by David Simon and Ed Burns.

15   Season 4, episode 12, "That's Got His Own," directed by Joe Chappelle, written by Ed Burns and George Pelecanos.

16   In season 4, episode 6, "Margin of Error, Prez says about Randy: "I don't want to see him get chewed up by the system." Alessandra Stanley's review of the last season of *The Wire* concludes that the broken system wins in the end. "So Many Characters, Yet So Little Resolution," *New York Times* (March 10, 2008), E1. Slavoj Žižek invokes "the system" in "The Wire: What To Do in Non-Evental Times," in *The Wire and Philosophy*, eds. David Bzdak, Joanna Crosby, and Seth Vannatta (Chicago: Court Press, 2013): 234. Jason Mittell writes: "Given the show's cynical vision of corrupt institutions, reform typically produces various forms of failure, as the parameters of the system are too locked in to truly produce social change or allow for an imagined solution to systemic problems." In "All in the Game: *The Wire*, Serial Storytelling, and Procedural Logic," electronic book review (March 18, 2011): http://www.electronicbookreview.com/thread/firstperson/serial.

17   Patrick Jagoda, "Wired," *Critical Inquiry* 38 (fall 2011): 198.

INDEX

Adjustment Bureau, The, 99
aesthetics, 2–3, 5–7, 11, 14, 16, 17, 22–25, 27, 28, 30, 53, 80, 93, 98
affordances, 6–11, 22, 97; of drama, 93; of hierarchies, 82, 83, 84; of narratives, 19, 40, 122, 125–27, 130, 134; of networks, 113–14, 117; of rhythms, 49, 58, 60, 64, 66–67, 68, 79; of wholes, 27, 31, 37, 39, 40, 47, 137
aging, 96–97
Aldington, Richard, 4
Amigoni, David, 151n2
Anderson, Benedict, 120, 121
antiformalism, 9, 22, 25, 28, 31, 35–36, 55
Antigone, 85–93, 122
Appadurai, Arjun, 155n9
Aristotle, 2, 24, 32, 152n8
Attridge, Derek, 159n13

Babel, 122, 127–28
Barthes, Roland, 152n8, 158n13
Becker, Howard, 161n55
Beetham, David, 163
Benjamin, Walter, 5
Bérubé, Michael, 161n36
Best, Stephen, 154n42
Bildungsroman, 1, 15–16
binary oppositions, 5, 7, 9, 18, 82–97, 104
biological clock, 8
blank verse, 4
Bleak House, 98–99, 115, 122–31
Boas, Franz, 115–16, 117
Bok, Derek, 157n48
Boniface VIII, 37
book history, 1. *See also* print culture
Bordwell, David, 122
Borges, Jorge Luis, 34–35
Bourdieu, Pierre, 50, 57, 66, 163n19
Bowden, Mark, 166n9
Brancusi, Constantin, 68–73
Brontë, Charlotte. See *Jane Eyre*

Brooks, Cleanth, 20, 27, 29–31, 33, 35, 36, 40, 46, 74
Brooks, Joanna, 155n10
Brooks, Peter, 24, 152n8, 158n13, 159n14
Brown, Homer, 56, 57
Brown, Marshall, 161n41
Brown, Wendy, 165n23
Browning, Elizabeth Barrett; 52, 74; "The Cry of the Children," 12; "The Young Queen," 74–81
bureaucracy, 87, 97–106, 132–33, 141–43, 149
Burke, Edmund, 157n36
Butler, Judith, 26, 83, 86, 94, 155nn4 and 12
Buzard, James, 116

Caldwell, Janis McLarren, 151n2
Canfield, James, 46
capitalism, 12, 17, 118, 144, 148, 159n16. *See also* economics
Castells, Manuel, 114
causation, 17–19, 113, 135
Chadda, Anmol, 134
Chave, Anna, 161n47
Christmas Carol, A, 96
Chu, Paula, 155n8
Clark, Beverly Lyon, 153n31
Clarke, Kamari Maxine, 165n20
class, 84, 107–8, 133
clausura, 37, 39, 43
Clifford, James, 116, 117
cloister, 37
close reading, 1, 4, 23
closure, 39–42, 129, 151n7
clusters, network, 120, 126
Cohen, Matt, 152n13
Cold War, 30, 34, 58, 60
Coleridge, Samuel Taylor, 24
collision, 8, 16–19, 80–81, 92–94, 96–97, 103, 132, 133, 137, 145, 147–48; of

collision (*cont'd*)
  hierarchies, 85, 92–93, 104, 109, 111; in narrative, 19–20, 42; of networks, 120; of rhythms, 8, 65, 67, 74, 139–40; of wholes, 37–39, 42, 44; of wholes and networks, 115–21
colonial power, 15, 43, 44, 50, 58–59, 107–8, 109–110, 120, 124–25
common law, 71–72
constitutive outside, 26, 31, 89
containment. *See* whole
Cooley, Alexander, 85
Craik, W. A., 41
Crane, Ronald S., 27
Crenshaw, Kimberlé Williams, 152n9, 163n16

Dames, Nicholas, 51–52
Danielson, Anne, 158n3
Daudet, Alphonse, 30
David, Deirdre, 109–110
Davidson, Cathy, 94–95, 164n3
deconstruction, 25–26, 83–85, 89
Deleuze, Gilles, 112, 153n20, 155n4
democracy, 30
Derrida, Jacques, 25–26, 63, 154–55n2, 164n9
description, 32, 93, 132
design theory, 6, 9, 152n15
dialectic, 18–19
diamonds, 10
Dickens, Charles, 96, 98–99, 101, 157n36. See also *Bleak House*
Dickinson, Emily, 118–19
DiMaggio, Paul, 160n28
Dimock, Wai-Chee, 4–5, 54, 153n28
Dinshaw, Carolyn, 153n20
Donne, John, 156n18
Dubrow, Heather, 5
Duchamp, Marcel, 68–69
Dworkin, Ronald, 161n53

Eagleton, Terry, 40, 151n7, 154n2, 156n19
economics, 12, 32–33, 41, 50, 57, 60, 70, 97, 102, 136, 153n26; networks and, 114–118, 121–22, 125–27, 131, 133, 144, 149. *See also* capitalism
Emerson, Ralph Waldo, 49
Empson, William, 27
enclosure. *See* whole
Engelstein, Stefani, 162n12

epic, 7, 12
Epstein, Jacob, 70–71, 73

Fabian, Johannes, 51
factory, 5, 12, 60
family, 13, 20, 43, 51, 63, 76, 87–93, 119, 133, 141, 157n36; as network, 117, 123, 125, 127–29, 145–46, 147
al-Farahidi, 152n8
Ferguson, Frances, 5, 13
Fink, Robert, 158n3
Finlay, Hugh, 120
formlessness, 9
Foucault, Michel, 5, 47, 57, 60, 63–65, 66, 94, 151n1
Fox, William Henry, 71
Freccero, Carla, 153n20
free indirect discourse, 5, 13
free verse, 4
Fuss, Diana, 118–19

Gallagher, Catherine, 32, 41, 53–54, 116, 117, 159n14, 166n33
Gallagher, Susan, 164n38
Gallop, Jane, 95
Gandhi, Leela, 114
Gascoigne, George, 78
Gaskell, Elizabeth, 96. See also *North and South*
Geissler, Karlheinz, 158n6
gender, 8, 9, 14–16, 19, 42–46, 54, 57, 62, 83, 84, 88–97, 104–6, 109–110, 143
Genette, Gerard, 152n8
genre, 13–14
ghetto, 36
Gibson, J. J., 152n15
Gigante, Denise, 54–55
Gissing, George, 45
Golston, Michael, 158n1
Graff, Gerald, 160n25, 161n38
Grafstein, Robert, 160n33
Granovetter, Mark, 112
Gray, Thomas, 156n18
Great Zimbabwe, 36
Greenblatt, Stephen, 27, 54, 116, 117, 151n7
Greene, Ronald, 165n21
Grossman, Allen, 160n27
Grossman, Jonathan, 114
Grosz, Elizabeth, 83, 86
Guattari, Félix, 112, 153n20

Harman, Barbara Leigh, 41
Harrison, Antony, 162n58
Hayot, Eric, 24, 159n17
Hayter, Alethea, 74
Hegel, G.W.F., 87
hierarchy, 5, 7, 20, 21, 82–111, 132–33,
   141–45, 147. *See also* affordances;
   collision
hinges, 113, 120, 121, 144, 146, 148
historicist criticism, 1, 5, 11, 27–28, 31–
   36, 39–40, 47, 52–56, 59, 63, 67–68,
   116–17. *See also* New Historicism
"holdover" forms, 12–13, 153n26
Homans, Margaret, 161n58
Honig, Bonnie, 162n13
Hope, Wayne, 159n16
hubs, 113, 121, 126–27
Hughes, Thomas. See *Tom Brown's
   Schooldays*
Hume, David, 19

ideology, 12, 14, 17–18, 39, 40–43, 85
intersectional analysis, 4, 11, 14, 94
Irigaray, Luce, 25, 151n7
iterability, 7, 10, 63–64, 67, 94, 141

Jackall, Robert, 100–104
Jackson, Stephen J., 158nn10 and 11
Jagoda, Patrick, 112, 148, 165n29
James, Henry, 51, 130, 152n10
Jameson, Fredric, 14, 24, 134–35, 154n37
Jane Eyre, 1–2, 20–21, 107–10
Jessop, Bob, 159n16
Johnston, Susan, 41
Jones, Rhys, 165n23
Joyce, Patrick, 112

Kanter, Rosabeth Moss, 104–6
Kaplan, Amy, 44
Keats, John, 156n18
Kennedy, Robert, 152n19
King's Dominion Law, 66
kinship. *See* family
Klaver, Claudia, 32
Koven, Seth, 45

Latour, Bruno, 19, 113, 153n22, 164n8
law, 2, 21, 55, 57, 62, 66, 80, 81, 88–93, 96,
   118, 123, 125, 126, 129, 133, 144, 145;
   common, 71–72; rhythms of, 68–73
Law, Jules David, 164n3

Lee, Hermione, 164n10
Lee, Julia Sun-Joo, 41–42
Leighton, Angela, 151n3
Lentricchia, Frank, 155n2
Lesjak, Carolyn, 18
Lessing, Gotthold Ephraim, 158n13
Lévi-Strauss, Claude, 82, 162n2
Liedman, Sven-Erik, 156n25
Little Dorrit, 98–99
Liu, Alan, 160n24
longue durée, 13, 67
López-Lozano, Miguel, 162n4
Loughran, Trish, 115, 120–21, 122
Love, Heather, 23
Lowndes, Vivien, 160nn28 and 30
Lubbock, Percy, 51
Lukács, Georg, 14, 30
lyric, 10, 11, 29, 74

Macherey, Pierre, 14
Major, Clarence, 49
Makowski, Elizabeth, 156n29
Malinowski, Bronislaw, 115–16
Mangum, Theresa, 96
Mann, Michael, 114
March, James, 58
Marcus, Sharon, 54–55, 154n42
Markovits, Stephanie, 10
marriage, 14, 41, 54, 56, 57, 63, 95, 109,
   117, 125–26, 128–29, 143
Marx, Karl, 18, 57, 84, 126
Marxist criticism, 4, 14–16, 24, 40, 62–63,
   108, 151n7
materiality, 1, 9–11, 29
May, Carrie, 45
McClintock, Anne, 43
McGann, Jerome, 153n25
McGill, Meredith, 34
McKee, Patricia, 164n36
Mecham, June, 37
meter, 4, 5, 49, 52, 73, 78–81, 152n8
Methodism, 38–39, 40
Michel, Jean-Baptiste, 123
Miller, D. A., 158n13
Millett, Kate, 154n2
Milton, John, 4
Mittell, Jason, 153n27, 167n16
monastery, 5, 60, 64–65
Moretti, Franco, 5, 14, 112, 123, 154n33,
   165n29
Munich, Adrienne, 161n58

Munro, Martin, 49, 159n15
music, 49, 51, 76

narrative, 6, 8, 10, 14–16, 19–21, 40–42,
    50–51, 93, 109–10, 127, 129, 135, 139;
    and networks, 122–31; theory of, 4,
    16, 24, 40, 122, 126, 152n8. *See also*
    closure; plot; suspense
nation, 58–60, 63, 69, 75–79, 131, 157n36;
    and networks, 118, 120–21, 122, 124–
    25; as whole, 3, 13, 21, 25, 26, 34, 36,
    38–39, 41–45, 48, 115
nationalism, 17, 30, 58–60, 124–25
network, 112–31, 133, 144–46; central-
    ized, 120, 146; chain, 127; distrib-
    uted, 120, 125, 127, 130; and narra-
    tive, 122–31. *See also* affordances;
    clusters, network; collision; family;
    hinges; hubs; nation; path length;
    "six degrees of separation"; "strength
    of weak ties"
New Criticism, 4, 11, 14, 20, 22, 24,
    27–31, 33, 35, 55, 74
"new formalism," 5, 11, 14, 16, 26, 74
New Historicism, 27, 34, 67, 116–17,
    160n24
New Institutionalism, 52, 57–68
Newman, Mark, 165nn11 and 29
New Women, 45
Norman, Donald, 152n15
North and South, 40–42
novel theory, 6; as spatializing, 40–42, 52

Oates, Joyce Carol, 164n37
Olsen, Johan, 58
organic form, 12, 26, 32, 54, 156n22
Owen, Stephen, 165n21
Oxenham, John, 156n31

panoptic spaces, 7, 47, 64
path dependency, 59, 67
path length, 113
Patmore, Coventry, 161n57
Pease, Donald E., 34
periodization, 52, 53–65
Perkins, David, 55
Pingala, 152n8
Piper, Virginia, 156n33
Plato, 2, 28, 33
plot, 5, 6, 20–21, 134–35, 146
poetry. *See* meter; rhyme; rhythm; sonnet

Poovey, Mary, 27–28, 31–34, 35–37, 46,
    48, 163n15
portability of forms, 4–5, 7, 10, 13–14, 23,
    64, 66, 86, 110
postal system, 8, 60, 119, 120
Powell, Walter, 160n28
print culture, 10, 13, 34, 114, 119, 121–
    22, 125
prison, 5, 8–10, 26, 60, 64–65, 114, 137,
    138–40, 149
Propp, Vladimir, 152n8
prosody. *See* meter
Proust, Marcel, 45

Qualls, Barry, 164n38

race, 5, 9, 11, 13, 17, 21, 38–39, 43, 44, 84,
    94, 107, 133, 136, 141, 143, 145, 149,
    166n12
Ramazani, Jahan, 165n21
Rancière, Jacques, 3, 17, 151n4
Rappaport, Helen, 162n60
replaceability. *See* surrogation
rhizome, 112
rhyme, 4, 6, 7
rhythm, 7, 8, 10, 20, 49–81, 96, 121, 127,
    132, 139–41, 144–45, 149; of gender,
    96–97; of labor, 7, 10, 21, 49, 51, 53,
    66. *See also* affordances; collision;
    meter
Richardson, Brian, 158n13
Roach, Joseph, 58, 164n3
Robbins, Bruce, 87, 107–10
Robert's Rules of Order, 141
Rossetti, Dante Gabriel, 152n16
Ruskin, John, 42–45

Sack, Graham Alexander, 164n7
scapegoat, 25–26
Schaub, Thomas H., 156n19
Schneiberg, Marc, 12–13
school, 1, 5, 7, 49, 60, 65–67, 133, 139–40,
    145, 147
Schor, Hilary, 159n14
Seligman, E.R.A., 47
seminar, 46–48
"separate spheres," 43–45, 94–96, 104, 105
Sewell, Margaret, 45
sexuality, 25, 26–27, 54–55, 95
Shakespeare, William; 155n17; *Romeo
    and Juliet*, 13

Shohat, Ella, 112, 115, 117
Siebers, Tobin, 156n19
Silva, Elena, 161n44
Simon, David. See *The Wire*
"six degrees of separation," 112
slavery, 41, 49, 96
sonnet, 6, 7, 11, 13
Sophocles. See *Antigone*
Spivak, Gayatri, 107–9, 154n41
Stalinism, 30
standardization of time, 50–51
Steichen, Edward, 68
"strength of weak ties," 112
structuralism, 5, 18, 82
sublime, 130
surrogation, 58, 128–30, 140–41, 147
suspense, 129–30, 145
Syriana, 122, 127–28

tenure clock, 8
theme parks, 66–67
Thomas, Dominic, 155n9
timetables, 5, 49–50, 60, 64, 65–66
Tom Brown's Schooldays, 14–16, 19
totality. *See* whole
Traffic, 122, 127–28
transportation, 113–14, 116–17, 118
Traynor, Roger, 161n54
Tucker, Herbert F., 12
Turner, Henry S., 10

Unger, Roberto Mangabeira, 17
unity. *See* whole
university curriculum, 58–59

Verdier, Nicolas, 161n1
Viswanathan, Gauri, 58

Warner, Michael, 120
Warren, Austin, 27
Weber, Max, 98, 99, 101, 102
Wellek, René, 27
White, Hayden, 14, 16
whole, 1, 20, 21, 24–48, 53–54, 80, 95
    96, 112, 115–21, 128, 130, 132, 137–
    39, 144, 148–49, 162n11. *See also*
    affordances; collision; nation
Williams, Carolyn, 153n28
Williams, Raymond, 62–63, 66
Wilson, William Julius, 134, 135
Wimsatt, William, 27
Wire, The, 23, 132–50
Wolfe, Cary, 155n12
Wolfson, Susan, 5, 12, 26
Woloch, Alex, 24, 151n7
Wood, Ellen Meiskins, 165n22

Yeats, William Butler, 7, 30
Yoder, Janice D., 164n33

Zerubavel, Eviatar, 50
Žižek, Slavoj, 136, 167n16